AFRICA AND THE WAR ON TERRORISM

Africa and the War on Terrorism

Edited by
JOHN DAVIS
Howard University, USA

ASHGATE

Published by
Ashgate Publishing Limited
Gower House
Croft Road
Aldershot
Hampshire GU11 3HR
England

Ashgate Publishing Company
Suite 420
101 Cherry Street
Burlington, VT 05401-4405
USA

Ashgate website: http://www.ashgate.com

British Library Cataloguing in Publication Data
Africa and the War on Terrorism
   1. War on Terrorism, 2001- 2. United States - Foreign
   relations - Africa 3. Africa - Foreign relations - United
   States 4. United States - Foreign relations - 2001-
   5. Africa - Foreign relations - 1960- 6. Africa - Politics
   and government - 21st century
   I. Davis, John, 1962-
   327.7'3'06'090511

Library of Congress Cataloging-in-Publication Data
Africa and the war on terrorism / edited by John Davis.
     p. cm.
   Includes index.
   ISBN 978-0-7546-7083-4
   1. Terrorism--Africa--Prevention. 2. War on Terrorism, 2001- I. Davis, John,
1962-

   HV6433.A35A34 2007
   363.325'17096--dc22

                       2007007985

ISBN 978-0-7546-7083-4

Printed and bound in Great Britain by Antony Rowe Ltd, Chippenham, Wiltshire.

Contents

List of Contributors

Dr. John Davis teaches International Politics at Howard University. He specializes in International Terrorism, International Relations, US Foreign Policy, National Security and Presidential Studies. Some of his publications include two books, *Presidential Policies and the Road to the Second War in Iraq: From 41 to 43* and *The Global War on Terrorism: Assessing the American Response* and over 25 book chapters, journal articles, and book reviews.

Dr. Judith A. Duncker is an Assistant Professor of International Politics on the faculty of City University of New York (CUNY) Brooklyn College and Lehman College campuses where she specializes in International Political Economy, US Foreign Policy and Modernization and Development and the Impact of Information and Communications Technology (ICT) on the political economy of development in Third World states.

Dr. Mohamed A. El-Khawas is a professor of History and Political Science in the Department of Urban Affairs and Social Sciences at the University of the District of Columbia, Washington, DC. He has published numerous articles, chapters, and monographs both in the US and abroad. His books include *Qaddafi: His Ideology in Theory and Practice*; *American Aid to Israel: Nature and Impact*; *Democracy, Diamonds and Oil: Politics in Today's Africa*; *Mozambique in the Twentieth Century*; *The Kissinger Study of Southern Africa*; and *American-Southern African Relations*.

Greg Mills is national director of the South African Institute of International , one of the top African scholars. His publications include *Big African States: Angola, DRC, Ethiopia, Nigeria, South Africa, Sudan*; *Affairs Security Intersection: The Paradox of Power in an Age of Terror*; *Future of Africa: A New Order in Sight?*; *Global Challenges and Africa: Bridging Divides, Dealing with Perceptions*; *Rebuilding Societies: Report of the 2004 Tswalu Dialogue* and is the author of a host of chapters and articles.

Dr. Samuel Moki specializes in International Relations, with particular interest in the sustainability of states in Africa. His publications include the *Bush and Gulf War II: A Study in Presidential Leadership*.

Dr. Raymond Muhula is with the Development Economics Data Group (DECDG) at the World Bank. His publications include: "Rogue Nations, States of Concern, and Axes of Evil: Examining the Politics of Disarmament in a Changing Geopolitical Context" and he recently completed a study on the role of contentious politics and social movements in Kenya's transition politics.

Andrew Othieno is a recent graduate from the London School of Economics (London) Development Studies Institute (DESTIN) and he has earned a Masters Degree in Development Studies. His current research interests involve regional integration with a focus on the East African Community (EAC), the economics and politics of conflict, and civil wars with a focus on the Great Lakes region.

Ronald D. Palmer served as US Ambassador to Mauritius and is Professor Emeritus at the George Washington University. His expertise includes US Foreign Policy and Southeast Asia.

Introduction

Africa's Road to the War on Terror

John Davis

Since the events circa 11 September 2001 African commentators have reacted to the US-led war on terrorism as either "a back to the future moment" or a grand opportunity to ensure that the continent performs more than an adequate role in the pivotal issue in international security. With respect to the back to the future moment, Adekeye Adebajo asserts that Washington changed its anti-colonial stance during the Cold War and shifted to articulating the priorities associated with the global struggle against containment.[1] In the midst of the new strategic realities the United States reduced the rhetorical pronouncements concerning "self-determination" and thereafter moved to undermine fledging democratic experiments throughout the continent.

In a further shift, successive US presidents supported authoritarian regimes that were willing to support their agenda, but when the Soviet Union collapsed the United States ended its association with its former proxies, leaving those governments to fend for themselves as many drifted to failed or collapsed state status. Though Adebajo accepts the realities of Africa's paramount role in the war on terror, he and others are concerned about what will happen when the war ebbs. At issue, will Washington become dismissive of its strategic partners when the war on terror concludes? Similarly, what will happen to continental priorities during the course of the war on terror? These are the issues that are of concern for Adebajo and others that support his observations.

Conversely, there are a host of scholars that assert the war on terror offers an opportunity for Africa to develop into and retain the unique global posture of "strategic relevance."[2] If and when Africa finds itself as a priority, say these scholars, it is when a state within the continent is embroiled in a host of negative events such as famine or starvation (Somalia and Ethiopia), genocide (Rwanda), civil war (Sudan, Sierra Leone, Liberia, or Democratic Republic of the Congo), or the HIV/AIDS pandemic (a host of states in the sub-Sahara region of the continent). In all cases these issues have the following commonalities: the world's attention span and its prescriptions have been woefully inadequate, the pledges unfulfilled, and Africa has always been perceived in a negative light.

The war on terror, as stated above, distinguishes Africa's strategic relevance and brings many of its states to "the fore."[3] In this realm the states within the Horn of Africa and those in the Sahel have emerged as critical "frontline states" in this new global conflagration. These states, along with others, have increased the attention to the aforementioned issues and moreover have focused the continent and the international community to the threat of terrorism.

There are still those that explicate the war on terror offers the region the opportunity to preclude the "emergence of another Afghanistan" and it permits the African Unity, working with the United Nations, or the United States, to rid the region of regimes that are listed as state sponsors of terror or those collapsed states (Somalia) believed to harbor senior al Qaeda operatives.[4]

Whatever the reason, negative or positive, Africa finds itself embroiled in yet another international conflict, and like the Cold War, the war on terror is not of its making. The task of this study is to provide a comprehensive introduction to illustrate Africa's road to the war on terror. In the sections that follow the objective is to explore some of the internal and external indices (collectively these indicators illustrate why Africa is both a target of terrorism and a place where it has flourished) that demonstrate Africa's growing participation in terrorism and to exemplify why it is a critical strategic partner in the war on terror. The final section concludes with "the structure of the study" providing the reader with a brief overview of the chapters in this study.

The Case for Terrorism in Africa

In understanding Africa's path to terrorism and why the continent remains a source for recruitment for al Qaeda, a source of terrorist financing, and equally significant, why the continent is replete with terror havens for bin Laden's "Afghan Arab" or his senior lieutenants, who roam the region in search of sympathetic clerics or indigenous groups to exploit, the next two sections provide an illustration of the internal and external indicators that symbolize why Africa is potentially the "next front in the war on terror."[5]

Internal Indices

According to African scholar Ted Dagne, a host of internal indicators are available to illustrate why the continent is now and will be a major player in the war in terror. The indicators are viewed this way: the "abject poverty and official corruption makes many parts of Africa a very attractive destination for terrorist organizations. Terrorist groups also see political, ethnic, and religious tensions in Africa as a favorable environment for penetration."[6] This is a very powerful statement and it illustrates the opportunities that have developed in Africa during the pre-9/11 and post-9/11 periods for the recruitment of terrorists, attainment of operational bases, and sources of funding for al Qaeda or its affiliated terror groups in the region. The section below examines some of the indicators listed by Dagne.

Islam

Religion is by far one of the critical variables that have induced fears of increased terrorist penetration throughout Africa. Nearly a third of Africa's 800 million people are Muslim. For most observers there has been an overemphasis on the al Qaeda threat. In reality much of the Islamic revivalism has its roots in Saudi Arabia and Pakistan. Saudi Arabia has built or refurbished numerous Mosques throughout Africa. Similarly, many Saudi conservative clerics, under pressure at home and exiled from their own country, have preached a host of anti-Western and anti-American Wahhabi laced messages throughout East Africa and beyond. Pakistan has endeavored to build mini-Madrasas in many of the Sahel countries, and many Pakistani and Saudi jihadists have inundated local bazaars with cassette tapes filled with messages calling for the "destruction of infidels" or jihad against US troops in Afghanistan and Iraq. In Mauritania and Chad, for example, this issue had become so prevalent that both countries have sought US assistance to stem the tide of what both states have described as increasing Islamic revivalism.[7]

In response to claims by the US and other countries about the increase of terrorism in the Sahel and elsewhere in Africa, the International Crisis Group launched a major study on the spread of and the threat of Islamic Revivalism. The report underscores the threat to Chad, Mali, Mauritania, and Niger. According to the report there is indeed reason for concern:

> While some observers have been skeptical of North Africa as a front in the war on terrorism, the battle with the GSPC in Chad appears to support US claims in this regard. The question is whether the GSPC case is an isolated incident or part of a larger trend. Each of the PSI countries suffers from a variety of threats that could easily trigger a rise in Islamism among the general population. While Niger and Mali are democratizing, with Mali having an excellent record on freedom of the press and Niger advocating separation of religion and politics as well as freedom of religion, Chad and Mauritania are very different stories. The Chadian government is dominated by one ethnic group and [is] irredeemably corrupt with the Darfur crisis having brought in more than 200,000 refugees…. An interest has been shown in all 4 PSI countries with respect to Sudanese controlled or backed Islamist missionaries or NGOs, with Chad in particular being subject to infiltration by Sudanese Islamists traveling under forged identities. Mali is the most clearly targeted, with a broad range of groups, some politicized, others apolitical, and some armed moving into the northern part of the country in large numbers. Algeria has been the main source of the GSPC influx, but others are coming in from South Asia and the Middle East.[8]

This excerpt illustrates the threat long conveyed by Sahel countries and the United States, but one often ignored by experts as an exaggeration and even a manipulation of events and facts by regional states in the Sahel to secure American military and economic assistance. While one may quarrel with the long-term necessity of assistance, both military and economic, the reality of Islamic revivalism cannot be dismissed.

Elsewhere in North Africa, the ever-increasing specter of terrorism in Nigeria, a major oil producing state, both before and after 11 September 2001, has been a cause of great concern. Terrorist attacks against oil refineries and Christians throughout the country, along with a host of religious-based killings, have heightened awareness in the region and elsewhere on the continent. The influx of radical Islamists from the Middle East is indeed alarming. Similarly, evidence abounds that Nigeria has become a target of aggressive, radical Sunni Muslim "agents with support from religious charities and other outreach (da'wa) groups headquartered in Saudi Arabia. In recent times, the main aim of Islamists in Nigeria has been the establishment of extreme Shari'ah, along the lines of the Wahhabi sect, as the exclusive law in the Muslim states of the north."[9]

Equally alarming is the presence of Taliban clerics in Nigeria preaching their brand of Islam and seeking to covert the indigenous population to their extremist sect. In an instructive example of the presence of radical Afghani clerics, consider the following:

> A "Taliban" cleric, Alhaji Sharu, told police he had received funds for the Nigerian network from al-Muntada al-Islami, an agency headed by Dr. Adil ibn Muhammad al-Saleem and based in Britain, but associated with the official Saudi state charitable and Da'wa institutions, the Muslim World League (MWL), World Assembly of Muslim Youth (WAMY), International Islamic Relief Organization (IIRO), and al-Haramain Islamic Foundation. All these groups are alleged by American and international investigators to be terror-financing bodies. Including al-Muntada al-Islami, they are together represented in the US by the "Friends of Charity Association," with a website at www.foca.net, and by the Washington attorney Wendell Belew.[10]

There is little doubt that the presence of "outsiders" in Nigeria and elsewhere on the continent continue to foment religious tensions among Africa's often marginalized Muslims. The question unanswered by the Nigerian government is how they will respond to the threat of Islamic fundamentalism.

Political Terrorism in Africa

Political violence is and continues to be a source of terrorism in the region. The use of political terrorism in this context is a synonym for state sponsored terrorism. No region of the continent is immune from this practice. One could select a host of recent examples, whether in Sudan, Somalia, Nigeria, Rwanda, Democratic Republic of the Congo, Sierra Leone, Liberia, and Mauritania, that provide a sense of the pervasive nature of this practice.[11]

In most cases the violence is associated with authoritarian regimes that desire to hold on to power and will kill indiscriminately to do so. Similarly, this form of terrorism is associated with ethnic, clan, tribal, and in some cases religious rivalries that have induced counter violence. Another form of political violence occurs in states where regimes have come to power and maintain relationships with their previous colonial masters, a practice that has spawned a host of anti-government movements that have caused rebel or insurgent violence. Incidences of insurgence, particularly those involving Islamic groups, are often penetrated or receive external support or direction by al Qaeda. Viewed collectively, al Qaeda utilizes political violence as a source of recruitment and propaganda, the result of which has increased instability and chaos in countries within the continent. It should be noted that this is a minority of cases; the vast majority of cases involve indigenous groups that have no connection to bin Laden. In the end the cycle of political terrorism has no end. Indeed many of these cases are historic whether in the case Rwanda, Algeria, or South Africa.[12] The war on terror continues apace; political terrorism at some point needs to be confronted. Unfortunately many of these states have partnered with the US in its war with al Qaeda, and Washington (in need of allies) has and continues to turn a blind eye to "the terrorism from within" that, at least in Africa, will preclude any long term success in the war on terror and will incessantly serve as reminder that this form of violence can only undermine an otherwise necessary war.

Failed States and Terrorism in Africa

Failed states dominate the landscape in Africa. These states have historically been corrupt, unable to govern, and have in some cases lost territory to rebels. African failed states have the following familiar characteristics. The typical African failed state is a country that is dominated by "factionalization of its ethnic and religious groups, [and] uneven access to and rewards from its economy and the absence of human rights."[13] On the historical legacy of African failed states, Franklyne Ogbunwezeh offers his take:

> The African continent is littered with failed states. Most of these states are economic backwaters, social apologies and political ruins. This landscape runs from the Casablanca to the Cape Town and from The Horn of Africa in the East to the Island of No Return in the West Atlantic. Most of these states true to type were the creatures of imperial convenience. To that end, they were meant to serve a purpose after which their ontological legitimacy or *raison d' etre* would then expire. At this expiration; the states, naturally not designed for self-propulsion; were condemned to tether on the brink, and finally implode upon the inglorious weight of their inherent contradictions. Colonialism designed and inspired the problems. But the decadence was then driven along by a horde of native pirates; trained in the fine art of piracy. These set of political actors were rogue personalities, weaned on selfishness. They were brilliant students of kleptocracy and political perversity. In about four decades they completely outclassed colonial perfidy and bested them in thievery. They did an inglorious job of mismanaging Africa, so much so that she is today the laughing stock of the world.[14]

Irrespective of this brilliant statement there are two controversies surrounding this debate. The first issue is a definitional one. Scholars have incessantly quarreled over the meaning of "failed states." The most acceptable definition has been this: a failed state "is one in which the government does not have effective control of its territory, is not perceived as legitimate by a significant portion of its population, does not provide domestic security or basic public services to its citizens, and lacks a monopoly on the use of force."[15]

As one would expect, the overwhelming majority of these states reside in the global south and are non-Western states. In a refutation to their negative status, many of these states have asserted that their status is historically connected to the old colonial era and is now resurfacing under a new neo-colonial impulse.

Second, failed states have been linked by the administration of George W. Bush to terrorism. The reason associated with the US president's view is a simple one: in the ungoverned territories of these states terrorists have carved out their own sanctuaries. In other cases, such as in Afghanistan or Sudan, terrorist entities (al Qaeda) have established special relationships with outlaw governments and thereafter established shelters in which a series of terrorist operational facilities were constructed and then used to launch devastating attacks on US and Western interests.

Among the current regions where failed states reside, Africa figures prominently in that many of its failed states have assisted al Qaeda directly or many of its affiliates have worked on behalf of bin Laden's transnational enterprise. Of these states Somalia has long been considered a target by the West, most notably the United States in the wake of the closure of al Qaeda's major operational base in Afghanistan. With its major strategic base closed, the view among US intelligence experts (and terrorist analysts the world over) is that bin Laden's legions would establish a new base in Somalia. Long before al Qaeda was evicted from its traditional home, US and NATO intelligence assets monitored Somalia from the air, via the Predator unmanned intelligence drone (and other platforms), on land via US Special Forces, along with those from Britain, and from the sea with naval forces utilizing sensors that were trained to monitor the communications of terrorists. Collectively, the US and NATO were prepared for a showdown with Somalia. Events in mid-December of 2006 when the Union of Islamic Courts (a group believed to harbor or is led by senior Al Qaeda operatives), or "UIC", assumed control Mogadishu, ended the debate over the "coming showdown." Thereafter, Ethiopia, with presumed backing from the United States, intervened and routed the forces of the Islamic Courts, and now occupies the country. Time will tell whether Somalia's long civil war has dissipated or if this is just a pause before returning to the renewal of clan dysfunction.

There are other examples of problematic failed states in Africa. In Central and West Africa, for example, a host of states figure prominently in support of al Qaeda or have knowingly or unknowingly provided refuge to its operatives. In a unique example the Democratic Republic of Congo (DRC), Sierra Leone, and Liberia were indicted as participants in bin Laden's criminal enterprises to fund his transnational network. This relationship was a long and profitable relationship for all participants:

> [Collectively they] have already provided opportunity for al Qaeda and criminal networks possibly affiliated with it to profit from the marketing of diamonds and other precious gems. Wars in the Democratic Republic of the Congo (DRC), Sierra Leone and Liberia opened this door and local warlords like Charles Taylor readily collaborated.[16]

In the wake of the strategic realities associated with failed states and the connection to terrorism, scholars have called for a dramatic influx of diplomatic activity along with increased economic investment. While the military option is often suggested it is a short term attempt at a quick fix in what is, in the case of African failed states, a long term problem.

External Indices

In this section the objective is to provide examples of the external variables that are critical indicators as to why Africa is ripe for terrorist penetration or how exogenous entities have already established themselves in various parts of Africa. This section examines the impact of the al Qaeda threat and additional threats in the form of other terrorist entities in the Middle East and elsewhere that have used African states as sanctuaries to launch terrorist attacks in the region and around the world.

The al Qaeda Threat

With few exceptions the principal external terrorist threat is al Qaeda. Bin Laden incessantly opined about an Islamic Caliphate. In the view of many Islamic militants, Africa is a natural focus of Wahhabist activity. In a vivid example, during the period 1991–1996 Sudan served as al Qaeda's central base of operations before intense pressure from the United States, Saudi Arabia and Egypt forced bin Laden to move his legions to Afghanistan.

Though Sudan represented a major safe haven for al Qaeda's presence and operational activity, East Africa remains the central target for jihadist penetration. To illustrate al Qaeda's strategy in the region, the words of Abul Bara' Hassan Salman, the Deputy Emir of Jamaat e-Jihad Eritrea (Eritrea Islamic Jihad Movement), an al Qaeda affiliate, are instructive:

> Politically, the African Horn refers to all the countries in East Africa. It includes Somalia, Djibouti, Eritrea, Ethiopia, and Kenya. The area is of particular importance as it links the East with the West through the Red Sea that is between the agrarian and industrial societies. The region is also an oil producer and a giver of mineral deposits in the Red Sea. The Horn's strategic security significance increased since the establishment of a Jewish nation in Palestine. These catalysts, along with some others, made the region a highly sought-after place particularly by the colonialists and imperialists, both past and present.[17]

Having set the stage for Western strategy, Bara' Hassan Salman asserted the region belongs to Islamists and not the West. In March of 1998 the Eritrean Islamist thereafter offered the following counter jihadist strategy:

> The external front ... is a very sensitive front from the aspect of our strategic security. In this respect we (a) liaise and exchange our experience and expertise with other Muslim organizations which also work to challenge the various corrupt regimes in the region; (b) concentrate our activities amongst Muslims through means which will enable them to see the conspiracies of the enemies and their plots to uproot Islam and Muslims; (c) strive to generate suitable opportunities to support our jihad through Islamic means; (d) move around neighboring countries and expose the corruption of the Eritrean regime and its danger over the entire region on the religious, security and political fronts.[18]

In the years since Bara Hassan Salman's statement a number of additional terrorist groups have worked to implement or carry out the aforementioned strategy. Those terrorist organizations include Al-Ittihad al-Islamia and later the Union of Islamic Courts, each of which exists in Somalia. The view by many experts is that the "suitable opportunities to our jihad through Islamic means" represents a clear reference to al Qaeda and its charitable worldwide support structure. Second, the use of middle level operatives within the transnational terror network to assist the local terrorist groups with their implementation of their agenda is another indicator of al Qaeda's presence in the region. In the end there are other determinants.

Islamic militancy is a hallmark of the region and it certainly predates bin Laden's network. That said, East Africa maintains the potential fertile breeding ground for al Qaeda's religious rhetoric.[19] One of the interesting barometers of al Qaeda's presence concerns the increase in radical anti-American messages and the burgeoning upswing in pro-bin Laden clerics. As a result of these twin activities, the transnational terror network "has had some success in recruiting East African Muslims to conduct guerrilla operations with transnational objectives. These operations have primarily been to attack US interests."[20]

It is noteworthy that several al Qaeda-sponsored attacks were carried out in the region. Those attacks include a significant strategy in Mogadishu that resulted in the withdrawal of US forces from Somalia. Mohammed Atef, the former leader of al Qaeda's military operations, undertook to privately train elements of Mohammed Farah Aidid's militia, resulting in the downing of two Black Hawk helicopters and the killing of 18 elite US military personnel. In the wake of the attack bin Laden hailed the success and offered these additional post-attack comments:

It is my companions that fought with Farah Aidid's forces against the US troops in Somalia. But we were fighting US terrorism. Under the cover [of the] United Nations, the United States tried to establish its bases in Somalia so that it could get control over Sudan and Yemen. My associates killed the American's in collaboration with Farah Aidid. We are not ashamed of jihad. In one explosion 100 American's were killed [a gross exaggeration of US troop deaths; this was an effort to kill US peacekeepers stationed in a hotel in Yemen, that were schedule to rotate in Somalia as a part of Operation Restore Hope, but none of the forces perished in the explosion. They left hours before its detonation], then 18 more were killed in the fighting [in Somalia].... After that 28,000 US soldiers fled Somalia. The American's are cowards.[21]

A number of other attacks—using al Qaeda cells from regional elements— occurred in the region. Those attacks include the 1998 East African Embassy bombings that destroyed US interests in Kenya and Tanzania that "coincided with the anniversary of the first deployment of US troops to Saudi Arabia in 1990."[22] In November 2002 the transnational terror group launched a deadly attack against a hotel in Mombassa, Kenya and was followed by a subsequent shoulder fired assault on an Israeli commercial jet that fortunately missed. Once again cells involving regional entities took part in the attacks.

Outside the region other associates of al Qaeda have been busy sponsoring their own terrorist attacks. In the Sahel, for example, the Algerian-based Salafist Group for Preaching and Combat (GSPC) has caused damage throughout the region, resulting in kidnapping of European tourists and the deaths of Mauritanian and Chadian soldiers among its numerous terrorist sprees.

Elsewhere in North Africa, Moroccan Islamists, also with long established relationships with al Qaeda, launched a series of attacks on 16 May 2003 in Spain that resulted in the deaths of 45 people. The method of attacks moved beyond the bombing of a restaurant but involved 12 suicide bombings. Similarly, additional attacks have been conducted against European interests, principally in Spain in March of 2004. This and a host of other planned attacks were inspired by bin Laden. As noted al Qaeda expert Rohan Gunaratna observes, "The threat of terrorism has shifted from al Qaeda to associated organizations." Gunaratna made this additional statement: "Al Qaeda has become a movement; it is no longer a single group."[23]

Evidence of this movement has resulted from bin Laden's appeal that Muslims worldwide participate in a renewed jihad against occupying US forces in Iraq. According to Central Command (CENTCOM) well over three hundred North Africans have been killed or captured. The fear among US military planners is that Iraq has become a training ground for terrorist groups, and worse many of the terrorist tactics used in Iraq—particularly the use of Improvised Explosive Devises (IEDS)—may be employed against US forces in the Horn and in North Africa.[24]

Lastly, in Somalia, the UIC as stated earlier, launched a takeover of Mogadishu and thereafter attempted to extend its control elsewhere in southern Somalia. The UIC movement, along with its alarming rhetoric, forced regional states, Kenya, Ethiopia, Eritrea, and Djibouti, to take note. With perceived US encouragement, Ethiopia in response to the UIC threat invaded the capital and currently occupies it. For now, the military occupation has temporary halted the Islamic revival in Somalia. To date troops from the Transitional government have assisted forces from Ethiopia in a joint effort to restore order to the capital.[25]

Additional External Threats

Al Qaeda is not the only external group that has thrived in Africa. Historically the Muslim Brotherhood, Hezbollah, Hamas and a plethora of Palestinian terrorists groups have been active in Africa or have sought sanctuary in Africa. In recent times Sudan has been the terrorist haven of choice. All of the aforementioned groups and others have received sanctuaries, many of which, including al Qaeda, have constructed terrorist training facilities and launched operations from Sudan.[26]

Libya is another well known terrorist sanctuary housing not only Arab terrorist groups, but was also home to many European, communist and other terrorist organizations from around the world. The leader of Libya, Muammar Qaddafi, used these, along with Libyan terrorist groups, to help finance terrorist operations against Israel, Egypt, Chad, Sudan, and most notably, the United States. Additionally, Libya was home to many terrorist training camps.

One of the interesting realities is that the Libyan sponsored terrorist organizations that maintained bases in the country dominated the headlines in the 1970s and early 1980s. The Libyan threat came to an unofficial end following former president Ronald Reagan's decision to launch a counterterrorist strike in the wake of the Berlin discothèque bombing that killed American military personnel.[27]

As far as terrorist havens go, the decade of the 1990s belonged to Sudan. The difference between Sudan and Libya is that it was Qaddafi's incessant terrorist operations against US interests that forced the closure of the bulk of Libya's terrorist related facilities. In time many of the terrorist groups that operated in Libya sought shelter elsewhere or invariably reduced their profile. In the case of Sudan the Islamic regime of Omar el-Bashir, aided by the National Islamic Front (NIF), was responsible for political terrorism against its own people both during the pre- and post-11 September period. By contrast, al Qaeda established a relationship with the regime that included financing of infrastructure projects in exchange for terrorist training camps. Within these facilities and elsewhere in Sudan, bin Laden and the el-Bashir government hosted a series of "terror conferences" that involved the "who's who" in terror groups. In the most significant of these conferences, al Qaeda and some 250 leaders of terrorist organizations formally agreed to a jihad against the United States. Prior to this, and certainly thereafter, a host of terrorist attacks were launched against the US and allied interests.

The historical record indicates that the tremendous pressure unleashed by the Saudis, Egyptians and the US forced al Qaeda to leave its sanctuary in Sudan. However, it took an additional counterterrorist strike by the Clinton administration to bring the attention of the West to the potency of the threat posed by and within Sudan. It would take the events of 11 September, however, for Sudan to formally join the war on terror and decrease its sponsorship of terrorism. In the post-9/11 world many of the terror groups that operated in Sudan sought sanctuary elsewhere rather than risk the wrath of the Bush administration.

Structure of the Study

In an effort to provide a comprehensive analysis of the multiple dynamics that set foundation for Africa's participation in the war on terror, this study begins with **Part I: Opening Perspective**. In the opening chapter, noted African scholar Greg Mills illuminates "Africa's New Strategic Significance." The author notes that Africa's strategic significance is manifested in a number of a ways: from the "lily pads", American access to countries that are strategically located, the mere fact that many of its countries have been designated as "frontline states in the war on terror", and finally, Mills provides an exhaustive examination of the efforts by the United States to build a host of integrated regional military and economic partnerships to ensure that participant states are prepared to confront local and international terrorists threats.

Part II: The Combined Joint Task Force and the War on Terror is designed to explore the role of two of the critical members of the combined joint force. In Chapter 2, Othieno and Davis examine the preeminent role enjoyed by Djibouti in the war on terror. As the "center of gravity" of the task force, this chapter explores the "extensive military activity" that continues at Camp Lemonier, a base that is home to over 1,200 US military personnel, with additional forces aboard ship, and with French forces stationed at the base camp as well. This chapter closes with an examination of the economic and political benefits to Djibouti in the wake of its partnership with the United States.

In Chapter 3, "Kenya and the Search for a New Role in a New War," Raymond Muhula asserts that since the East African embassy bombings in August of 1998 Kenya and Tanzania have each established separate relations with the United States to preclude future acts of terrorism within their respective countries. In the case of Kenya the author asserts the relationship underwent a dramatic change following the events of 11 September, offering bases to US army and naval forces and the long established joint US–Kenya military relationship has dramatically increased. Since that tragic day Kenya has been elevated to the status as a "frontline state." Moreover, internally the government of Kenya has worked to introduce and implement a host of counterterrorist bills to ensure that they are prepared to address internal threats on their own. According to the author these counterterrorist measures have produced an anti-Muslim backlash because such legislation dramatically increased the number of detentions and deaths of Muslims throughout Kenya.

Part III: Regional Dynamics examines the external and internal indices that have increased, rather than decreased, the likelihood of terrorism within Africa. As an attendant consequence regional organizations such as the African Union (AU) and select regions have come under increasing pressure to move proactively to deal with the burgeoning issues that produce or have accelerated regional and external terrorist threats. Chapter 4—"Globalization and its Impact on the War on Terror"—by Judy Duncker opens this section. The author endeavors to explicate how a number of "globalization currents"—from terrorist chat rooms, integration of regional military organizations that have developed in response to the al Qaeda threat, the evolution of a host of new entities (African Coastal and Border Security Program, Terrorist Interdiction Program, Personal Identification Secure Comparison and Evaluation System, and a other measures)—have been developed by the US and its African coalition partners to confront the transnational terrorist threat posed by al Qaeda and its regional affiliates. Additionally, the author examines the regional (AU) and supranational (UN) efforts to interdict terrorist financing, what all experts assert is a critical measure to ending the threat posed by terrorism.

Mohamed A. El-Khawas begins this section with an examination of the first of two critical regions. In Chapter 5 "North Africa and the War on Terror," El-Khawas explores why North Africa has long been considered a haven of terrorism. Among the countries within the region, several figure prominently in terrorism; they include Morocco, Algeria and Tunisia, each of which are major hubs of transnational terror which has seen participant terror group involvement in Iraq, Afghanistan, and—equally troubling—many cells from various North African organizations have participated in bombings in Europe, most notably in Spain. Additionally, this study examines how these countries have cooperated with the Bush administration in the war on terror, and finally, the response of the aforementioned countries to the US-led war in Iraq.

Examining another region, Ambassador Robert Palmer, in Chapter 6, "Political Terrorism in West Africa", makes a bold statement: while al Qaeda is indeed a threat to the region, the greater threat is internal. That threat is the ever-present specter of state sponsored terrorism in a region that continues to disrupt the development of mass political participation. Surveying critical countries—Nigeria, Liberia, Senegal, Sierra Leone, to name a few—the author explores the historical legacy of colonialism and how it is manifested in a host of authoritarian leaders within the region who, in order to stay in power, unleashed a reign of political terror against their political foes. In an interesting twist, the author asserts that the combination of political terrorism is as much a threat to the outbreak of terror in a region teaming with Muslims as is al Qaeda's presence. To exacerbate the situation "firebrand clerics" have used this threat to increase Islamic revivalism in the region.

In the final chapter in this section—Chapter 7 "The Role of the African Union: Integration, Leadership and Opportunity"—Sam Moki explicates that of all of the institutions in the region, the African Union (AU) receives little attention in its efforts to work with member states and their efforts to confront terrorism. The nature of this chapter involves the examination of the role that the AU has performed in dealing with continental terror; this study explores the multiple rivalries of member states that affected the organization's ability to deal with terrorism. Lastly, this chapter considers another fascination: why the AU's efforts to pass or implement regional measures to deal with terrorism are often eclipsed by the Western countries and the actions by the UN.

The final section, **Part IV: Clinton and Bush: Impact on Africa**, examines two US presidential administrations and their disparate efforts to deal with terrorism in the region. In the initial study, Chapter 8 "The Clinton Approach: Sudan and the Failure to Capture bin Laden", the editor asserts that the signature events of the pre-11 September era occurred in Sudan, the alleged terror capital of Africa and Clinton's failure to capture Osama bin Laden before his departure to Afghanistan. Equally fascinating, this chapter argues that Clinton's war on terror preceded the simultaneous destruction of the US embassies in Kenya and Tanzania. This essay endeavors to illustrate that it was Clinton's "silent war" with Sudan that informs us as about the president's post-embassy approach to terror in the wake of the East African embassy bombings.

In Chapter 9, "The Bush Model: US Special Forces, and the War on Terror", the editor explores the Bush administration's radical decision: the president's approach used coalitions to minimize the US military footprint. To that end the administration decided that in order to preclude Africa from becoming the next front in the war on terror it was important to use intelligence and US Special Forces to redefine American relationships with a host of critical states in the region. Similarly, this chapter explores the bureaucratic politics that set in motion the Combined Joint Task Force in the Horn of Africa, The Pan Sahel Initiative, and Trans-Sahara Counterterrorism Initiative, coalitions that symbolized the Bush administration's strategy to include Africa in the US-led war on terror. This chapter closes with an assessment of these coalitions.

This study concludes with "Africa and the War on Terror: An Assessment." In this conclusion, the editor uses aspects of the aforementioned chapters to identify the strengths and weaknesses of the Africa phase of the war on terror. In this chapter a host of additional issues will be examined. These issues include the growth of anti-Americanism in the wake of the US-led war on terrorism; the on-going problem of reciprocal intelligence sharing; the decline of African issue prioritization; political terrorism in Africa; and the impact of the US indifference to anti-terrorist training, among other issues.

Notes

1. Adekeye Adebajo, "Africa and America in an Age of Terror," *Journal of Asian and African Studies*, Vol. 38, No. 2–3, 2003, pp. 175–176.
2. The opening chapter, "Africa's Strategic Relevance" by Greg Mills will provide this perspective for the reader.
3. J. Stephenson Morrison, "Somalia's and Sudan's Race to the Fore in Africa," *Washington Quarterly*, Spring 2002, p. 201.
4. Jeffrey Herbst and Greg Mills, "Africa and the War on Terror," *Royal United Services Institute (RUSI) Journal*, October 2003, p. 46.
5. There are those that believe that Africa is already the next the front in the war on terror. There are several measures to support this supposition: the presence of US forces, which while in the region to train regional partners, is nonetheless a "magnet" for recruitment for radical groups, both indigenous and external (al Qaeda), and will increase the already high anti-Americanism in the region. Second, many groups or radical Islamists have joined the jihad in Iraq and have subsequently taken their new found terrorist skills back to their home states and "will soon foment" trouble, whether in targeting US troops, those of regional partners, or a host of "soft targets" throughout Africa.
6. Ted Dagne, "Africa and War on Terror," in *The Global War on Terrorism: Assessing the American Response* (New York: Nova, 2004), ed. by John Davis.
7. Craig Smith, "US Training African Forces to Uproot Terrorists," *New York Times*, May 11, 2004, p. A4.
8. Dan Darling, "ICG Report on the Sahel Region," April 11, 2005. http://www.windsofchange.net/archives/006649.php. The site was accessed on December 8, 2006.
9. Stephen Schwartz, "Islamic Extremism on the Rise in Nigeria," *The Jamestown Foundation*, October 21, 2005. http://jamestown.org/terrorism/news/article.php?articleid=2369814. The site was accessed on December 8, 2006.
10. Ibid.
11. Much more will be said about political terrorism in Chapter 6.
12. A few books illustrate the point. See General Paul Aussaresses, *The Battle of the Casbah: Terrorism and Counterterrorism in Algeria 1955–1957* (New York: Enigma Books, 2004) and John A. Berry and Carol Pott Berry, eds, *Genocide in Rwanda: A Collective Memory* (Washington, DC: Howard University Press, 1999), and Samuel Decalo, *Coups and Army Rule in Africa: Studies in Military Style* (New Haven, CT: Yale University Press: 1979), are but few examples of political terrorism in Africa.
13. Jeffrey Young, "Failed States Foster Terrorism," November 6, 2006. http://www.voanews.com/english/archive/2006-11/failed2006-11-09-voa3.cfm. The site was accessed on December 8, 2006.
14. Franklyne Ogbunwezeh, "Africa: The Ontology of Failed States," http://www.dawodu.com/ogbunwezeh1.htm. The site was accessed on December 8, 2006.
15. "The Failed States Index," *Foreign Policy*, May/June 2006. http://www.foreignpolicy.com/story/cms.php?story_id=3420. The site was accessed on December 8, 2006.
16. Testimony before the House Committee on International Relations Subcommittee on Africa Hearing on "Fighting Terrorism in Africa" by Princeton N. Lyman Ralph Bunche Senior Fellow and Director of Africa Policy Studies, April 1, 2004. Council of Foreign Relations. http://www.cfr.org/publication/6912/terrorist_threat_in_africa.html?breadcrumb=default. The site was accessed on December 8, 2006.
17. Rohan Gunaratna, *Inside al Qaeda: Global Network of Terror* (New York: Columbia University Press, 2002), pp. 151–152.
18. Ibid., p. 154.
19. "Do al Qaeda's East Africa Operations Pose a Threat to US Interests?" *Power and Interests News Reports* (PINR), December 1, 2004. http://www.pinr.com/report.php?ac=view_

report&report_id=240. The site was accessed on December 8, 2006.

20. Ibid.

21. Simon Reeve, *The New Jackals: Ramzi Yousef, Osama bin Laden and Future of Terrorism* (Boston: Northeastern University Press, 1999), p. 182.

22. "Do Al Qaeda's East Africa Operations Pose a Threat to US Interests?"

23. Peter Ford, "Terrorism Web Emerges from Madrid Bombing," *Christian Science Monitor*, March 22, 2004. http://www.csmonitor.com/2004/0322/p01s02-woeu.html. The site was accessed on December 8, 2006.

24. Warren P. Strobel, "Iraq Emerges as a Terrorist Training Ground," *Seattle Times*, July 5, 2005. http://www.commondreams.org/headlines05/0705-10.htm. The site was accessed on December 9, 2006.

25. Jeffrey Gettleman, "Somali Government Seeks to Tighten Its Grip Amid Chaos," *New York Times*, January 5, 2007, p. A9.

26. See Edgar O' Balance, *Sudan, Civil War and Terrorism, 1956–99* (New York: Palgrave Macmillan, 2000).

27. David C. Martin and John L. Walcott, *Best Laid Plans: The Inside Story of America's War Against Terrorism* (New York: Harper & Row, 1988), pp. 251–259.

PART 1
Opening Perspective

Chapter 1

Africa's New Strategic Significance

Greg Mills

Introduction

As international attention in the war on terrorism continues to focus primarily on the Middle East, it is easy to forget that al Qaeda's most extreme terrorist attacks prior to September 11 were the August 1998 bombings of US embassies in Dar es Salaam and Nairobi. These attacks cost the lives of 224 people (including 12 Americans) and injured 4,574 more. Since that time, Africa has been again struck, on 16 May 2003, when 14 suicide bombers killed 44 people and injured more than 100 in a coordinated attack on five targets in Casablanca. In May 2004, South Africa's police commissioner announced that authorities had arrested several al Qaeda suspects "who had evil intentions against this country"[1] just five days before the country's mid-April democratic election, the second ever. While in the spotlight of international attention, al Qaeda's African activities have nevertheless paled in comparison to the continent's homegrown, domestic sources of insecurity and violence.

Terrorism is also a tactic that guerrilla armies and warlords in Africa have adopted for decades during wars predating and unconnected to the larger global terrorist threat. If terrorism is defined as violent acts against a civilian population by non-state actors, then it is employed by many African groups, including paramilitaries in the Democratic Republic of Congo, where probably more than three million citizens have lost their lives in the last half-decade; the Revolutionary United Front in Sierra Leone; all the warring parties in Liberia; militias in the Republic of the Congo; warlords in Somalia; and many other participants of Africa's numerous civil wars. So-called armies, which often resemble loose confederations of armed gangs, regularly use terrorist tactics, including abduction of children, amputation, rape, and indiscriminate killing, to coerce local populations into supporting their causes or to garner resources to continue fighting. Domestic terrorists in Africa's civil wars have killed a far greater number of Africans than have terrorists motivated by international causes. Ongoing African conflicts afflict approximately 20 percent of the continent's population, with most of its victims being innocent civilians.[2]

The post-September 11 US-led war on terrorism targets terrorist acts that, although horrific, have claimed relatively few lives by the standards of violence in Africa. The real terrorist threat on this continent remains internal. Importantly, however, September 11 highlighted the conditions of governance and economic growth necessary not only for African stability, but also prosperity. While al Qaeda was plotting the attacks on the World Trade Center and the Pentagon, African leaders were devising a plan for African economic recovery, deemed the New Partnership for Africa's Development (NEPAD), formally adopted by the then Organization of African Unity (OAU) in October 2001. NEPAD offers a partnership to end African sources of insecurity, proposing a new global aid and development regime for Africa in response to what is essentially an African-imposed structural adjustment program. This coincidence in timing also marks shared Western and African interest to strengthen local initiatives to deal both with continental and global terrorism through building state capacities.

Raising Africa's Profile

Had there never been a September 11, 2001, President George W. Bush arguably never would have made a visit to Senegal, South Africa, Botswana, Uganda, and Nigeria in July 2003—the first visit by a sitting Republican president to Africa. At the very least, the September 11 attacks added urgency to his visit. Prior to his departure, the president stated that "many African governments have the will to fight the war on terror ... we will give them the tools and the resources to win [this] war.[3]

According to the September 2002 *US National Security Strategy*, the attacks taught the United States "that weak states ... can pose as great a danger to our national interests as strong states. Poverty does not make poor people into terrorists and murderers. Yet poverty, weak institutions, and corruption can make weak states vulnerable to terrorist networks and drug cartels within their borders."[4] Long recognized by the international community as the single most-impoverished continent and for its weak governmental institutions, Africa's clear potential to become a breeding ground for new terrorist threats thus landed it a new place on the US foreign policy agenda. Air Force Gen. Jeffrey Kohler, the director of plans and policy at the US European Command, which has responsibility for Africa, added, "What we don't want to see in Africa is another Afghanistan, a cancer growing in the middle of nowhere."[5]

The September 11 attacks, moreover, have brought new international, not just US, attention to the potential security threats posed by failed or collapsed states as epicenters of crime, disease, terrorism, and instability more generally, demonstrated by NATO deputy supreme allied commander Admiral Sir Ian Forbes's assertion that "the strategic context in which we find ourselves has changed dramatically since 11 September 2001. Future threats come not from conquering states, but from failed or failing ones and from catastrophic technologies in the hands of embittered minorities."[6] This rationale goes a long way to explain why Bush, arguably more than any other US president, has elevated Africa in his rhetoric and in the more concrete terms of aid and access to trade with the proposed $5 billion increase in annual aid through the establishment of the Millennium Challenge Account (MCA) and the United States' $15 billion initiative to fight AIDS. The Bush administration has also overseen efforts to integrate Africa's economies into the global economy through the extension of the African Growth and Opportunity Act (AGOA) beyond 2008; the June 2004 signing of the free-trade agreement (FTA) with Morocco; and the proposed FTA with the member states (Namibia, South Africa, Lesotho, Botswana, and Swaziland) of the Southern African Customs Union.

Following his meeting with President Festus Mogae of Botswana during his trip, Bush commented, "We both understand that we must work together to share intelligence, to cut off money, to forever deny terrorists a chance to plot and plan and hurt those of us who love freedom."[7] Yet understanding the relationship between Africa and terrorism so that effective policies can be established to address it will require that US and African policymakers go beyond simple platitudes about shared interests and that they engage in difficult discussions about how to increase the ability of African states to command their own territories.

While the White House continues to pledge more aid to fight terrorism and steadily increases its military footprint on the continent, Africa's actions to deal with terrorism have been both slow and limited. Unsurprisingly, African leaders have preferred to equate the war against terrorism primarily with the war to end poverty and, to this end, to receive greater assistance. As Tanzania's president, Benjamin Mkapa, has argued, "It is futile, if not foolhardy to think there is no link between poverty and terrorism."[8] Nevertheless, the relationship between poverty and terrorism is not as clear as African leaders might prefer. Poverty alone does not foster terrorist movements, and extraordinary poverty is something with which Africans have long managed to cope. Rather, a sense of growing frustration with the lack of opportunity is inevitable on a continent that has failed to keep pace with global economic growth, even compared to other areas of the developing world.

Moreover, strict conditionalities, long a source of contention between Africa and the West, will remain on new aid disbursements. During his Africa tour, Bush said that the MCA would provide aid to countries with governments "that rule justly, root out corruption, encourage entrepreneurship, and invest in the health and education of their people." Countries making these changes, he said, would get more help from America: more foreign investment, more trade, and more jobs.[9] Dealing with the problem of poverty in Africa is key to providing long-term security to Africans. This begets a key question in the relationship between Africa and the West: What forms of intervention are most appropriate in securing Western interests and satisfying African demands? In so doing, how can external parties, as well as African recipients, avoid the corrupting psychology and limited benefits of traditional forms of aid? Extending state authority and governance must be the principal response to Africa's internal and external forms of terrorism, but this may demand giving African militaries and police forces greater resources to defeat insurgents, local as well as foreign.

Beyond Poverty: Addressing State Weakness

The defining characteristic of many African states, and a critical issue in combating terrorist activity, is their weakness. By the 1990s, reportedly one-third of sub-Saharan African states were afflicted by low state capacity[10] and inability to exercise control and authority over their rural regions or their borders. The boundaries of African countries have never been determined by how far these states can extend their power; they were imposed by colonial rulers and have been retained by African political elites.[11]

Globalization has, at least temporarily, exacerbated the weakness of African states, not least because it has generated new debates within countries, exposing government failure and corruption, increasing pressure on government to reform, and creating a cause around which opposition can rally. The spread of such openness and transparency poses challenges to the client-oriented and autocratic nature of many African economies.

Key to establishing a strong partnership between Western powers and African governments to combat terrorism is the fact that addressing the pervasiveness of state weakness on the continent tackles the conditions that give rise both to domestic and international terrorist movements. Yet there is no exact correlation between state weakness or failure and terrorist activity; indeed, it may be argued that terrorism requires key governance and infrastructure attributes (such as regular air flights and reliable communications and banking systems) to operate effectively beyond just simply offering lawless safe havens. Moreover, the conventional wisdom is that such states play host to terrorists beyond the reach of the law is subject to debate. Collapsed states also play host to drug lords and warlords who may be competitors rather than collaborators. Their lawlessness and violent nature makes them inevitably difficult environments from which and in which to operate. They are dangerous especially for foreigners, are exposed to international counterterrorist action, and are difficult settings in which to maintain neutrality and partisanship, without which outsiders can themselves become embroiled in local disputes and politics.[12] Although complete state failure can create anarchic environments that are not ideal for terrorists, weak states, quasi-states, or those in crisis can provide the ideal environment for terrorist organizations. In other words, working out of Nairobi is preferable to working out of Mogadishu, or Dakar to Monrovia.[13]

Given the pervasiveness of state weakness, there is, however, overlap between the conditions that give rise to domestic terror and the international movements. First, Africa's weak states offer sanctuary and succor to terrorist movements from within Africa and without. In addition to offering stopover points and safe havens for terrorist movements, Africa's weak central government authority can provide a route for bypassing international banking systems and financial scrutiny. The relative absence of local authority not only allows external actors to use African territories as safe havens but also permits indigenous paramilitary groups to terrorize local populations. Many African states are so weak that non-state actors terrorizing civilians is a viable military strategy and is easier than developing an army to fight states. At the same time, some international terrorists may also see ungoverned parts of Africa as safe havens or as places that provide opportunities for attacking Americans and other Western targets on the continent.

Second, beyond the sanctuary that weak states provide, widespread conditions of conflict and poverty create a breeding ground for alienation and radicalization, thereby providing potential recruits to the cause of terrorist groups. Finally, Africa has 250 million Muslims, comprising 40 percent of the continent's population. Until now, the key terrorist threats in Africa have come from areas where African states adjoin the Arab world. Despite this fact, the United States remains particularly concerned about states with large Muslim populations such as Nigeria, Tanzania, and Ivory Coast. Traditional African religions, however, are historically the ones that are more closely linked to insurgent warfare on the continent, such as with the Lord's Resistance Army in Uganda. By comparison, sub-Saharan Africa's Muslim communities largely draw on the moderate Suwarian tradition of Sufi Islam, although new strains and influences are present.[14] As one commentator has noted:

> It is alarming [to see] the spread of rigid forms of Islam, which are historically rare south of the Sahara and which are creating division, chaos, and violence in both East and West Africa. Islamists in Kenya are pushing to expand Islamic law, or *shari'a*, to include sentences of amputation in certain crimes, as well as stoning in cases of adultery, practices already in place in Nigeria. The chairman of Kenya's Council of Imams and Preachers, Ali Shee, has warned that Muslims in the coastal and northeastern provinces will break away if *shari'a* is not expanded. Tanzania is experiencing a similar push for Islamic law.[15]

All these forces—a large number of weak and failing states, porous borders, widespread poverty, political frustration, religious radicalism, and repression—combine to create an environment in which the kind of alienation and radicalism that can foster both domestic and international terrorism thrives. The war on terrorism waged since the September 11 attacks has brought the implications of such conditions for global terrorism to the attention of Western policymakers. Former Clinton administration assistant secretary of state for Africa Susan Rice testified before the US Congress in November 2001 that "Africa is unfortunately the world's soft underbelly for global terrorism."[16]

How to toughen the African state remains problematic, particularly given the poor record of aid delivery on the continent and the resistance of Africans to external conditionalities. The fact that the weak nature of the African state and the corruptibility of the African political class have over time made the continent a soft target for all kinds of terrorist groups is further complicated in an environment where wars of liberation have left a certain residue of ambiguity about the distinction between terrorists and freedom fighters and a latent hostility toward the West over colonial and postcolonial policies. Whatever the debates about the links among weak states, poverty, and terrorism, can the policies of the Western and African states intersect to fight both local and global terrorism?

Prospects for Cooperation against Terrorism

What Has Africa Contributed to the War on Terrorism?

African countries were quick to condemn the September 11 terrorist attacks. South African President Thabo Mbeki said at the time, "The South African government unreservedly denounces these senseless and horrific terrorist attacks and joins the world in denouncing these dastardly acts."[17] Others from Sudan's Omar el-Bashir to Nigeria's Olusegun Obasanjo and even Robert Mugabe in Zimbabwe were also quick to offer their cooperation to combat global terrorism.

Nevertheless, rhetoric has not matched reality. Some initial, token measures were certainly taken immediately. Pretoria quickly forwarded a list of the names of individuals with possible links to the September 11 suspects. Earlier, in June 2001 the extradition and mutual legal assistance treaty between South Africa and the United States signed in 1999 had come into force, signaling closer legal and criminal cooperation. Elsewhere, the Algerian government immediately forwarded two lists to US authorities: one with the names of 350 suspected Islamic militants linked to al Qaeda and another with 1,000 known Algerian terrorists active in the West.

The reality of African actions in cracking down on terrorism has not entirely matched this early promise. Of 53 North and sub-Saharan African countries, only seven—Egypt, Eritrea, Kenya, Djibouti, Uganda, Morocco, and Ethiopia—have joined the global war on terrorism; and as of April 2004, only five—Botswana, Ghana, Kenya, Mali, and Sudan—had signed all 12 international conventions and protocols relating to terrorism.[18] After the 1998 bombings of the US embassies in Kenya and Tanzania, African states adopted the African Convention on Terrorism, but the signing and ratification process has been slow. African countries apparently lack resources as well as political will in dealing with external terrorism, reflecting alternative priorities.

It is critical to understand that African leaders are primarily concerned about fighting local terrorists, whereas Westerners are often more concerned with those terrorists who threaten Western interests and happen to operate in Africa. These positions are not necessarily contradictory, but they produce nuances that must be understood in the context of African domestic priorities.

On a visit to the United States in November 2001, Algerian president Abdelaziz Bouteflika remarked, "Terrorism is one and indivisible. If we are going to combat terrorism, we must do it together."[19] Although this statement may be diplomatically expedient, any strategy to deal with terrorism in Africa should distinguish between local terrorism and the kind carried out through international links, between the terrorism and coercion of a civilian population carried out by local armies or militias and the operations of movements such as al Qaeda. Although strengthening and extending local state authority and improving governance should contribute to dealing with local and external forms of terrorism, any approach must recognize the danger that the pretext of counterterrorism could subvert domestic democracy.

Wanted: State Support

In the short term, military action informed by sophisticated analysis of the domestic situation is pivotal. The US military has already targeted key African countries to provide austere camps or airfields for US troops, currently stationed in Europe, to rotate more frequently into the African continent. Such antiterrorism-based "lily pads" would enable US troops to deploy readily and quickly into African trouble spots where US interests are threatened.

Yet cooperation must go beyond military measures and extend to intelligence gathering and information collection as well as management, training, and networking with African militaries. Appropriate national legislation will also need to be drawn up and coordinated, both between African states themselves and in their relationship with key external partners such as the United States. The creation of the African Union initiative—the African Institute for the Study and Research on Terrorism—is a step in this direction. Established in Algiers in September 2002, the institute aims to "centralize information, studies, and analyses on terrorism and terrorist groups and develop training programs by organizing, with the assistance of international partners, training schedules, meetings, and symposia."[20]

Ultimately, a truly effective campaign against the domestic sources of terrorism in Africa requires enhancing the ability of African states to wield authoritative force—the very defining characteristic of the state. Fighting terrorism in Africa thus demands not only the capacity of the West to mount the occasional spectacular raid but also to manage the much more mundane task of rebuilding the police forces in African countries. African leaders are much more concerned about this issue than they are about the deployment of US special operations units on their territory.

Most African police forces are in dismal shape: they lack funding, have large cadres of untrained personnel, rely on outdated methods, are tasked with repression, and are intent on extortion rather than detection. Yet local police are critical in the fight against terrorism, both to collect intelligence to prevent attacks and, if attacks do occur, as first responders. Western agencies have shied away from helping Africa's police forces because of their poor human rights records. Indeed, African statistical agencies, central banks, and trade ministries have often received far more Western assistance than local law enforcement agencies have, even though many of these agencies would be unable to function without police security protection against terrorist acts.

More generally, the West finally will have to come to grips with the profound domestic and unique security threats that many African countries face. Africa's internal forms of terrorism require foreign engagement that builds the security forces of the state as the most effective responses to the problem of weak states in a time of global terrorism. Until peace in Africa can be secured and local government authority strengthened, global efforts to deal with terrorist networks will continue to toil.

To avoid empowering states that might abuse their power to govern or to wield force, not just any capacity should be built; to rid the continent of the kinds of conditions that breed the societal alienation and radicalism that give rise to terrorism in the long term, democracy and civil society must be promoted in Africa. It is astonishing how quickly and with how comparatively little fanfare African states have embraced multiparty democracy as the only acceptable form of government over the last decade. More than 40 African countries regularly hold multiparty elections, although less than half this number has passed the ultimate test of democracy: a peaceful change in government through the polls. Indeed, Africa needs further democratization, a goal fully endorsed by the African polity but one that will meet with greater resistance from those elites who are either not elected or elected in contests that are obviously not fully free and fair.

Historically, Western governments have limited their military assistance to African states to peacekeeping efforts. European nongovernmental organizations, which increasingly dictate that continent's foreign policy toward Africa, approach every war with the assumption that the only solution is conflict resolution. Fighting terrorists, however, should not exclude the same military logic used by the West when fighting terrorists who threaten Western interests. Bush's $100 million commitment made in 2003 to fight terrorism in Africa has to be backed up by a commitment to building state capacity, including the continent's militaries and police forces.

Thus, Bush's East Africa Counter-Terrorism Initiative has dedicated resources to improve police and judicial counterterrorist capabilities in Kenya, Uganda, Tanzania, Djibouti, Eritrea, and Ethiopia. This program provides training and some equipment for counterterrorism units, as well as support for senior-level African decision makers and legislators concerned with drafting legislation on terrorist financing and money laundering. Similarly, the aim of Washington's $7 million Sahel initiative is to assist Mali, Mauritania, Chad, and Niger "in protecting their borders, combating terrorism, and enhancing regional stability" and to "encourage the participating countries to cooperate with each other against smuggling and trafficking in persons, as well as in the sharing of information."[21] The form of such assistance will be crucial in determining its success at creating local capacity. The use of embedded foreign support of local police forces, militaries, and bureaucracies may offer a sustainable, more effective, and less expensive option for long-term capacity building.[22]

There are, moreover, dangers that such security measures may, at least in the short term, exacerbate the conditions that give rise to external and internal terrorism in the first place. For example, the welfare of thousands of Somali families has been affected by the United States' November 2001 decision to freeze the assets of Somalia's largest financial company, al-Barakaat, because of its alleged association with al Qaeda through links with the local Islamic movement, Al-Ittihad al-Islamiya. Given the Somalis' dependence on remittances from the Somalia Diaspora, the measure has proved to be hugely damaging to Somali families and the image of the United States alike.[23] The danger also exists that certain US-led initiatives, such as the container security initiative inspection scheme[24] constitute a major and highly intrusive intervention into the way states run their affairs. Such measures may provide an incentive for African leaders to improve governance conditions but could also fuel anti-American and anti-Western sentiment in the process.

In the longer term, however, dealing with terrorism in Africa requires fundamentally changing the conditions of lawlessness and alienation that empower leaders to terrorize their own citizens and enable movements such as al Qaeda to acquire a substantial following. The United States will find Africa a somewhat receptive partner to demands for changes in fundamental conditions. NEPAD's focus is in accord with efforts to address the roots of terrorism. African countries will also be happy to accept the additional foreign aid that the Bush administration has promised in the proposal. The administration's aforementioned $5 billion increase in annual aid through the 2002 MCA program and the $15 billion initiative to fight AIDS—potentially the greatest, future single source of state collapse and lawlessness in Africa—is a first step in the right direction.

Finally, the promotion of democratic values and state capacity should go hand in hand with a diplomatic strategy to reach out to Africa's Muslim communities and negate the stereotyping prevalent, particularly the perception that Islam is a force only for militancy. Islam is far from a monolithic religious force throughout the continent. Rather, distinct Islamic practices characterize Africa's various regions, reflecting their historical traditions and origins. Radical Islam may have minimal resonance in Africa, but its continued moderation will require a need to enhance enduring traditions of tolerance among the continent's religious communities to avoid division and radicalization through outside influence, including that of Saudi-sponsored mosques encouraging a more extreme Wahhabi interpretation of Islam in Nigeria and South Africa. With around 70 million Muslims and fed by outside influences along with local ethnic and regional rivalries, relations between these communities in Nigeria in particular remain fragile. There have been several localized outbursts of internecine violence in northern Nigeria, including the attempts to stop the November 2002 Miss World pageant.

Whatever their differences in emphasis, the United States has found Africa a somewhat receptive partner to demands for changes in fundamental conditions that give rise to domestic terrorism sources and allow external forms of terrorism to take root. The events of September 11 have led to greater engagement on the problems of African development and the related challenges of Western engagement. For all of the problems of poverty, violence, and corruption in African countries, the importance of the policy reforms and achievements that have been made on the continent should not be understated.

Post-9/11 Prospects for State Building

Although African responses toward US policies in the war on terrorism (including the US decision to go to war in Iraq) have been mixed and African and Western leaders maintain disparate priorities when it comes to combating terrorism, the September 11 terrorist attacks and the emergence of the global war on terrorism initially brought unprecedented international attention to Africa's problems that seemed bound to prove beneficial to the continent.

Subsequently, the US-led war in Iraq has threatened to remove Africa and especially NEPAD, its homegrown governance and development plan, from the international spotlight and the assistance its challenges require. Events in Iraq and the war on terrorism elsewhere around the globe have highlighted the importance of not allowing African states to collapse. Thus, continued and expanded access to global markets through initiatives such as the US AGOA has improved the prospects for African development and stability, though questions still remain about the economic sustainability of preferential market access. Despite the schizophrenic nature of Western responses to Africa's development needs—vacillating between protectionism through domestic subsidies and greater access to trade and more aid— there has arguably been much more generous and proactive engagement by the Bush administration than by any of its predecessors, the Clinton administration included. Clearly, the September 11 attacks also reshaped the administration's view of Africa's strategic value.

Overall, Washington's hunger for allies and its recognition of the need for African stability, in light of the potential for the wider spillover of transnational terrorism generated in Africa, has created a unique opportunity for African states to use the new attention to and comprehension of Africa's strategic importance to increase assistance and help realize NEPAD's ambitious goals of enabling Africa's stability, prosperity, and renaissance.

Notes

1.   Jeremy Michaels, "Al-Qaeda Ring Bust in SA," *Star* (Johannesburg), May 27, 2004,
        http://www.thestar.co.za/index.php?fSectionId=129&fArticleId=2091054. The site
        was accessed on July 8, 2004.
2.   Adam Lusekelo, "Africa's War on Terror Targets Poverty," *BBC News*, February 27,
        2003, http://news.bbc.co.uk/1/hi/business/2797405.stm. The site was accessed on July
        8, 2004.
3.   Kristina Nwazota, "President Bush to Visit Five African Nations," *Online NewsHour*,
        July 2, 2003, http://www.pbs.org/newshour/extra/features/july-dec03/africa_7-2_
        printout.html. The site was accessed on July 8, 2004.
4.   For the full text, see http://www.whitehouse.gov/nsc/nss.html. The site was accessed
        July 8, 2004.
5.   Eric Schmitt, "US Military Wants to Increase Its Presence in Africa," *Sydney Morning
        Herald*, July 7, 2003, http://www.smh.com.au/articles/2003/07/06/1057430078697.
        html. The site was accessed on July 8, 2004.
6.   Ian Forbes, "Transformation towards Future Warfighting," *RUSI Journal* (October
        2003): 56.
7.   Office of the Press Secretary, The White House, "President Discusses AIDS
        Initiative, Iraq in Botswana," July 10, 2003, http://www.whitehouse.gov/news/
        releases/2003/07/20030710-3.html. The site was accessed on July 8, 2004.
8.   Nwazota, "President Bush to Visit Five African Nations."
9.   Susan Ellis, "Bush Says Peoples of Africa Will Build Their Own Future of Hope,"
        July 14, 2003, http://usinfo.state.gov/regional/af/potus2003/a3071201.htm. The site
        was accessed on July 8, 2004.
10.   Joshua Forrest, "State Inversion and Non-State Politics," in *The African State at a
        Critical Juncture*, eds. Leonardo Villalon and Phillip Huxtable (Boulder, CO: Lynne
        Reinner, 1998), p. 45. See also John Mackinlay, "Globalisation and Insurgency,"
        Adelphi Paper, no. 352 (London: International Institute for Strategic Studies [IISS]
        and Oxford University Press, 2002), p. 109.
11.   Jeffrey Herbst, *States and Power in Africa* (Princeton: Princeton University Press,
        2000), pp. 252–253.
12.   Ken Menkhaus, "Somalia: State Collapse and the Threat of Terrorism," *Adelphi Paper*,
        no. 364 (London: IISS and Oxford University Press, 2003), pp. 72–75.
13.   Ibid.
14.   For an analysis of the influence of Islam on Africa, see "Africa: Islamist Terrorism
        Thrives on Weak States," *Oxford Analytica Daily Brief Services*, January 15, 2004,
        http://www.oxan.com/db/item.asp?NewsItemID=DB97142. The site was accessed on
        July 9, 2004.
15.   Paul Marshall, "Radical Islam's Move on Africa," *Washington Post*, October 16, 2003,
        p. A25.
16.   House Committee on International Relations, *Africa and the War on Global Terrorism:
        Hearing before the Subcommittee on Africa of the Committee on International
        Relations*, 107th Cong., 1st session, 2001, http://commdocs.house.gov/committees/
        intlrel/hfa76191.000/hfa76191_0f.htm. The site was accessed on July 8, 2004
        (testimony of Susan Rice).
17.   "Africans Condemn September 11 Terrorist Attacks on the United States," September
        20, 2001, http://www.usembassy.it/file2001_09/alia/a1092028.htm. The site was
        accessed on July 5, 2004.
18.   US Department of State, *Patterns of Global Terrorism 2003*, April 29, 2004, http://
        www.globalsecurity.org/security/library/report/2004/pgt_2003/pgt_2003_31578pf.
        htm. The site was accessed on July 8, 2004. (hereinafter "Africa Overview").
19.   Ofeibea Quist-Arcton, "Algerian President Says Terrorism Must Be Fought
        Equally   Worldwide"   *AllAfrica.com*,   November   5,   2001,   http://allafrica.com/

stories/200111050631.html. The site was accessed on July 8, 2004.
20. See "Plan of Action of the African Union High-Level Inter-Governmental Meeting on the Prevention and Combating of Terrorism in Africa," Algiers, September 11–14, 2002, p. 10, http://www.iss.co.za/AF/RegOrg/unity_to_union/pdfs/oau/keydocs/PoAfinal.pdf. The site was accessed on July 8, 2004.
21. "Africa Overview." See also "Out of Africa," *Air Force Link*, http://www.af.mil/photos/story_photos.asp?storyID=123007344. The site was accessed July 8, 2004.
22. See David Richards, "Sierra Leone: Pregnant with Lessons," in *Global Challenges and Africa*, eds. Richard Cobbold and Greg Mills (London: Royal United Services Institute for Defense and Security Studies, 2004).
23. Rakiya Omaar, "Peace-Building and Democracy: The Lessons of Somalia and Somaliland," in *Global Challenges and Africa*, eds. Richard Cobbold and Greg Mills (London: Royal United Services Institute for Defense and Security Studies, 2004).
24. "US Expands Container Security Initiative to South Africa," December 2, 2003, http://hongkong.usconsulate.gov/csi/2003/120201.htm. The site was accessed on July 6, 2004.

PART 2
The Combined Joint Task Force and the War on Terror

Chapter 2

Djibouti's Pre-Eminent Role in the War on Terror

John Davis and Andrew Othieno

Everything is moving everywhere. There is not going to be a place in the world where it is going to be the same as it used to be. We are going to rationalize our posture everywhere.

Douglas Feith, Under Secretary of Defense, for George W. Bush

Introduction

On 11 September 2001 the US, and indeed the world at large, was dealt an unexpected blow by radical fanatics whom the Western world (and those who subscribe to the same view) consider nothing more than evil murderers and desperate ideologues. Given what one would consider to be a reasonable definition for terrorism, that is, "premeditated politically motivated violence perpetrated against non-combatant targets usually intended to influence an audience"[1] the logical conclusion is that these were voiceless individuals who knew no better way of gaining attention to address their concerns.

The World Trade Center (WTC) bombing of the 1993 and the Oklahoma bombing that followed some years later had already brought the United States of America within the circle of vulnerable states. The Middle East, Europe, Asia, and Latin America had previously witnessed a wave of terrorist attacks. The attacks of 11 September and the ripple effects that spread globally made it clear that even the US is no longer a safe zone. Africa, potentially the most vulnerable part of the globe, had not been a victim of the mayhem, fierce destruction and volatile terrorism, until the attacks in August of 1998 that destroyed the US embassies in Kenya and Tanzania. Although political violence was prevalent in the northern part of the continent, much of Africa had not generally been associated with terrorism on such a scale other than the experiences of countries like Uganda (northern Uganda) and Rwanda (the 1994 genocide).

Since the attacks on US embassies in East Africa, combating international terrorism in Africa has become a major objective of the United States. Strong statements have been in made in the past. President Clinton stipulated in 1998 that: "The US is in a long ongoing struggle between freedom and fanaticism, between the rule of law and terrorism."[2] In a recent expression, in 2001 President George Bush expressed similar sentiments when he told the UN General Assembly that terrorism is at the top of the US agenda, and should be at the top of the world agenda. He echoed his predecessor by stating that: "This is a different kind of war that requires a different type of approach and a different type of mentality."[3]

African countries overwhelmingly expressed their support for the US-led efforts in the war against terrorism. Even the leader of Sudan's National Islamic Front (NIF) government, President Omar el-Bashir, who once "provided a safe haven to Osama bin Laden between 1991 and 1996, condemned the terrorist attacks."[4] President Yoweri Museveni of Uganda reaffirmed that governments' condemnation of terrorism but, seeing it from a different perspective, was quick to point out that it was US reluctance that created bin Laden. For the past twelve years there has been terrorist activity in northern Uganda. The country had initially sought assistance in confronting terror but the international community remained indifferent to requests by Uganda. However, events circa 11 September 2001 altered the political landscape. In the words President Museveni "The people who have been terrorizing us have now woken up the big guys!"

In the wake of the attacks Africa, consistent with the world at large, empathized and rallied behind the United States. With respect to the administration's response, President Bush fell short of swearing an outright oath to the American people that the perpetrators would be found and brought to justice.

Currently the war on terrorism has taken many drastic and rather interesting turns for those who have been keen observers. What was initially a war cry for support from all corners of the globe has now been labeled the 'so-called' war against terrorism by several contrasting schools of thought. Dozens of theories have been spun about the real intentions of the Bush administrations, the most prominent involving the increasing capacity of national resources (oil) among a number of select states. The states within Africa have gained validity because the US military footprint has been extended to some of the most unexpected parts of the world.

For the purposes of this essay, one important theme, which has gained prominence but still remains overshadowed, only to be found by those who have delved deep enough with a quest to thoroughly understand the war on terrorism, is "Africa and its role" in this conflict. Although America's national security and Africa in the same sentence has historically been consistent with the Cold War association, the war on terrorism may be a replay of that relationship. This new partnership emerged after the Bush administration's decision to establish a military base in Djibouti, a small and little known country in the Horn of Africa, which is also a crucial transit point between the Red Sea and the Gulf of Aden, mere miles across the water from the Arabian Peninsula.[5] The establishment of this base represents a dramatic shift for US security policy in Africa since the closure many years ago of the Wheelus Air Force Base in Libya and Kagnew communications station in Ethiopia.[6]

Considering the plethora of weak and failed states in Africa, their vulnerability, and their susceptibility to terrorist infiltration, the Bush administration has recognized the continent's importance to the war on terrorism. As this study will attempt to explain in some detail, state instability on the African continent has been elevated to a high priority. Their strategic importance, and that of the continent as a whole, cannot be ignored. Bush administration officials and leaders around the world have come to understand that Africa is a potential breeding ground for terrorists. In recent years Africa has emerged as an important staging area, offering training facilities and a location from which to target US interests. As previously mentioned, this was clearly illustrated by the US embassy bombings in Kenya and Tanzania on 7 August 1998. Consequently, US officials are closely monitoring countries vulnerable to terrorist penetration and influence as well as countries that are sympathetic to terrorist organizations.[7]

The fact that the partnership between selected African states and the United States has slowly gained traction, especially with regard to Djibouti (which would have initially been considered to be of no significance at all to US interests) indicates a transformation of US national security policy. Creating a launching pad designed to project power in and around that specific geographic area has long-term consequences for Djibouti and the Middle East, to which the US now has easy access via this route. The trends of the war, and the countries that immediately surround the Horn, including Sudan, Somalia, the Great Lakes, and the Sub-Saharan African region as a whole, are all indications of the growing significance of Djibouti to preventing or combating terrorism. Indeed, it has now become clear that Washington views the Horn of Africa as al Qaeda's second theater of operation after Central Asia.[8]

The object of this study is to examine the following: the importance of Djibouti to terrorists pre- and post-11 September; the establishment of the Combined Joint Task Force within this country and its principal function to illustrate the economic benefits that have accrued to Djibouti since the time of its classification as a "frontline state" in the war on terror; and finally to explore the means by which the US-Djibouti partnership may be sustained.

The Importance of Djibouti to Terrorists in the Past

Djibouti, like Kenya, Eritrea, and other countries within the region, remain targets of terrorism. The largely unsecured borders of each country provide easy access that permits terror groups to establish a platform to conduct terrorist activities. As reported by experts, "Djibouti's importance to terrorists derives from its transit capabilities rather than its potential as a base for international terrorist organizations."[9]

Accessing the activities and the organizations that utilize Djibouti remains a difficult process for a number of reasons. First, many of these terror groups such as al Qaeda and along with a host of Palestinian terrorist organizations, used Djibouti as one of several African transit points (another being Sudan) to carry out terrorist related activities against Western interests throughout Africa. These groups rarely stay long and retain a low profile. Second, throughout the 1990s, the height of terror activities in the region, numerous terror groups (such as Al Qaeda, Hezbollah, Islamic Group, and the Palestinian Islamic Jihad, to name a few) transited through Djibouti en route to Sudan to attend a plethora of conferences on terrorism that were sponsored by Khartoum during the 1990s. Third, few if any terrorist activity occurred within the tiny country; rather, its location enhanced the logistics capabilities of al Qaeda and its affiliates. Fourth, beginning in 1999, regional realities have increased Djibouti's attractiveness to foreign terrorist activity. Additionally, according to Deborah West, well into the year 2001, Djibouti remained "a thoroughfare for terrorists for any incidents to be staged there"[10] and later implemented in places within East Africa and elsewhere. Finally, a major dilemma confronting Djibouti and which may enhance terror within the country is found in the following quote:

> The groundwork to support such groups has expanded: in the last five years a new Islamic Center has been opened, supported by Saudi Arabia; reportedly, the number of mosques has grown from approximately 35 to over 100, financed and often staffed from outside Djibouti. The young cleric in the most important mosque in Djibouti City reportedly was trained at the Cairo theological Center known for its radical Islamist doctrine. Economic links to individuals in the United Arab Emirates (U.A.E.) and Somalia are close as are communal links to families in Yemen.[11]

In the final analysis the potential for an indigenous Islamic movement may yet prove threatening to Djibouti's efforts of democratic governance. Equally significant, it is unknown how many terror cells have developed as a result of the radical mosque. Nonetheless, this remains a real dilemma but one in which the government in Djibouti and Western states as well as regional intelligence networks have been monitoring.

Have Things Changed? Response to New Realities

In the wake of the events circa 11 September, Djibouti has a strong interest in preventing terrorism, primarily because its economy is entirely service-based and dependent on the foreign use of its port.[12] The government of Djibouti has taken considerable strides in recent years to combat terrorism, including an aggressive immigration campaign to remove illegal aliens from Djibouti.[13] Second, in recognition of post-11 September realities the government of Djibouti signed three international conventions and protocols relating to terrorism. Third, they signed the Convention for the Suppression of the Financing of Terrorism on 15 November 2001. Fourth, President Guelleh closed down terrorist-linked financial institutions and shared security information on possible terrorist activity in the region.[14] Consistent with this move, the counterterrorism committee established under President Guelleh moved to enhance coordination and action on information concerning terrorist organizations (and those transiting through the country).[15]

Djibouti's counterterrorist efforts are very much in keeping with the multilateralism that is associated with the global war on terrorism. A statement by Defense Secretary Donald Rumsfeld is instructive. The war on terrorism "absolutely requires the cooperation of countries of all sizes on each continent on the face of the earth, if we're going to be successful in tracking, finding, and dealing with terror cells."[16] The secretary made these remarks during a 9 December DOD news briefing while en route to Eritrea on the first leg of a trip to the Horn of Africa that included stops in Ethiopia and Djibouti.[17]

In response to and acceptance of the new realities, Djibouti is now subject to attacks from al Qaeda or its affiliated groups from Yemen or those groups that operate in Sudan and Somalia. Possible terrorist threats include attacks on US (and French) personnel and facilities and disruption of the port and the Addis-Djibouti rail link, which would damage Djibouti's major economic asset and thereby impact regional transportation. Another potential target involves the return of disaffected opposition groups, the goal of which would be to cause instability forcing coalition troops to exit the country. Lastly, another possible soft target may involve a major attack on Inter Governmental Authority on Development (IGAD) headquarters, which is a symbol of regional cooperation and supported by Western donors, including the US.[18] Either way the increasing Western footprint in Djibouti poses short and long-term threats to the country.

Djibouti and the Combined Joint Task Force

The relationship between Djibouti and the United States is by no means a new one. Indeed, beginning with assistance to the George H.W. Bush administration during the first Gulf War, and providing subsequent assistance to the same administration during the United Nations Operation in Somalia (UNOSOM), and similar support to the administration of Bill Clinton during the Unified Task Force in Somalia (UNITAF), the two countries have had cordial relations throughout this period.[19] The problem with the relationship is that the benefits during theses periods largely accrued to the United States and the relationship was one that fulfilled the strategic objectives of the superpower, rather than one that concerned itself Djibouti's national interests.

The US has since established the Combined Joint Task Force in Horn of Africa (hereafter referred to as CJTF-HOA) at Camp Lemonier in Djibouti. This project started in October 2002, with the expectation that this facility would serve primarily as a staging area for conducting raids on al Qaeda targets in the region, particularly Somalia. Another US intention concerned obtaining the strategic presence in the region to assist in intelligence collection to forestall future terrorist attacks.[20] Finally, the American military presence in Djibouti offers the US the capability for rapid deployment against terrorist targets in Somalia and Yemen.

Following the terrorist attacks in New York and Washington, in September of 2001 the US sought friends in the Horn of Africa. Upon receiving wind of news that US Special Operations Forces (SOFs) had been sighted in Djibouti, the media pressed for information. Considering the importance of the project, which at that time was in its infancy, the media was fed disinformation. By the middle 2002, the US base in the former French colony just miles across the Red Sea from Yemen and within striking distance of Iraq was no longer a secret. The Pentagon acknowledged that it has sent 800 SOFs to the new base with nothing being said about the 1,500 Marines training at Obock, 30 miles north of Djibouti across the Gulf of Tadjoura. Djibouti officials also denied that their country would serve as a base for any action in the Middle East. President Guelleh told the *Associated Press*: "If we give some facilities to our friends, Americans or French, to use our climate conditions for conditioning their troops, that doesn't mean it's for a specific operation. This is normal bilateral relations with those superpowers."[u] By the end of the year the Pentagon claimed that no operation had been launched but it was obvious, given the military training exercises that were taking place, that American influence over government forces in Ethiopia, Eritrea, Kenya, and Yemen was increasing.[22]

By the middle of 2003 the US base had grown steadily and even established a semblance of permanence. On 7 April 2004, in a speech (pertaining to the war on terrorism and its implications for Africa) at the Howard University's Ralph Bunche International Affairs Center, H.E. Roble Olhaye, the Djibouti Ambassador to the United States, acknowledged that his country "serves as the only US military base in Africa, with ground and naval forces positioned."[23] Additionally, Olhaye asserted that

> The US together with other forces stationed in Djibouti, namely; French, German, and Spanish, have established in Djibouti the military headquarters [that are] responsible for northeast Africa and Yemen, and covers land and airspace areas of Kenya, Djibouti, Ethiopia, Somalia, Eritrea, Sudan and Yemen, including the coastal waters of the Red Sea, Gulf of Aden and Indian Ocean.[w]

Given the strategic location and the military hub, it is now clear the CJTF-HOA's central mission is to deter, pre-empt, and disable terrorist threats emanating from within and around that region.

The base in Djibouti may serve another salient operational purpose: intervention. In September of 2002, for example, the international press speculated the US, utilizing forces stationed in Djibouti, was preparing to launch a mission to target al Qaeda forces and elements of a well known affiliate, al Abyan, in the lawless region of Hardramawt in Yemen.[24] The type of naval vessels and other significant US military activity in the region supplemented the increasing conjecture of an impending attack. A few examples are instructive. The first example involved the presence and continuous military preparations aboard the *USS Belleau Wood,* a Marine amphibious assault ship that began to patrol just off the coast of Yemen. The second measure of speculation developed over the activity surrounding the *USS Mount Whitney*, which serves as the nerve centre of the Central Command's (CENTCOM's) counterterrorist operations in the HOA. The movements of Army and Marine units in Djibouti only increased anxieties. The latter activities and speculation forced a denial on the part of the government of Djibouti.[25] Interestingly, as the Bush administration was poised to launch a special forces-led attack into Yemen, the mission was halted not from objections from the government in Djibouti but rather from the government in Yemen which had not authorized or sanctioned such a campaign.[26] Though no military mission commenced what is clear is that no US counterterror response will be initiated without the use of the base in Djibouti.

Economic Gains Made by American Presence

Initially, the tangible benefits for the stationing of US and other coalition troops in the tiny African country were relatively small until the US formally responded to the words of President Guelleh, who stated "it is normal that we should get something"[27] in return for the use of Camp Lemonier military facility. Following extensive negotiations in 2003 the Bush administration agreed to pay $31 million per year for stationing its forces in Djibouti (the French agreed to pay $34 million per year).[28]

For Djibouti, a sleepy Muslim country that normally subsists on port fees, base rentals, and foreign aid, the whole burgeoning military presence promotes business within the country and has certainly enhanced Djibouti's stature throughout Africa. In total Djibouti receives more financial benefits from the war on terror than any other country in Africa. A few examples are instructive. The CJTF-HOA public works project called for the expenditure of US$2 million. Some thirty-eight projects have been completed; these projects range from the renovation of thirteen schools, the completion of six water and well projects, and the completion of numerous medical clinic projects. Specific examples exhibited are a well in the Djiboutian village of Andangalina. Another project involved the construction of a school dormitory in Tadjourah, Djibouti's.

Second, in an effort to spread the word on efforts to ensure a balanced bilateral relationship, the US Embassy in Djibouti released the following data to support US claims of a reciprocal relationship: in 2004 USAID budgeted more than $20 million in direct assistance for Djibouti. The distribution of the funds is as follows:

12 million has been dedicated to the health sector to increase access to equitable health care and improve quality of care to support reductions in infant, child and maternal mortality. This takes the form of training programs for medical professionals and education programs through the Ministry of Health.

$8 million has been dedicated to the education sector to assist the Ministry of Education in implementing education reform program, increase access to basic education, improve quality of teaching and learning, increase opportunities for girls' education and develop a strategy for sustainable employment for school graduates. This academic year USAID donated 40,000 school kits to Djibouti, providing supplies for every child enrolled in Djiboutian schools. USAID also works closely with the U.S. military to identify school renovation projects in Djibouti.

$0.4 million for an IFESH (International Foundation for Education and Self-Help) Teachers for Africa Program. IFESH is a non-profit program based on the premise that in order for emerging democracies to be sustained in Africa and for law and order to be upheld, a country's citizens must be literate and capable of making informed choices.[29]

In addition to the above, former secretary of state Colin Powell orchestrated efforts that have produced supplemental assistance in the form of two regional projects totaling $5 million. The first project called for the establishment of the Famine Early Warning System Network (FEWSNET) office in Djibouti. The second program required spending $4 million to develop a livestock holding and export facility in Djibouti. This private-sector livestock program assists in the export of livestock from Djibouti to the Gulf and Middle East. Finally, the injection of financial assistance enables Djibouti to pursue the war on terrorism with greater veracity and resources.[30] Equally significant, the burgeoning economic partnership "enables Djibouti to undertake infrastructure and social programs essential to its medium and long-term survival."[31] Viewed collectively, the Bush administration has made a genuine attempt to "to win the hearts and minds" of the people of Djibouti. The result of US efforts and President Guelleh's leadership have worked to transform the country's economy. Though much has been accomplished, a far greater infusion of economic assistance is required to end the poverty in Djibouti.

Sustaining and Solidifying the Partnership

In order to sustain and solidify the US-Djibouti partnership, the Bush administration (and subsequent US administrations) will have to overcome several significant obstacles that impact all "frontline" African states in the war on terror. The obstacles include the following: sharing of intelligence, more training in anti-terrorism and counterterrorism, self sufficiency for the government of Djibouti, and mechanisms to ensure the relationship exists long past the conclusion of the war on terror.

The issue of intelligence sharing is critical to the government of Djibouti. With the Camp Lemonier base serving as a major intelligence weigh station, the Guelleh government remains concerned that intelligence collection may lead to missions against its neighbors (Somalia or Yemen) that may be launched without its approval. Thus direct involvement provides more control over US military forces, a point of great emphasis since Djibouti does not wish to find itself in conflict which it has no direct influence over the decisions to engage a potential enemy. From another perspective, the regional states comprising the CJTF-HOA share intelligence on terror groups. However, intelligence gathered by the US (and other coalition forces stationed) in Djibouti is not always provided to the host government. This is a trend the host government is attempting to reverse. Second, while the Bush administration has launched the East Africa Counterterrorism Initiative (EACTI), a program dedicated to "improving police and judicial counterterrorist capabilities in the East African countries of Kenya, Uganda, Tanzania, Djibouti, Eritrea, and Ethiopia" as well as providing "training and some equipment for special counterterrorism units for senior-level decision makers,"[32] the efforts to assist Djibouti in this venue (counterterrorism) still require more attention from the Bush administration. In particular, to secure soft targets, a larger police and military force is needed. This will eliminate terrorist financing (a minor problem currently) and money laundering. Though the US participates in a number of counterterrorist and anti-terror operations within Djibouti, Central Command (CENTCOM) concedes that at some point the government of Djibouti must become self-sustaining. Additionally, increasing the country's military forces will assist in the securing of Djibouti's porous borders. On the third point, to ensure that Djibouti is not left twisting in the wind if and when the war on terror concludes that process must begin now. That is, if and when the government of Djibouti positions itself to protect its own borders and is able to handle all forms of anti-terrorist and counterterrorist activity, the need for foreign reliance will dissipate. It is during this period that will dictate when all foreign troops may leave the country, or put another way, the host country will be in a greater position to determine the parameters of the strategic partnership. The US military is prepared for these realities. As Marine Colonel Ed Holst told a reporter in Djibouti, "The population needs to see that it is not just Americans but see their own government doing something."[33] In this case "something" is a reference to preparing the country for self-sufficiency, thereby cutting the umbilical cord to the West.

Finally, one of the great disappointments for countries that form partnerships with the US during international crises is that once the incident, war or crisis concludes, the Untied States is too quick to terminate relationships with partners or allies. This was true with the US in Pakistan when the Carter, Reagan and eventually, the first Bush administration, used Pakistan as a base of operations until the Soviets withdrew from Afghanistan; thereafter the US concluded the relationship leaving the Pakistani government to confront the increasing presence of radical Islam, dealing with the power vacuum in Afghanistan, and bin Laden's access and eventual influence over the ISI, Pakistan's intelligence services. Djibouti is well acquainted with this US attitude, having experienced this behavior during the senior Bush administration following the conclusion of the Operation Desert Storm, Operation Provide Hope and following the Clinton administration's debacle in Mogadishu, Somalia in 1993. Long-term sustainability of the US-Djibouti relationship is critical in a country that borders Somalia.[34] This point is all the more important in an environment where Islamists have seized control of the capital of the country, which endangers not only the stability elsewhere in Somalia, but threatens stability elsewhere in the Horn. Action is needed to prevent the establishment of an enclave of terrorist activity in a country whose Islamic practices are far more conservative than those in other countries. That action came in the form of military intervention by Ethiopia, which defeated and then forced the dispersal of the Union of Islamic Courts (UIC) and al Qaeda operatives that had received safe haven in southern Somalia.

Conclusion

In this chapter the authors have endeavored to illustrate the evolution of Djibouti's role as a major player in the war on terror. There are three striking aspects of the country's function as a frontline state in the war on terror. The first concerns the ability of this tiny African state to assume a role of such prominence. Second, we often forget that this is a role the government of Djibouti lobbied for and received. Third, once the negotiations concluded on the terms of usage of its military facilities—and the attendant status of forces agreement—the government of Djibouti reaped substantial political and financial benefits and, of equal significance, this once-obscure entity is now the envy of the continent.

Fourth, not only has Djibouti benefited politically from the relationship, it is continuing to receive other financial benefits to include investment that assists in the diversification of its economy; considerable direct aid on the part of the US government for needed infrastructure improvements; and lastly, that the government receives more financial assistance than any other member of the combined joint task force.

Fifth, Bush and Guelleh have worked to sustain the relationship. Equally important, in the case of Djibouti, Guelleh is working to ensure reciprocal benefits for his country. With respect to the long-term assessment of the relationship, the government of Djibouti is working overtime to preclude the replication of previous efforts. In short, Guelleh is determined that what occurred after the senior Bush and Clinton administrations is not repeated, namely that the US does not simply use its relationship solely for the benefit of American interests, and once those interests have been met then terminate the relationship. Thus the leader of Djibouti is working assiduously to include the national interests of his country into the long-term strategic calculations of its relationship with regional neighbors remain a part of any negotiations on the future of US-Djibouti ties.

In spite of the rapid and advantageous changes that have occurred within the US-Djibouti relationship, there are two troubling aspects regarding Djibouti's participation in the war on terror. Human rights violations have dramatically increased following the country's acceptance of a leading role in the combined joint force. First, it is patently clear that President Guelleh has used the war on terror as a means to crack down on opposition leaders, many of which were imprisoned without the identification of any charges. Second, in a practice that should worry the Bush administration, who wants to promote the virtues of democratic governance as an alternative to radical Islam, the US administration has turned a blind eye to the banishment of many of the country's non-state run newspapers. Additionally, beginning in September of 2003 the Guelleh government expelled over 100,000 of the country's residents, about fifteen percent of Djibouti's population. Amazingly, the international community failed to halt this practice. Viewed collectively, in the words of Saunders, a major US ally in the war on terror is "using its new funds and legitimacy to do things that may themselves be worse than terrorism."[35]

Djibouti's function as a major ally in the war on terror, for now, is secure. What remains unclear is whether the human rights abuses have been eradicated. As all Africa watchers are well aware, the abuses are reminiscent of another Western practice established during the Cold War, one that when the superpower conflagration concluded, left African states (many former allies with the US) to pick up the pieces of a host of internal crises. These crises developed as eventual "blow back" that haunted the host country and at times US interests. In the future all countries within the Horn have to diligently work to prevent the return of such outcomes again. Ending such abuses will go along way to evaluate or measure victory in the war on terror and regional stability.

Notes

1 Brian Whitaker, "The Definition of Terrorism," *Guardian Unlimited*, May 7, 2001. http://www.guardian.co.uk/elsewhere/journalist/story/0,7792,487098,00.html. Retrieved on April 4, 2006.
2 D. Bender, *Terrorism in Africa* (New York: The Progressive Inc, 1999).
3 P. Pillar, "Terrorism and the Western Foreign Policy" (Washington, DC: Brookings Institute Press, 2001), pp. 69–74.
4 Ted Dagne, "Africa and the War on Terrorism." *The Congressional Research Service*, 2002, p. 4.
5 Thomas Donnelly and Vance Shuck, "Toward a Global Cavalry: Overseas Rebasing and Defense Transformation," National Security Outlook, American Enterprise Institute for Public Policy Research, Washington, DC, July 1, 2003.

http://www.ciaonet.org/pbei/aei/nso/dot08/. Retrieved on April 4, 2006.

6   David Shinn, "Fighting Terrorism in East African and Horn," *Foreign Service Journal*, September 2004, p. 41.

7   Theodros Dagne, "Africa and the War on Terrorism: The Case of Somalia," *Mediterranean Quarterly*, Fall 2002: 62–73. The authors accessed the online version, see http://muse. jhu.edu/journals/mediterranean_quarterly/v013/13.4dagne.html. Retrieved on April 4, 2006.

8   Jean-Louis Peninou, "Horn of Africa Al Qaeda Group?" *Le Monde Diplomatique*, December 6, 2001.

9   As reported in "Terrorism in the Horn of Africa," *Special Report 113*, United States Institute of Peace, Washington, DC, January 2004, p. 1. http://www.usip.org/pubs/ specialreports/sr113.html#djibouti. Retrieved on April 9, 2006.

10   Deborah L. West, "Combating Terrorisms in the Horn of Africa and Yemen." Belfast Center for Science and International Affairs (BCSIA), John F. Kennedy School of Government, Harvard University, Cambridge, MA, 2005, p. 9. http:// bcsia.ksg.harvard. edu/BCSIA_content/documents/Yemen%20Report%20BCSIA.pdf. Retrieved on April 24, 2006.

11   See "Terrorism in the Horn of Africa,"

12   West, "Combating Terrorisms in the Horn of Africa and Yemen," p. 9.

13   Ibid.

14   "Patterns of Global Terrorism, 2003." Released by the Office of the Coordinator for Counterterrorism. Retrieved on April 29, 2004, www.state.gov/s/ct/rls/crt/2003/31578. htm.

15   See Africa Overview, Department of State. http://www.stateusa. gov/miscfiles.nsf/1b90098fa85d7c3585256e60000eb74d/ 9aa5b226c86acd7985257003006d4f38/$FILE/2003terror_africa.pdf.

16   Defense Department transcript: US Department of Defense News Briefing, Secretary of Defense Donald H. Rumsfeld. Monday, December 9, 2002. http://www.globalsecurity. org/military/library/news/2002/12/mil-021210-usia04.htm. Retrieved on April 29, 2006.

17   Staff writers, "Djibouti Turns into US Long-term Africa Intelligence Base." Afrolnews. http://www.afrol.com/articles/10789. Retrieved on May 2, 2006.

18   See "Terrorism in the Horn of Africa,"

19   Robert Rotheberg, Editor, *Battling Terrorism in the Horn of Africa* (Washington, DC: Brookings Institution Press, 2005), pp. 49–50.

20   Staff writers, "Djibouti Turns into US Long-term Africa Intelligence Base."

21   Andrew England, "US Military Grows in Djibouti," Free Republic, September 30, 2002, p. 1.

22   See Statement by H.E. Roble Olhaye, Ambassador of Djibouti, Dean of the African Diplomatic Corps, "The War on Terrorism: Its Impact and Implications for Africa," Howard University Ralph Bunche International Affairs Center, Washington, DC, April 7, 2004.

23   Ibid.

24   John Davis, *The Global War on Terrorism: Assessing the American Response* (NY: Nova Science Publishers, 2004), pp. 203–204.

25   "U.S. Military Grows in Djibouti," Associated Press, September 29, 2002.

26   Davis, *The Global War on Terrorism*, p. 206.

27   Mark Fineman, "Destitute Djibouti Pines for U.S. Aid," *Los Angeles Times*, December 28, 2002.

28   "Djibouti's Port and Its Ties with Ethiopia," *The Somaliland Times*. August 4, 2004. http://www.somalilandtimes.net/2003/134/13406.shtml. Retrieved on May 17, 2006.

29   See "Developing a Stronger Djibouti." http://djibouti.usembassy.gov/ development_aid_to_djibouti.html. Retrieved on May 19, 2006.

30   Ibid.

31   See "Terrorism in the Horn of Africa,"

32. See the following website: www.globalsecurity.org/security/library/report/2004/pgt_
     2003/pgt_2003_31578pf.htm. Retrieved on May 23, 2006.
33   See Doug Saunders, "A Terrifying War on Terror," Global Policy Forum.
     www.globalpolicy.org/empire/terrorwar/analysis/2004/1030terrify.htm.
34   Rotheberg, *Battling Terrorism in the Horn of Africa*, p. 60.
35   Saunders, "A Terrifying War on Terror,"

Chapter 3

Kenya and the Global War on Terrorism: Searching for a New Role in a New War

Raymond Muhula

Introduction

In August 1998 Kenya and Tanzania suffered two devastating attacks of terrorism. The twin attacks on the US Embassies in Nairobi and Dar es Salaam were masterminded by Osama bin Laden and his al Qaeda network. The two countries have had close relations with the United States, but the attacks may also have been the result of a growing disenchantment with the internal socio-economic and political marginalization of the Muslim communities in both countries. For the US, it was the first sign that the international security debate was about to shift in unprecedented proportions. A new war was about to begin with a non-state actor with vast international networks and resources. Soon, a similar attack on US soil, in New York and Washington DC—America's financial and political capitals—confirmed it. The puzzle was now complete. America would need allies in the war on terror from all corners of the world. Kenya and Tanzania had unwittingly been drawn into a new war. Both had to search for their role, embrace America's emerging unilateralism, or face isolation.

Kenya endured another attack by al Qaeda operatives which operated cells along the East African coastline. In November 2002, a bomb exploded in Kenya's coastal town of Mombasa resulting in the death of fifteen people. This coincided with the firing of anti-aircraft missile on a departing chartered Arkia airlines aircraft en route to Tel Aviv. In May 2003, Kenyan authorities received credible threats of terrorist attacks on Western targets such as diplomatic missions. Major airlines such as British Airways cancelled flight operations to Nairobi for several weeks following these reports. The United States renewed a travel advisory issued after the 1998 embassy bombings, warning its citizens against non-essential travel to Kenya. The Kenyan government suspended flights to neighboring Somalia, the perceived source of the majority of the terrorist elements. In August 2003, a suspected suicide bomber detonated a hand grenade outside a police station in Mombasa, killing himself, a policeman and another civilian. One factor was now firmly established: Kenya was both a terrorist node and a terrorist hub; it was both a victim and a source of terrorism.[1]

Islam, Terrorism and the War on Terror

Several reasons have been advanced to explain the resurgence of Islamic-related terrorism in recent years. Indeed, from the divergence in the literature it is difficult to explain terrorism using a single causal factor. Mair, for instance, notes the complexity of the causes of terrorism, while others such as Newman suggest that a focus on "root causes" of terrorism is not useful in explaining terrorism as a general phenomenon.[2] However, the most identified causes of terrorism include ideology (Drake); religion (Rapoport, poverty (Bush) and human rights (IPA), state failure and weak institutions (Mills). Other researchers have challenged extant thinking on the causes of terrorism, suggesting that they do not go far enough in explaining repeated attacks on a target. Otenyo suggests an emphasis on both external and internal factors.[3] An emphasis on external factors allows researchers to understand the extent of symbolic representation of a dominating power as an important motivation for terrorist target selection. Moreover, as Rees and Aldrich note, the line between external and internal security has been blurred by international security.[4] As has been observed recently, terrorists commit crimes in countries that are not necessarily their homelands.[5]

One of the most salient features of terrorist target selection is ideology. Ideology shapes the terrorists' morality regarding the consequences of their actions. It provides them with justification for attacking a particular target perceived as threatening.[6] Drake observes that ideology "allows terrorists to justify their violence by displacing the responsibility onto either their victims or other actors, whom in ideological terms they hold responsible for the state of affairs which the terrorists claim led them to adopt violence."[7] Because they are rational actors, terrorists attack targets that provide the most optimal benefits of their actions. Nevertheless, target selection is determined by availability of resources in the group, reaction of the society to terrorist actions and the security environment of terrorist operations.[8] The attack on Western countries and their perceived allies elsewhere is a manifestation of this phenomenon.

Crenshaw concurs observing that socio-political and economic factors that constitute the environment in which terrorism occurs are important analytical variables in understanding what makes certain localities susceptible to terrorist attacks.[9] Mills argues that the real terrorist threat in Africa remains internal.[10] However it is important to understand that the majority of the factors identified as causes of terrorism merely play a catalytic role and are not necessarily causal factors. States with inadequate structural strengths or the absence of legitimate governments enable terrorist elements to penetrate adherents.[11] For this reason, a critical examination of the factors such as state failure, statelessness, institutional weakness, and porous borders are important analytical issues in understanding the vulnerability of countries to terrorist attacks. It is this combination of factors that has been significant in the recent terrorist attacks in Kenya and other non-Western countries.

In addition to looking at purely internal factors that states have control over, other accounts have called for an examination of external factors, notably the geopolitical factors that contribute to terrorist retaliation. The most salient argument in this regard is that the geopolitical imbalance existing in the Middle East and the perceived Western support for Israel and its Zionist ideology has fuelled much of the resistance to the Judeo-Christian foundation of the international state system.[12] The extension of such associations between Israel and African countries on the one hand, and Western countries and Africa on the other, has provided the ideological *raison d'être* for the recent attacks on African countries.

The intensification of this chasm has produced the incessant conflict between Palestine and Israel, fuelled animosity between the government of Lebanon and Hezbollah, provided justification for the US-led invasion of Iraq, and more recently precipitated the conflict between Israel and Hezbollah. Muslim extremists have interpreted these occurrences as a provocation, and have therefore been on the defensive. The single most visible manifestation of this animosity has been in the repeated attacks of Western countries and their allies.

To be sure, attacks on US interests as retaliation for its perceived support of Israel are not new. Long before the 1998 twin embassy bombings, US interests had been targeted. The most memorable attack was the 1988 terrorist bombing of US-bound Pan Am Flight 103 over Lockerbie, Scotland. In recent years, the theater of this ideological conflict has shifted to countries with vast US interests. In this sense Kenya is a victim, but the war has also been taken to America itself, as demonstrated by the multiple attacks on American cities on 11 September 2001.[13]

The most important aspect of Muslim fundamentalism has been the emergence of a domino effect through isolated attacks in various corners of the world. Such attacks have elicited retaliatory attacks by concerned countries, and received vast media coverage. This has kept terrorist organizations and their key leadership in the news. Indeed, most of the world heard about al Qaeda and Osama bin Laden from the extensive media coverage after the twin embassy attacks.[14] Even more startling is the fact that the post–September 11 crackdown on terror networks has dispersed them around the world, and even strengthened their resolve.

Nevertheless, the view that the jihad ideology as a basis for Muslim extremism is founded on traditional Muslim thinking has been faulted. Recent scholarship suggests that "the rise and spread of jihad networks is not a reaction to the West derived from tradition but rather a symptom of Islam being transformed by Western globalization."[15] The neo-jihadist movements in the West merely an attempt to assert their existence in Western communities that are majority non-Muslim, and do not reflect the mainstream thinking within traditional Muslim societies. The link between the extremist Muslims and the formal institution of Islam remains weak as is the agenda of the jihadists.[16] Thus there is a difference between the Hamas and Hezbollah, for instance, which are principally engaged in nationalist struggles, and groups such as al Qaeda, which are more interested in Islamist revival, and even global hegemony.[17]

This difference is manifested more in Africa, where terrorist attacks have been retaliatory for the perceived support of Western countries by some African countries. Even in countries with Muslim majorities such as Mali, Senegal, and Nigeria it is difficult to talk of an authentic Islamic fundamentalist sentiment that embodies a distinct terrorist threat. The majority of terrorist groupings are mere cells of external terrorist organizations such as al Qaeda. But, this is not to say that it is impossible to have an authentic African terrorist regime, since the conditions that drive the growth and spread of terrorism are present in most of these African countries.

Nevertheless, it is also puzzling why some countries have become more susceptible to terrorism than others. Why for instance would terrorists repeatedly target Kenya, with only a small number of Muslims, compared to other countries? What structural conditions of the Kenyan socio-economic and political landscape support the development of an incipient terrorist network capable of masterminding major attacks not only in the country, but also in the region? How has the government responded to undermine the use of its territory for terrorist actions? How has the United States (perceived as an accomplice) supported Kenya's efforts in the war on terror?

In this chapter we chronicle Kenya's role in the war on terror, arguing that Kenya suffers from both a geographical and geopolitical curse. It is for this reason that Kenya is both a haven for and victim of terrorism. Any effort to design a counterterrorism strategy should be cognizant of this duality. To date Kenya's counterterrorism mechanisms have concentrated on the first curse: its victim status caused by geography, and ignored the most fundamental reason for these attacks: the geopolitical underpinnings of its susceptibility to terrorist anger. This study examines both.

Kenya as a Source of Terrorism: The Geographical Curse

Kenya lies between Somalia and Tanzania with a border that stretches along the 536-kilometer Indian Ocean coastline. Together with Djibouti, Somalia, Ethiopia, Eritrea and Sudan, it is regarded as high risk for terrorism.[18] This coastline is shared with Tanzania and stretches from Lamu to Mombasa on the Kenyan side and from Tanga through Dar es Salaam to Mtwara towards the Tanzania–Mozambique border. The Somali coastline joins Kenya's at Ras Kamboni to the South, and stretches all the way to Djibouti. This proximity to the coastline and the substantial Muslim presence in the region makes it easy for radical elements to infiltrate and blend with local Muslim and Arab communities from where operations can then be initiated.

Kenya's main neighbors are Ethiopia (North), Somalia (East), Sudan (Northwest), Tanzania (South) and Uganda (West). Of all Kenya's neighbors, Tanzania is the only peaceful country. Sudan, for instance, has been involved in a long civil war with the Sudan People's Liberation Army (SPLA) for over three decades. At the end of the war in 2004, a new war emerged in the Darfur region of Sudan. Both conflicts have created easy passage for weapons into Kenya. Two weeks after the attacks US President Bill Clinton ordered military strikes on a Sudanese chemical factory linked to bin Laden.[19] Like Sudan, Uganda has been embroiled in a conflict with the Lord's Resistance Army (LRA) in the Northern part of the country for more than two decades.

While there is no evidence of collusion between the LRA and Muslim extremists in Kenya or Tanzania, Uganda has repeatedly accused the Muslim-led Sudanese government of arming the LRA. Because of the proximity of both countries to Kenya, it is difficult to rule out the possibility of cross-border transfer of both weapons and extremist military personnel into Kenya. Both Somalia and Ethiopia have witnessed several years of internal conflict, with worrying spillover effects on

Kenya and Tanzania. Somali, for instance, has not had any central authority since the fall of Siad Barre's government in 1991. The recent rise to prominence of the Islamic Courts is disturbing.

The substantial Muslim population of Somali descent in Kenya makes it difficult to identify genuine Kenyan Somalis. As a result of the porosity of the Kenyan border with these countries, it is very easy for arms to be transferred into Kenya across the border. Finally, the Ethiopian government's conflict with the Oromo Liberation Front (OLF) has also made the Kenya–Ethiopian border a favorable avenue for arms transfer.[20] It is not inconceivable that some terrorist accomplices have entered Kenya through this border, since Oromo fighters have repeatedly crossed the border into Kenya. In nearby Eritrea, a jihadist movement continues its war with Eritrea. Kenya's counterterrorism strategy is therefore imperiled by the country's proximity to weak and insecure neighboring states.

Because of proximity to some of East Africa's most volatile states, Kenya has become a very important partner in the global war on terror. In a way, it is the gateway to the Horn of Africa, both for the terrorist network and for the US pursuit of terrorist masterminds. Kenya has a long-standing agreement with the United States for use of its military bases, air and sea ports for US military training, and passage to delicate spots in the Indian Ocean coast and the Horn of Africa. Indeed, the fact that the United States military entered Somalia through Kenya's sea port of Mombasa exposed Kenya to the wrath of fundamentalist Islamic movements then taking hold in Somalia. Soon after the withdrawal of US military from Somalia, Kenya became a target of al Qaeda.[21] By 1993, the network was already operating in Kenya.[22]

Kenya's attractiveness to terrorists is exacerbated by the fact that it also boasts the best infrastructural facilities in the region. It is far easier to operate a cell in Kenya than in any of the other Horn countries. Connected through a vast road and railway network, it is easier to move from Kenya into Tanzania, or Uganda. Moreover, the Jomo Kenyatta International Airport (JKIA) is the largest and busiest one in the region, making it easy for terrorists to move from one country to the other, both within and outside the region. For instance, al Qaeda cells believed to have set up in Nairobi as early as 1992 were expanded after the US invasion of Somalia, and would be useful as a conduit for weapons transfer in the region. This was probably due to the ease of movement into and outside Kenya, on account of its well-networked international air transport system. Mohammed Odeh, the convicted al Qaeda operative for the 1998 embassy bombings, was arrested in Pakistan en route from Nairobi.[23] Moreover, the Tel Aviv–bound chartered aircraft targeted by shoulder-fired missiles in the 2002 attack had just departed Moi International Airport in Mombasa.

Kenya is also home to almost 300,000 Muslims, who mainly live along the coast that borders Tanzania and Somalia. These Muslim communities share a common ancestry with those in the countries of the Arabian Peninsula and are therefore enjoined both ideologically and physiologically. Incidents of anti-Western sentiments in the Arab world normally resonate within the Kenyan coast either in pronouncements by significant Muslim clergy or in overt public protest by the people. Moreover, because Kenyan coastal Muslims are mostly of Arab descent, it easy for extremists from the Arab world to blend in with the locals, intermarry and operate their terrorist cells.

Indeed it has been established that the terror network in Kenya draws its leaders from the Gulf States, Somalia, Pakistan, and Comoros Islands.[24]

Both the Kenya government and key political leaders for a long time believed that Kenya was merely a victim of terrorism and not a source of terrorism. The fact that the 1998 bombing was masterminded by non-Kenyans informed much of the government's thinking regarding Kenya as a victim. This in spite of the fact that Kenya's vulnerability to international terrorism had long been established when terrorists linked to the Popular Front for the Liberation of Palestine (PFLP) bombed the Norfolk Hotel in downtown Nairobi, following the use of Kenya's facilities by Israeli forces during the Entebbe hostage rescue of passengers on a Paris-bound Air France Flight 139 from Tel Aviv.

In recent years, following the attack on the Paradise Hotel in 2002 and the arrest of a few terrorist suspects, the government has become aware of the need for a counterterrorism strategy, and has worked closely with the Bush administration and both regional partners and the international community in insulating the country from repeated attacks.[25] The aforementioned attacks were too coordinated to have been the work of temporary extremists. As it were, the attacks would later be linked to Al Ittihad al Islamiya, a terrorist network with roots in Somalia, and linked to al Qaeda.

It is for this reason that the government has responded in various ways. For instance, the government of Kenya (GoK) created the Anti-Terrorist Police Unit in 2003, published the Suppression of Terrorism Bill in 2003, the Proceeds of Crime and Money Laundering (Prevention) Bill in 2006, and a supplemental Anti-Terrorism Bill in 2006. Additionally, the GoK has worked jointly with the United States, in programs such as the Terrorist Interdiction Program (TIP), Joint Counter-Terrorism Task Force (JCTTF), East Africa Counterterrorism Initiative (EACTI), and the Safe Skies Initiative. At the regional and international levels, the GoK is party to numerous regional agreements such as the suppression of terrorism, and has to date ratified all twelve conventions and protocols related to the suppression of terrorism.

Kenya as a Victim of Terrorism: The Geopolitical Curse

Geopolitics explains a state's ordering of priorities in relation to other states with respect to their national interests.[26] It "explains the utility of strategic locations to the bargaining powers of states and their relation with others in geographically contested spaces."[27] While some state partners are viewed as important to the national interest, others are considered less important or even inconsequential.[28] Consistent with this argument, Otenyo identifies four factors that justify a geopolitical understanding of the terrorist threat to Kenya. First, Kenya's close association with the West and with Israel; Kenya's self-definition as an oasis of peace in a conflict ridden region, and finally an elite association with polarizing elements from the Muslim world such as Turkey's Abdullah Ocalan and Somali's Siad Barre.[29]

The argument that Kenya is a merely a victim of terrorist attacks because of its diplomatic relations with Israel and the United States is perhaps the most dominant. Political and religious leaders have argued that Kenya would not be a target of radical Islamic terrorism if it were not too close to these countries. For instance, during a memorial for the 1998 bombing victims, Paul Muite, the chairman of the parliamentary committee on Administration of Justice and Legal Affairs, criticized the US for inadequately compensating bomb victims. According to Muite, "The attacks on the US embassy were targeted at the Americans. Kenyans were regarded as collateral damage."[30]

Kenya's relations with the United States and Britain since independence lend credence to such arguments. The British military has operated bases in Nanyuki town, in Kenya's Rift Valley province. Kenya is also the only country in East Africa with a formal agreement—since April 1980—with Washington for the use of its local military facilities. This agreement permits US troops the use of the port of Mombasa, as well as airfields at Embakasi and Nanyuki. Kenya also provides its airspace for military maneuvers by the United States, and for reconnaissance missions in the region, and has served as an important gateway to the Horn of Africa. For instance, American troops invading Somalia in the ill-fated Operation Restore Hope entered Mogadishu through the port of Mombasa, a move that was heavily criticized by then US Ambassador Smith Hempstone.[31] This geo-strategic importance of Kenya is heightened by the fact that in 1992 the US lost access to two key military bases of Mogadishu and Berbera following the fall of Siad Barre.

It is noteworthy that the emergence of Kenya as a terrorist target began with the disintegration of Somalia, and the subsequent anger of radical Muslims. In February 1998, Osama bin Laden issued a fatwa calling for the killing of Americans in any country. Specifically, it noted that "in compliance with God's order, we issue the following fatwa to all Muslims: the ruling to kill the Americans and their allies, including civilians and military, is an individual duty for every Muslim who can do it in any country in which it is possible to do it."[32] The embassy attacks in Nairobi and Dar es Salaam followed only months later. It is believed that this call provided the rationale for these attacks. According to the FBI, Mohamed Sadeek Odeh, the convicted embassy bomber discussed these fatwa with Mustafa Mohamed Fadhil in Kenya.[33]

Kenyan facilities have also been useful in US counterterrorism operations in the region. The US Navy has participated in numerous counterterrorism drills along the Indian Ocean coast, sometimes jointly with their Kenyan counterparts. For instance, in 2003 the US Navy participated in the Combined Joint Task Force Horn of Africa (CJTF-HOA) operation with Kenyan forces. The combined forces focused on guarding the Indian Ocean coastline against terrorist attacks.[34] According to US Navy officials, the joint exercise was meant to "detect, disrupt and defeat transnational terrorist groups in the region."[35] In recent years, the US has stepped up its assistance to Kenya to improve the capacity of the country to deal with the terrorist threat, and to forestall similar attacks as the ones recently witnessed in the country.

Kenya is a major beneficiary of US funding, which has continued to increase since the embassy bombing in 1998. The International Military Education and Training (IMET) funding is useful to countries in the region and has been identified as a foreign policy tool for countries playing a vital role in the global war on terror.[36] Kenya received $486,000 in 2002, and requested $600,000 more in 2003 and 2004 in military assistance.[37] Additional financial support obtained from US covers the improvement of security apparatus in the national coastline, borders, airports, and ports.

Kenya and Terrorism: A Tale of Three Atrocities

Kenya suffered its first terrorist attack in 1980. This attack was allegedly organized by the Popular Front for the Liberation of Palestine (PFLP) to avenge Kenya's permission to Israeli soldiers to refuel in Nairobi during the Entebbe hostage crisis. Following the hostage taking of an Air France Flight 139 en route to Paris, the terrorists forced the plane to land in Uganda, with President Idi Amin's permission. In the subsequent raid to rescue the hostages, Kenya allowed Israelis to use facilities at the Jomo Kenyatta International Airport. On New Years Eve in December 1980, a bomb exploded at the Norfolk Hotel, in downtown Nairobi. The hotel, owned by a Jewish family, was a popular tourist destination. Thirteen people died in the blast, which also injured 87 people and partially destroyed the building. Later, Kenyan sources revealed that the mastermind of the terrorist activity was 34-year-old Qaddura Mohammed Abdel al-Hamid, a Moroccan citizen and a member of the PFLP, who fled for Saudi Arabia shortly after the bombing.[38] The movement denied GoK statement that it was responsible for the attack, and cautioned that "Israel might use such reports as justification for raids against guerrilla bases in southern Lebanon and 'terrorist activities' against the Palestinians."[39]

Kenya did not enact any legislation to address terrorist crimes after this incident, and no organized terrorist related attacks occurred in Kenya in the interim period. The next two terrorist attacks redefined the government of Kenya's understanding of the threat of terrorism to its national security. It had to rethink its national security strategy, and place counterterrorism at the center. First, it was the terrorist attack on the US embassy in downtown Nairobi on 7 August 1998 and then the twin attacks of the coastal resort Paradise Hotel and the departing Israeli aircraft en route to Tel Aviv in 2002 that provided the impetus for this shift.

Bloody Friday 7 August, 1998: US Embassy Bombing

By far the single largest attack on American interests before September 11 involved the unfortunate terrorist attacks on the US embassies in Kenya and Tanzania. In many respects such attacks were the opening round of the global war on terrorism. Following these attacks, the United States bombed a Sudanese-based chemical factory, suspected to have links with al Qaeda mastermind Osama bin Laden. It also fired missiles into Afghan–Pakistan border where Taliban militia and Osama bin Laden allegedly operated from. These would be the first shots of what has become known as the global war on terror.

On 7 August, 1998 suicide bombers drove a truck bomb into the basement of the American embassy in downtown Nairobi. At almost the same time, a similar operation was underway at the US embassy in Dar es Salaam, Tanzania. Investigators revealed that a similar attack planned for the US embassy in Kampala failed. The combined embassy death toll neared 5,000 people, with a dozen US casualties. It emerged later that the mastermind behind these attacks was the al Qaeda terrorist network, whose leader Osama bin Laden had lived in Sudan in the years immediately before these attacks. The main planners and executors of this attack had arrived in Kenyan almost two years earlier, and disguised themselves in various forms, including operating as charity workers.[40]

The period immediately after the bombing, the GoK made major pronouncements regarding the pursuit of terrorists in the country, and vowed to bring the masterminds to justice. President Moi of Kenya even hinted that the government had a clue as to who the attackers were.[41] Both Kenyan and US intelligence agencies intensified the search for the mastermind, and within a week arrested Mohammed Sadeq Odeh, one of the suspects in the terror plot.[42]

Nevertheless, in spite of the attack and the arrest of the terrorist suspects, the national mindset was still steeped in denial. The dominant argument within the country was this: Kenya is a peace-loving nation; one that does not harbor terrorists. For the most part, the government only employed its diplomatic arsenal: meeting with US Secretary of State Madeline Albright, and cooperating with the US investigative agencies. However, no efforts were made by the government of Kenya to initiate a broader national counterterrorism strategy that would inform its own war on terror. Nor did it cooperate with regional countries in crafting a joint program for counterterrorism. The ideological basis of this lax approach was premised on the assumption that Kenya was merely a victim of, not a source of terrorism.[43] This and other factors such as inadequate intelligence system, a corrupt law enforcement and immigration system, poor financial reporting mechanisms, and inadequate legislation to deal with terrorist related offences contributed to the continued use of Kenyan territory as an incubator for further terrorist activity in the country, and possibly elsewhere in the region. It was against this background that the second terrorist attack occurred in Kenya.

Paradise Lost: The 28 November 2002 Attacks

In the morning of 28 November 2002, a suicide bomber drove a vehicle into the reception of the Paradise Hotel in Kikambala on the Kenya coastal region, and detonated a bomb. Consistent with al Qaeda's signature, this attack was first phase of a twin attack; the second attack targeted a departing Arkia airlines aircraft. The aircraft dodged a shoulder fired Strella 7 missile shortly after its departure en route to Tel Aviv with over 200 passengers on board.

Unlike the terrorist attacks on the US embassy four years earlier, these attacks were not surprising. They occurred 2 1/2 months after the first anniversary of the September 11 attacks in New York and Washington, DC. Moreover, shortly before attacks, there had been warnings of an impending attack on Western targets, prompting countries such as the US, Britain, and Australia to issue travel warnings to their citizens traveling to Kenya.[44]

An important outcome of these attacks was that they confirmed to the GoK that the country indeed harbored terrorist cells. For instance, in May 2003, the government admitted the presence of a terrorist network in the country, releasing credible intelligence regarding an impending terrorist attacks on Western targets. Moreover, it renewed its commitment to an effective counterterrorism regime by creating the Anti-Terrorism Police Unit to handle only terrorist related crimes. This unit was headed by the senior commissioner of police and brought together law enforcement officials trained in counterterrorism.

Government Response: The Challenge of Counterterrorism

Livingstone identifies three categories of counterterrorism measures: military, regulatory (legal), and appeasement. Military approaches mix preemption with deterrence and retribution, while judicial responses create penalties for terrorist activities.[45] The last strategy—the appeasing option—encompasses accommodation and concession.[46] Kenya government's counterterrorism policy can be viewed through three lenses: legislative, policy, and diplomatic.

In spite of the initial lethargy in responding to the challenge posed by renewed terrorist threat to its territory, the government of Kenya has responded vigorously in creating the necessary infrastructure for an effective counterterrorism strategy. This laxity in crafting an anti-terrorism strategy was informed by a general feeling that even though there was a significant Muslim population in the country, it had always been moderate. The threat of extremist tendencies arising from this group was therefore remote. This changed with the second attack in 2002 and allegations in 2003 of another terrorist plot.

While to date there is no stand-alone anti-terrorism legislation, the government has been able to disrupt terrorist related planning, including arresting terrorist masterminds. For instance, in October 2005 four men suspected of funding terrorist activities were arrested. An additional person was arrested in Northern Kenya for possession of a rocket launcher and rocket propelled grenade that were allegedly being smuggled to Mombasa.[47] The policy and the diplomatic aspects of Kenya's counterterrorism strategy have progressed much faster than the legislative one. The Suppression of Terrorism Bill has not been passed after a draft bill was rejected in 2003. A revised bill (2006) has met equal resistance from law makers and Muslim communities within Kenya. On the judiciary front, seven terror suspects that were arrested in connection with the 2002 bombings in Kikambala were acquitted in 2005. The closest Kenya has come to strengthening the prosecution of terrorist suspects is in the amendment of the Evidence Act to make confession taken before a police officer admissible in a court of law. This led to a recent successful prosecution of a terrorist suspect.

Legislative Initiatives

Suppression of Terrorism Bill 2003

In 2003 the government of Kenya published the Suppression of Terrorism Bill with wide ranging provisions on what constituted terrorism. In this bill terrorism was broadly defined, *inter alia*, as "the use of threat or action" where:

(a) the action used or threatened: (i) involves serious violence against a person, (ii) involves serious damage to property (iii) endangers the life of any person other than the person committing the action (iv) creates a serious risk to the health or safety or the public or a section of the public or (v) is designed seriously to interfere with or seriously disrupt an electronic system; (b) the use or threat is designed to influence the government or to intimidate the public or a section of the public; and (c) the use or threat is made for the purpose of advancing a political, religious or ideological cause.[48]

The definitional problem that bedevils the global quest for a precise operationalization of the concept of the term "terrorism" was evident in this definition and in the bill in particular. Like most counterterrorism legislation, the bill has been described as riddled with vague and broad parameters that open them to abuse by the state.[49] The bill immediately encountered opposition from all quarters including parliament, civil society, and transnational human rights organizations.[50] As a result, the Suppression of Terrorism Bill 2003 was withdrawn pending further consultation. It was revised and presented to parliament for discussion.

Suppression of Terrorism Bill 2006

The Suppression of Terrorism Bill 2006 is a revised version of the Suppression of Terrorism Bill, 2003. If passed by parliament, it would be known as the Anti-Terrorism Act, 2006. While by far a better version, it has not been passed owing to the political implications of the bill. In this bill terrorism is defined as:

(a) An act of omission in or outside Kenya which constitutes and offence within the scope of a counterterrorism convention; (b) An act or threat in or outside Kenya which, *inter alia*, involves serious bodily harm to a person; involves serious damage to property; endangers a person's life…"[51]

One significant addition to the definition is the reference to counterterrorism conventions. Over the years, twelve key international conventions have been developed within the United Nations to address the threat of terrorism, and the obligations of state parties under those conventions and protocols. Kenya is party to all the conventions. Moreover, the bill distinguishes between free speech acts such as protests, demonstrations, or work stoppages, and overt acts of terrorism.[52] An important provision of this bill is that it addresses issues of international terrorism. Under the bill, the incitement to commit a terrorist offence does not have to take place in Kenya for it to be an offence under the proposed act. Section 8 (2) of the bill notes that "it is immaterial whether or not the person incited is in Kenya at the time of the incitement."[53] This part of the bill recognizes that Kenya is a critical partner in the global war on terror. It also signals the government's acknowledgement that Kenya is no longer merely a victim of terrorism, but a harbor of terrorists.

Another important provision of this bill that relates to the global war on terrorism is the provision for mutual assistance and extradition. Under section 33(1) of the proposed act, Kenya's Attorney General may share information regarding terrorists with a foreign state. Such information might include details of movement, travel documents, communication technologies, or terrorist related offences committed. However, under section 34 (1) of the proposed act the Attorney General can only do this with the permission of the High Court.[54] The act would also allow Kenya's Attorney General to make similar requests to a foreign state.

Even though the proposed act is a somewhat relaxed version of the original Suppression of Terrorism (2003) Bill, it has also attracted numerous criticisms, particularly from the Islamic community in Kenya. Critics of the anti-terrorism bill argue that the war on terror is not Kenya's war, and that any laws that are written specifically as part of a counterterrorism program are written at the behest of the US government. The second argument is that the laws are discriminatory and that they target the Muslim community. This is buttressed by the fact that the Kenyan police have arrested and detained, sometimes incommunicado, many people from the Muslim community on suspicion of involvement in terrorist activities.[55]

The Terrorism Suppression Bill (2006) has not been passed, and the government has been making overtures to the Muslim community to support it. In spite of promises by the government that Muslims would be involved in the process before the bill is enacted, and that the act would not target the Muslim community, Islamic leaders have remained adamant in their opposition to the bill.[56]

While the government's work on the legislative aspects of its counterterrorism policy has been undermined by an assertive parliament, a vibrant civil society, and a determined Islamic religious community, its work on both bilateral and multilateral initiatives on counterterrorism has been more productive.

Diplomatic Initiatives

Following repeated threats to Kenya and the impact of these threats on the national economy, the GoK has initiated both multilateral and bilateral initiatives to build partnerships with affected countries both inside and outside the region. As part of its regional counterterrorism initiatives, the GoK has participated in numerous discussions under the auspices of regional organizations such as Inter Governmental Authority on Development (IGAD), the African Union (AU), the Commonwealth and the United Nations. Nevertheless, the most prominent diplomatic initiative is the bilateral cooperation with the United States government on improving Kenya's counterterrorism readiness. For the United States, it has been described as a "high priority" in the fight against terrorism in the region.[57]

Military Training and Counterterrorism Strategy

At the bilateral level, Kenya's greatest partner has been the American government, whose support for counterterrorism operations in Kenya has been on the rise since

1998. Even with the seemingly high profile cooperation between the US government and Kenya, the former still views Kenya's efforts as inadequate. According to the Bush administration, there has been little progress on the war on terror in Kenya. In its annual *Patterns of Terrorism* report, the US State Department faults Kenya for disbanding the Joint Terrorism Task Force established in 2004 with US funding to improve cooperative work on counterterrorism among the police and armed forces. According to the report, the GoK did not complete the National Counterterrorism Strategy, nor did it sensitize the country on the terrorist threat.[58]

The nature of support from the US government has varied. It ranges from provision of military hardware to counterterrorism training. For instance, among the highly publicized counterterrorism joint exercise was in June 2003 when the US military's Combined Joint Task Force–Horn of Africa (CJTF-HOA) personnel arrived in Mombasa to conduct joint training with the Kenyan military as part of the counterterrorism preparation.[59] A press release from the CJTF-HOA secretariat indicated that "The goal, for what will be an extended period of operations in coastal and international waters between Kenyan and CJTF-HOA forces, is the integration of a variety of advanced technologies into coastal and maritime counterterrorism plans and operations."[60] The CJTF-HOA area of operation includes the total airspace, land areas, and coastal waters of Kenya, Somalia, Sudan, Djibouti, Ethiopia, Eritrea, and Yemen. Additional joint operations occurred in June–July 2003 when the Kenya Navy and the USS Joint Venture (HSV-XI) undertook joint coastal and interdiction operations. Other training operations were jointly conducted with the USS Jarret (FFG33) and Kenya's Shupavu in January 2004. Kenya's Defense Department and the US Central Command signed a memorandum providing for joint maritime operations at least two times a year under the US military's Combined Joint Task Force–Horn of Africa (CJTF-HOA).

According to top commanders of the Kenyan Navy it is anticipated that these training operations will enhance both the operational and tactical capacity of the Navy to protect Kenya's coastline. Ultimately, this will "produce and increase Kenyan counterterrorist capability, deter cross-border movement, and create credible pressure on terrorist activities within Kenyan waters and in Somalia from the south."[61] Apart from joint counterterrorism training of military personnel, Kenya is also a major beneficiary of the US $100 Million East African Counterterrorism Initiative that was launched by President Bush in 2003.

Initiative of 2003 East African Counterterrorism

Kenya is a central partner in the East African Counterterrorism Initiative (EACTI). The EACTI was announced by President Bush in 2003 with a view to strengthening the capacity of East African countries to fight terrorism. Under the program, Kenya has participated in joint military exercises with neighboring countries in counterterrorism readiness. As part of the EACTI, there has been joint military training in maritime and coastal border security, and purchase of equipment for patrol.[62] Under the initiative, Kenya received funding to improve the National Counterterrorism Center and to fund the joint counterterrorism task force. The joint task force was established to improve interagency communications and information sharing to better target and disrupt terrorist activities in the country and the regions. The task force was later disbanded in 2004. Additionally, as part of the initiative, Kenya received funding for police training and to modernize its communication equipment. In addition to these more visible programs, with support from the United States government, the government of Kenya has recently become part of the Terrorist Interdiction Program (TIP). Through this program, custom officials can identify terrorist suspects entering the country. The data can then be shared among countries for effective monitoring of suspected terrorists.

Another important aspect of border controls is the Export Control and Related Border Security Assistance project that has received substantial funding by the US. Under this program, the Kenyan government is provided with funds to improve border controls to prevent transfer of weapons of mass destruction through the country's borders. These and other programs such as the Safe Skies Initiative (SSI) remain some of the most important outcomes of bilateral work between Kenya and the US in the global war on terror. On its own, the government of Kenya has also initiated policy measures to undermine the terrorist threat. The three most important outcomes in the policy front are Anti-Terrorism Police Unit established in 2003, the National Counterterrorism Center (NCTC) established in 2004 and, the Kenya National Counterterrorism Strategy that was drafted in 2004.

The Anti-Terrorism Police and the NCTC have been very instrumental in assisting local assets in arresting and disrupting the activities of potential terrorist masterminds. Both units have an important role in the war on terror given that their mandate covers not only counterterrorism but also money laundering, narcotics trafficking, and proliferation of illicit arms. However, the anti-terrorism police unit have been criticized for the indiscriminate arrest of Muslims and various incidents of human rights violation.[63]

Conclusion

The 11 September 2001 attacks on the United States effectively marked a turning point in the global war on terrorism. At the regional level in Africa, the 1998 twin embassy bombings in Nairobi and Dar es Salaam demonstrated the consequences of Africa's geopolitical relations with the West. The recent bombings in some African and Asian countries precipitated a renewed focus on the causes of terrorism. More significantly, the debate raised questions about what is the best counterterrorism strategy in the wake of the US military invasion of Iraq.

It is, however, clear that a military solution alone is not sufficient as a counterterrorism strategy: a combination of strategies is necessary to win the war on terror. This is because, even with the launch of the global war of terror by the United States, there has been a substantial increase in terrorist related incidents. The US Department of State estimates that incidents of international terrorism increased from 175 in 2003 to 655 in 2004.[64]

Terrorism continues to be among the most salient national security concerns for Kenya today. There is no doubt that the threat of terrorism will define a sizeable portion of national security debates for some time. As the global war on terrorism proceeds in other parts of the world, Kenya must be wary of the factors that make it vulnerable to terrorist attacks. As one of the countries with the lowest number of Muslims, and by far among those with the most moderate of Muslim factions, it is still possible to reverse its perceived soft target status to create a formidable national security platform that can sustain terrorist penetration.

The initial attacks in 1998 and the subsequent attacks in 2002 have proved that Kenya is not only a victim of terrorism, but also a source. It is for this reason that an effective counterterrorism strategy must deal with both the source as well as the victim related factors. As noted above, the source related factors are not largely immitigable. Measures such as tighter administrative checks on entry and exit procedures across the borders, eligibility for national identification documents, as well as public awareness are necessary aspects of such a strategy.

At the same time, Kenya cannot underestimate the important geopolitical role it plays in the East Africa region, first as a gateway to the region, and also as a mediator in regional conflicts. Kenya's national security is affected by the insecurity in surrounding conflict affected states such as Sudan, Somalia, Uganda, and Ethiopia. The resultant cross-border exchanges pose enormous implications for Kenya's national security. Kenya must continue to play its traditional mediation role in the region. Domestically, it must begin to systematically engage the coastal Muslim communities in governance and equitable distribution of national resources. Such programs would isolate the unscrupulous Muslim charities (for example, the disbanded Al-Haramain) that have inserted themselves in Muslim communities to provide social services usually provided by government.

Geopolitically, Kenya must redefine its foreign policy strategically to isolate aspects of external relations that have potential ramifications for domestic security. It is clear that all three terrorist attacks have been preceded by the government or ruling elite with unfavorable implications for volatile non-state actors. The formal agreement with the United States regarding the use of Kenyan facilities for US military operations needs to be reviewed in line with the changing realities of post–11 September geopolitical interests. The emergence of non-state actors as key players in global political decisions, while confounding, nonetheless requires that states rethink not only their national security strategies, but also their geopolitical relations to incorporate non-state actor interests, even if symbolically. More importantly, Kenya must appreciate its unique position as both source and victim of terrorism. Such pragmatism must therefore inform not only the national counterterrorism strategy, but also guide policy makers and legislators in its design. This is what will ultimately produce an effective counterterrorism regime, and shore up Kenya's role in this new war.

Notes

1. Marc Sageman, *Understanding Terror Networks*. Philadelphia: University of Pennsylvania, 2004. Cited in Thomas Dempsey, *Counterterrorism in African Failed States: Challenges and Potential Solutions*. Carlilse, PA: Strategic Studies Institute, April 2006. Available on the internet at: http://www.strategicstudiesinstitute.army.mil/

pdffiles/pub649.pdf. Accessed on October 25, 2006.

2. Stefan Mair, "Terrorism and Africa: On the Danger of Further Attacks in Sub-Saharan Africa", *African Security Review*, 12(1), 2003, p. 1; Edward Newman, "Exploring the Root Causes of Terrorism", *Studies in Conflict and Terrorism*, 29(8), December 2006, p. 36.

3. Eric, E. Otenyo, "New Terrorism: Toward an Explanation of Cases in Kenya", *African Security Review* 13(3), 2004, p. 77.

4. "Contending Cultures of Counterterrorism,"

5. Ibid., p. 907.

6. C.J.M. Drake, "The Role of Ideology in Terrorist's Target Selection," *Terrorism and Political Violence*, 10(2), Summer 1998, p. 1.

7. Ibid., p. 1.

8. Ibid., p. 2.

9   Martha Crenshaw, "The Causes of Terrorism Past and Present" in C. Kegley, Jr (ed.), *The New Global Terrorism: Characteristics, Causes and Controls*. New Jersey: Prentice Hall, 2003, pp. 92–106.

10 Greg Mills, "Africa's New Strategic Significance", *The Washington Quarterly*, 27(4), p. 157.

11 Ibid., p. 161.

12 See, for instance, Raymond Muhula, "Rogue Nations, States of Concern and the Axes of Evil: Examining the Politics of Disarmament in a Changing Geopolitical Context. *Mediterranean Quarterly*, Fall 2003, pp. 73–95.

13 Since the embassy bombings, other attacks outside the United States have included the USS Cole in Yemen, and so on.

14 The emergence of Al Jazeera TV, and the vast number of internet sites dedicated to Muslim extremism have been of immense use in communicating the message of the Islamists.

15 Ibid., p. 131.

16 Ibid., p. 137.

17 bid., p. 136.

18 Karl Wycoff, "Testimony before the House International Relations Committee", Subcommittee on Africa, Washington, DC, April 2004.

19 BBC "Special Report: US Strikes" http://news.bbc.co.uk/2/hi/special_report/1998/08/98/us_strikes/155347.stm. August 28, 1998. Accessed October 3, 2006.

20 "Kenyan armed forces arrested 63 members of the Oromo Liberation Front (OLF) in northwest Kenya, reports the Ethiopian News Agency. Fifteen of the detainees reportedly said they were trained in Eritrea to fight with the OLF. Security forces also recovered ammunition and anti-tank land mines in the operation. *ETHIOPIAN NEWS AGENCY*, "Kenya - Military Captures 63 militants (JUN 23/ENA)." June 23, 2004. http://global.factiva.com/ha/default.aspx. Accessed on October 3, 2006.

21 International Crisis Group. "Counterterrorism in Somalia: Losing Hearts and Minds", *Africa Report* no. 95, July 11, 2005.

22 Thomas Keane et al., *The 9/11 Commission Report: Final Report of the National Commission on Terrorist Attacks upon the United States*, New York: New York, 2005, p. 68.

23 BBC, "Americas Bomb Suspects Linked to bin Laden" Available: http://news.bbc.co.uk/2/hi/americas/160512.stm. August 29, 1998. Accessed on October 3, 2006.

24 Gilbert Khadiagalla, "Kenya: Haven or Helpless Victim of Terrorism", in *United States Institute of Peace, Terrorism in the Horn of Africa*, Washington, DC: USIP, January 2004, p. 2.

25 Even though some key political and Muslim leaders still see this as an American problem, and vow to block any anti-terrorism legislation.

26 Brennan M. Kraxberger, "The United States and Africa: Shifting Geopolitics in an 'Age of Terror'," *Africa Today*, 52(1), Fall 2005, p. 49.

27 Muhula, "Rogue Nations," p. 81.

28 Kraxberger, "The United States and Africa," *Africa Today*, pp. 47–68 and p. 49.

29 Otenyo, "New Terrorism," p. 82.

30 Standard Reporter, "Compensate Blast Survivors, MP Tells America," *East African Standard*, August 7, 2006. Available on the web at: http://www.Eastandard.net/print/news.php?articleid=1143956449. **Downloaded August 17, 2006.**

31 Smith Hempstone, *Rogue Ambassador*. Memphis: Sewanee University of the South, 1996.

32 T.J. Caruso, "Al Qaeda International." Testimony of J.T. Caruso, Acting Assistant Director, Counterterrorism Division, FBI Before the Subcommittee on International Operations and Terrorism, Committee on Foreign Relations, United States Senate December 18, 2001Available on the internet at: http://www.fbi.gov/congress/congress01/caruso121801.htm. Accessed on October 25, 2006.

33 Ibid.

34 Bradley Shaver, "High Speed Naval Vessel Surfs African Region." Available on the internet at: http://defendamerica.mil/articles/jul2003/a072203a.html. Downloaded August 14, 2006.

35 Ibid.

36 US *Military Assistance*, p. 151. Available on the internet at: http://www.state.gov/documents/organization/17783.pdf. Accessed on October 25, 2006.

37 Ibid., p. 153.

38 *New York Times*, "Official Kenyan Sources Assert Arab Radical Mohammed Akila was Responsible...." Available on the web at: http://global.factiva.com/ha/default.aspx.

39 Associated Press, "Arab Guerrillas Deny Accusation by Kenya on Bombing of a Hotel", 9 January 1981. Available on the web: http://query.nytimes.com. Accessed on October 3, 2006.

40 Hared H. Adan, "Combating Transnational Terrorism in Kenya." Unpublished Masters Thesis, US Army Command and General Staff College, Fort Leavenworth, Kansas, 2005, p. 33.

41 Agence France Presse, "Kenya has Clues to Bombing: Moi" 9 August 1998. Available on the internet at: http://global.factiva.com/ha/default.aspx. Accessed October 5, 2006.

42 BBC, "Bombing Suspect Returns to Nairobi", Available on the internet at: http://news.bbc.co.uk/2/hi/africa/152860.stm. Accessed on October 5, 2006.

43 Adan, 2005, p. 39. Also see: Gilbert Khadiagalla, "Kenya: Haven or Helpless Victim of Terrorism," in United States Institute of Peace, *Terrorism in the Horn of Africa*, Washington DC: USIP, January 2004, p. 2.

44 Ibid., p. 47.

45 Neil C. Livingstone, "Proactive Responses to Terrorism: Reprisals, Preemption and Retribution," in C.W. Kegley, ed., *International Terrorism: Characteristics, Causes and Controls*. New York: St. Martin's Press, 1990, pp. 219–227.

46 Ibid. Cited in Wynn Rees and Richard J. Aldrich, "Contending Cultures of Counterterrorism:
Transatlantic Divergence or Convergence?" *International Affairs*, 81(5), 2005, p. 907.

47 United States Department of State (Office of the Coordinator for Counterterrorism), *Country Reports on Terrorism 2005*. Washington, DC: 2006, p. 50.

48 Government of Kenya, "Suppression of Terrorism Bill, 2003", *Kenya Gazette Supplement* No. 38 (Bills No. 15), Nairobi: Government Press, April 2003.

49 Kathurima M'Inoti, "Combating Terrorism in Africa." Paper prepared for the Annual Conference of the Association of Law Reform Agencies of Eastern and Southern Africa (ALRAESA), Entebbe, Uganda, 4–8 September 2005, p. 13.

50 Amnesty International, "Kenya: Memorandum to the Government of Kenya on the Suppression of Terrorism Bill, 2003." Amnesty International, September 2004, p. 1.

51 Government of Kenya, "The Anti Terrorism Bill, 2006" (Draft), p. 3.

53 Ibid., p.4.

54 Ibid. p. 6.

55 Ibid. p. 23.

56 Amnesty International has documented some of these arrests in a recent memorandum to the GoK.
57 Nation Correspondent, "Muslims to Have Say on Proposed Law on Terror, Says DC," *Daily Nation*, October 13, 2006. http://www.nationmedia.com/dailynation/nmgcontententry. asp?premiumid=0&category_id=1&newsid=82890. Accessed on October 13, 2006.
58 USAID, "Kenya: USAID's Strategy in Kenya." Available: http:// www. usaid.gov/ locations/sub-saharan_africa/countries/Kenya/.
59 United States Department of State (Office of the Coordinator for Counterterrorism), *Country Reports on Terrorism 2005*. Washington, DC: 2006, p. 50.
60 The total CJTF-HOA contingent numbers more than 1,800, representing all branches of the U.S. armed services, coalition military members, and civilian personnel.
61 Combined Joint Task Force–Horn of Africa (CJTF-HOA), Press Release, June 15, 2003. Available on the web: http://usembassy.state.gov/nairobi/wwwhrel14.html. Accessed on October 17, 2006.
62 Major General Pasteur P. Awitta, "The Commanders Respond," Proceedings 130, No. 3 Washington, DC: United Nations Naval Institute, March 2004, pp. 53–63.
63 United States Department of State (Office of the Coordinator for Counterterrorism), *Country Reports on Terrorism 2004*. Washington, DC: p. 29.
64 On this see for instance: Amnesty International, "The Impact of 'Anti-Terrorism' Operations on Human Rights", AI Index: AFR 32/002/2005. http://web.amnesty.org/ library/Index/ENGAFR320022005. Accessed on October 30, 2006.
65 S.B. Glasser, "US Figures Show Sharp Global Rise in Terrorism: State Dept. Will Not Put Data in Report," *Washington Post*, 27 April, 2005. Cited in Neil J. Melvin, "Islam, Conflict and Terrorism." In Stockholm International Peace Research Institute (SIPRI). *SIPRI Yearbook 2006: Armaments, Disarmaments, and International Security*, Oxford: Oxford University Press, 2006, p. 123.

PART 3
Regional Dynamics

Chapter 4

Globalization and Its Impact on the War on Terror

Judy Duncker

Introduction

7 August 1998 marked a significant historical landmark for the continent of Africa in the Global on Terror (GWOT) when a car bomb detonated behind the US Embassy in Nairobi, Kenya, killing 291 people and wounding approximately 5,000. Among them were twelve dead and six wounded US citizens. Almost simultaneously a second bomb detonated in Dar es Salaam, Tanzania. The destruction in both sites in Africa and the subsequent destruction of the World Trade Center (WTC) on September 11th 2001 signaled to the US and the world that terrorism was no longer restricted to the Middle East, but now, like other significant aspects of global relations, that it too had been globalized and necessitated global attention.

Since 1998 the Horn of Africa—Kenya, Ethiopia, Djibouti, Somalia, Eritrea, and Sudan—have emerged as the major source of terrorism on the continent, with Sudan providing safe haven for terrorists, the most famous of which is Osama bin Laden's al Qaeda transnational terrorist network. Since September 11, the Horn became a "strategic focal point in the American war against terrorism."[1] The instability in the region has been attributed to the "inability of the weak, 'failed' or 'failing states' in the region to police effectively its borders, maintain law and order, and protect Western strategic economic interests."[2] In addition to the Horn of Africa, closer examination has also revealed that the threat of terrorism has persisted in West Africa in two regions: Muslim Sahara and the Sahelian Belt. Similarly, in the North African country of Algeria, US troops have been engaged in military maneuvers due to the presence of terrorist groups who infiltrate the area as a result of unprotected borders to plan and execute their agenda. Other countries such as Niger and Mali also pose a security risk to the interests of the United States and the West. As a result the continent has been the center of attention, particularly in the East and West Africa regions.

Africa's role in the globalization of terror is more pervasive and troublesome and poses several pressing questions regarding the stability of existing world order. This chapter identifies the overlap of three distinct global processes that have occurred, the sum total of which have created a new security dilemma that threatens the security and stability of the international system. These processes are: the decline in the benefits of globalization accruing to states in Africa, the globalization of Islam, and the dissemination of information technology throughout the continent.

The chapter argues that the rise in global terror is less a reaction to deteriorating circumstances on the continent, but rather the result of the creation of a new regional hegemonic system intent on destroying the old. The globalization of radical Islam has resulted in the creation of increasing financial assistance to replace deteriorating global opportunities. This alternative assistance is provided by the Saudi state and is accompanied by an alternative religious, cultural and ideological base (Wahhabism), whose ideology attributes blames the West for the increasing decadence and declining economic base and one that calls for their destruction.

The availability of information technology, *in the wrong hands*, serves two purposes. First, it helps to facilitate the globalization of radical Islam. While Islam has been around for centuries, what is new is presence of a new "benevolent" whose financial support justifies allegiance from an "exploited" that sees themselves as the victim of the larger globalized system. Second, the availability of information technology has aided in the destruction of the existing hegemonic order established and controlled by the West as demonstrated by the steady increase in global terrorism.

The Global War on Terror (GWOT) is handicapped in two dimensions. First, Africa's deteriorating economic conditions pose a challenge in the availability of the information infrastructure needed to detect, halt, and destroy the proliferation of terror organizations within its borders. Second, while the dissemination of information and communication technology is important to minimize terrorist activities, it does very little to address the transfer of allegiance which this chapter argues is a significant factor in fighting the GWOT. While attacking the instruments of terror, the GWOT has failed to address the trappings of the existing global economic order and its existing configuration of global economic interdependence which lies at the heart of the transformation of hegemonic allegiance.

Africa and Globalization of Terror

The 1998 incidents of terror in Kenya and Tanzania signaled to the United States' foreign policy apparatus that al Qaeda had indeed penetrated the continent in order to facilitate its international operations. Consequently, three major al Qaeda trouble spots threaten the stability of the continent. In West Africa radical al Qaeda groups can be found in Nigeria and Niger. Other al Qaeda linked groups such as the Salafist Group for Preaching and Combat (GSPC) have developed a stronghold in Algeria and have developed some influence in eastern Mauritania, Northern Mali, northern Niger, and northern Chad. A third area in which al Qaeda has some influence is in the terror financing networks in Sierra Leone, Liberia, and the Democratic Republic of the Congo, where the trade in diamonds has been a profitable enterprise for the financing of international terror activities. In addition to the trafficking of diamonds in West Africa, other troubled spots have included the rise of Islamist movements in northern Sudan, northern Nigeria and in Somalia with the rise of Al-Ittihaad and the Union of Islamic Courts (UIC). Susan Rice argues before the US Congress that

Africa is unfortunately the world's soft underbelly for global terrorism. Al Qaeda and other terrorist cells are active throughout East, Southern, and West Africa, not to mention North Africa. These organizations hide throughout Africa. They plan, finance, train for, and execute terrorist operations in many parts of Africa, not just from Sudan and Somalia. They seek uranium, chemical weapons components and the knowledge of renegade nuclear, chemical and biological weapons experts from Libya to South Africa. Terrorist organizations take advantage of Africa's porous borders, weak law enforcement and security services, and nascent judicial institutions to move men, weapons, and money around the globe. They also take advantage of poor, disillusioned populations, often with religious or ethnic grievances, to recruit for their jihad against the civilized world. In short, terrorist networks are exploiting Africa thoroughly. And in the process, they are directly threatening our national security.[3]

While these incidents occurred inside of the continent, the effect of African terrorism would be felt around the globe. On 25 July 2005 four young assailants attempted what turned out to be a botched bombing of five points in the public underground rail system in Britain and one public bus line. Two of the perpetrators were African: Yassim Hassan Omar, a Somali native; and Muktar Said, an Eritrean. Likewise, a Tanzanian native, Ahmed Khalfan Ghailani, was captured and arrested in Pakistan, charged with the bombing of the US embassies in Kenya and Tanzania.[4]

While Rice identifies the importance of porous borders and the organizational effectiveness of al Qaeda in penetrating these borders, Marc Sageman argues that the effectiveness of global terror requires a pre-established set of structural relationships that facilitate and expedite the activities of the al Qaeda global network. Sageman argues that this global structure is one that consists of "hubs" and "nodes." Dempsey argues that this distinction is significant in defining the threat posed for the international system. The threat level created by "nodes" remains limited to location, and within the countries that have access to the system. "Hubs," on the other hand, have a wider international reach, creating a greater threat to the global community.[5]

Hubs are those organizational units that provide overall direction, guidance, funding, ideological support and leadership for Islamist groups throughout the globe. Nodes, on the other hand are typically small groups of individuals who operate in isolation from their communities and are isolated from each other. They conceive and implement the plans on the ground. They are internally very cohesive. This cohesiveness is enhanced through the use of information technology. Sageman argues that central to the operation of the hub–node structure is information technology, which provides the link between hubs and nodes which facilitates the movement of peoples, finances and communication of information. Node operations are hard to detect even with the most sophisticated technology of the international law enforcement community. They find their targets and plan their operations independent from the hubs, but benefit from the financial resources of the hubs.[6]

Since September 11, the relationship between "hubs" and "nodes" has been quite malleable and ever-changing. Jessica Sterns describes this changing relationship as "protean": designed to prevent detection.[7] Prior to September, the relationship between "hub" and "node" appeared to have been stronger. However, post-September 11 ties between the hub and nodes appear more illusive and weaker. After September

11 al Qaeda operations became more decentralized and connections to hub appear to be weak or non-existent.[8]

Using Sageman's framework, Dempsey argues that the al Qaeda structure was quite malleable in expediting terror on the African continent. In Liberia and Sierra Leone, al Qaeda operations functioned as hubs. Likewise, in Somalia, the Al-Ittihaad al-Islamiya (AIAI) serves as a regional hub for the infiltration of political Islam throughout East Africa, providing financial, ideological encouragement throughout Ethiopia; whereas the Jihadist group Ayro functions as a node, functioning independently to carry out its Jihadist missions in the region. In Kenya al Qaeda cells operated as nodes rather than hubs in carrying out the bombing of the US embassy.

A string of effective global organizational structures has the ability to deploy terror on the African continent and maintains the ability to spread terrorist activities elsewhere around the world. One important issue in understanding the role played by Africans concerns the causal factor that determines Africa's involvement in terror and the level of its involvement and commitment to al Qaeda and its agenda. To provide a more comprehensive analysis of this issue, the next section explores the role of Africa and the globalization of Islam.

Africa and the Globalization of Islam

One common denominator in the attacks against US interests in Africa, and the growing instability in the Horn of Africa, concerns the growth of Islam in the region. Islam continues to be the fastest growing religion on the continent as well as throughout the world.[9] Of the nearly one billion Muslims that exist throughout the world, approximately 700 million reside on the continent of Africa.[10]

Wahhabism is a radical form of the Islamic faith which has its roots in Saudi Arabia. It is also found in Pakistan, Afghanistan, Indonesia, and Sudan. Its ideological tenets consist of three elements: the spread of the faith with missionary zeal; political jihad and jihad; the commitment to use violence to preserve Islamic rule and the global community of believers (*umma*) from the infidel enemy. Wahhabism is the religion of the ruling families of Saudi Arabia who finance the global spread of this faith from the sale of oil. Strict Wahhabi adherents believe that those outside of the faith that fail to practice its principles are heathens and enemies of the Islamic people and the Islamic state. Critics point to its most famous adherent, Osama bin Laden and the radical al Qaeda organization; a network that beliefs in an sect of Islam that is misinterpretation and distortion of Islam.

The Saudi royal family undertakes its obligation to spread Islam globally with tremendous zeal. With contributions from both state coffers and personal financial resources, it financed the establishment of a number of Islamic centers throughout the world. In Africa it established the King Faisal Center in N'djemena, Chad; the Islamic Center in Abuja, Nigeria; and the Islamic African Center in Khartoum, Sudan. The Kingdom established more than 1,359 mosques throughout the world at a cost of SR 820 million. In Africa the Islamic Solidarity Mosque was established in Mogadishu, Somalia. In Gabon the Saudi's built four mosques, two of which are in Burkina Faso. From his personal resources King Fahd funded the King Faisal Mosque in Chad; the

Farooee Mosque in Cameroon; Zanzibar Mosque in Tanzania; al Azhar Mosque in Egypt; Yaoundi Mosque in Cameroon; Grand Mosque in Senegal; and the Islamic Institute in Djibouti.[11]

The globalization of Islam is empowered by what Strange identifies as the "center of gravity." He identifies two power sources: the Islamic cell and the *madrassas* or religious schools. The cells reflect the structure that was identified by Sageman to carry out its global objectives. The madrassas, however, are the centers of learning based on the *sharia* legal code. This is where indoctrination and transmission of anti-globalization, anti-American and anti-Western sentiments occur and where students prepare for the worldwide jihad and the creation of a global Islamic community (*ummah*).

The critical requirement for the center of gravity necessitates an ideology to inspire recruits; a fertile environment in which to recruit; command and control leadership; legitimacy—sponsorship from either a state, political party or media outlet, funding; sanctuary, and access to supplies.[12]

The globalization of Islam rested heavily on the spread of madrassas, which remains the locus of indoctrination. The Kingdom undertook to facilitate the state-sponsored spread of Islam to the continent. In addition to funding of mosques, Islamic Centers and madrassas, the Kingdom underwrote travel for the purpose of *Hajj* (pilgrimages); educational exchanges; humanitarian aid and charitable contributions; and financial support for Wahhabi groups and organizations. It vigorously recruited and financially supported and rewarded hard line clerics that articulated the most virulent anti-American rhetoric and who strongly proclaimed and urged the destruction of the West. For those religious leaders outside the faith, inducements were provided for those willing to abandon their non-Islamic beliefs and convert to Islam. [13]

The globalization of Islam necessitated two sets of conditions. The first involved an elaborate and sophisticated financial system that allows ready access to finances. Second, it requires the utilization of quick and efficient methods of global communications that facilitates instant global communications. The former resulted in the establishment of a system of Non-Government Organizations (NGOs) to finance the operations of global Islam. The latter required the access to Information and Communications Technology (ICT) that would enhance the level of global interdependence.

Three Islamic institutions were created by the Kingdom's global spread of Islam. The first was the Muslim World League. Funded by the Saudi government, more than half of its affiliates were located in Africa: a total of sixteen. A subsidiary of the League, the International Islamic Relief Organization (IIRO) was also created. The mission of the IIRO was to train religious leaders and distribute the Koran for purposes of conversion. Of its 70 global affiliates, 36 were located in Africa. The third institution that was established was the World Assembly of Muslim Youth (WAMY); the objective of the WAMY was to provide support to fund over 48 mosques in sub-Sahara Africa. The Saudi government also provided developmental assistance through the Saudi Fund for Development (SFD) in the amount of $750 million in grants and $1.9 billion in loans between 1975 and 2002 to sub-Sahara Africa.[14]

As the issue of globalization of terror gained international traction, the Saudi global financial structure became intertwined with the global structure of terror. Islamic organizations were charged with allowing resources to fund global terror. A list of Islamic charities associated with terrorism was created. The list includes the World Association of Muslim Youth, the Muslim World League and the International Islamic Relief Organization, all of which are stationed in Saudi Arabia. There are two additional charitable organizations that have been linked to terror: Al Wafa Charitable Organization and Al Haramayn Islamic Foundation (See Appendix).[15]

US Foreign Policy and Africa's Global War on Terror

On June 2002, in his address to the graduates at West Point, President George W. Bush set the course for the new direction that the US would take in fighting the GWOT:

> Defending our nation against its enemies is the first and fundamental commitment of the Federal Government. Today, that task has changed dramatically. Enemies in the past needed great armies and great industrial capabilities to endanger America. Now, shadowy networks of individuals can bring great chaos and suffering to our shores for less than it costs to purchase a single tank. Terrorists are organized to penetrate open societies and to turn the power of modern technologies against us. To defeat this threat we must use every tool in our arsenal—military power, better homeland defenses, law enforcement, intelligence and vigorous efforts to cut off terrorist financing. The war against terrorists of global reach is a global enterprise of uncertain duration. America will help nations that need our assistance in combating terror. And America will hold to account nations that are compromised by terror, including those who harbor terrorists.[16]

There are presently a variety of US foreign policy initiatives that attempt to protect American interests. The Terrorism Interdiction Program (TIP) computer system was established in 2003 in select airports in Kenya, Tanzania, and Ethiopia. A year later Djibouti and Uganda were also equipped with the technology. Using this technology, airport security agencies are able to more accurately detect terrorists in transit. The computer hardware and software provide the capability of performing name and other identity checks from a global terrorist watch list. The point of the system is to increase the probability of spotting and detaining a terrorist immediately after a crime has been perpetrated. It further allows nations to collect, analyze and compare, and distribute terrorist information, resulting in a greater likelihood of detaining terror suspects.[17]

The African Coastal and Border Security Program (ACBSP) was established in 2003 to set aside funding for specific African countries to provide intelligence data, special equipment, and training that would eliminate cross-border threats, to combat piracy, smuggling, and other illegal transborder activities. Recipients of this program are Angola, Chad, Djibouti, Eritrea, Ethiopia, Gabon, Kenya, Nigeria, Uganda, and Sao Tome. The program receives approximately $4 million from the US each year for Africa's border security. Additionally, Nigeria has also been the recipient of seven US Coast Guard cutters to assist in the protection of offshore oil installations and oil tankers.[18]

A second US foreign policy initiative, the Trans-Sahara Counter Terrorism Initiative (TSCTI), was established in June of 2005 to prevent Africa from becoming a safe haven for terrorists. TSCTI is an inter-agency endeavor of the Department of State, USAID, and the Treasury and Defense Departments designed to combat Islamic terrorism, instill political and economic development, and to enhance regional security by enhancing the integrity of each nation's borders. In the interagency collaboration several bureaucratic entities were tasked with appropriate responsibilities: the State Department assumed the responsibility of airport security, responsibility for military operations was given to the Department of Defense, money laundering was placed under the purview of the Department of the Treasury, and finally, USAID undertook development and educational issues.

TSCTI is the reformulation of a previous policy, the 2002 Pan Sahel Initiative (PSI), a US$8.4 million program with a regional focus of border protection for states in the Sahel (Mali, Chad, Niger) against terrorist groups stationed in Algeria. TSCTI has expanded to include the broader Sahara region as well as to cooperatively extend to states in the Maghreb (Algeria, Morocco, and Tunisia). Participant countries received assistance from the US European Command (EUCOM) to control its vast borders so as to stem the illegal movement of arms, people, and goods that might otherwise go undetected. A large component of the program is the provision of border safety as well as aviation security.

The US Department of Transportations Safe Skies for Africa Initiative (SSAI) provides African states with the training and facilities to evaluate their aviation systems to enhance aviation safety. This program established a virtual training symposium where African aviation specialists can share, exchange and post information concerning aviation security and training needs. Additionally, this program has also reviewed the aviation systems of nine participating members and offers technical assistance to assist participating countries to meet the aviation safety standards of both the Federal Aviation Administration as well as the International Civil Aviation Organization.

Collectively, the Bush administration moved to integrate critical states in several regions as a "preemptive move" strategy to prepare African states for the expected relocation of al Qaeda to suspected safe havens. This policy oddly enough represented the administration's inadvertent understanding of the globalization terror.

Information Technology and the Global War on Terror

Central to the Bush administration's strategy to defeat global terrorism was the recognition of an enhanced role for information and communications technology. Jakkie Cilliers observes that globalization is a significant factor in the spread of terrorism in three ways: First, he argues that global interconnections through the internet, cell phones, and international travel create a facilitating environment that assists in the facilitation of the spread of terrorism. Second, communications technology, such as television and other media, create the kind of media extravaganza surrounding the bombings and hijackings which in turn mobilizes and instigates other terrorists worldwide to action. Third, globalization facilitates the global movement of labor and the creation of diaspora communities. These communities, Cilliers argues, become a breeding ground for and lend support to the internationalization of terrorism.[19]

Globalization provides the equipment and the connections that create fertile ground for insurgent terrorist activities. ICT, which emerged as the instrument for the ascendancy of capitalism to yet another level, has wielded its double-edged sword to become the potential for its very demise. The ICT infrastructure that facilitates the globalization of commerce and the movement of capital also facilitates the spread of terror through regions otherwise untouched by the specter of terrorist violence. Thus from this perspective terrorism in the current highly integrated world creates a security dilemma of enormous proportions.

As a result of the ensuing security dilemma, one can expect the emergence of a new hegemonic discourse articulating a new security agenda which attempts to protect the vulnerabilities of international capital from the looming yet ephemeral presence of the terrorist whose very power comes from the ability to use the access to information technology to reproduce by recruiting other likeminded ideologues for the execution of the deadly strategy to influence and undermine the hegemonic order. This chapter endeavors to explicate how complex interdependence and the use of information technology by terror groups created a global security dilemma that posed a threat to the economic interests of the West. Winning the GWOT can only occur with the assistance of the West to transform Africa's aging infrastructure to one that can compete with the information challenges posed by global terrorist groups. The gauntlet has been thrown down and both Africa and the West are forced to meet the challenge.

Since September 11th, information technology has been given significant attention in the GWOT in every agency that has been charged with addressing the issue of global terror. As the war on terror becomes a global endeavor, the role that IT plays becomes crucial to its success. The success of US military abroad in protecting America's far flung interests require a superior ability to communicate essential details as swiftly as possible in a format in which only the essential personnel are able to translate and utilize in operation. The US Defense Advanced Research Project Agency (DARPA), the research and development arm of the US Department of Defense, played a critical role in streamlining the IT instruments to assist the administration's implementation of a strategy to win GWOT.

David Holtzman posits that "the administration is currently at work planning a new information system—one capable of anticipating terrorist acts using artificial intelligence, or 'data profiling' technologies."[20] Holtzman argues that a successful counterterrorism strategy should consist of the following:

> Connecting government databases containing *information* from customs, immigration, law enforcement, military and tax files, state and local records, political contribution lists, and education and voting records; Building software that bridges government and commercial databases.; Connecting the system to millions of real-time sensors for up-to-the-minute threat assessment. Sensors include chemical and radiation detectors and cameras in public

places such as storefronts, highways and airports; Requiring that everyone carry a national ID card, and tying it into a database of biometric *information* such as fingerprints, retinal scans, face measurements, blood type and DNA; Tracking phone calls, e-mails and the like and generating diagrams of social groupings using "traffic analysis" tools. Predicting behavior based on social interactions and "networks" of individuals who communicate with one another within a group; Building *technology* that will "guess" what people are thinking and what they might do, using rules-based analyses similar to those used by credit scoring systems; [and] Giving people a secret "threat score" or "loyalty rating" using *technology* similar to that used by credit card companies.[21]

The technology that has emerged from this constellation of needs has been the Terrorism Information Awareness (TIA) system. TIA is the brainchild of DARPA and was designed to utilize information technology in a security context as a tool to effectively detect foreign terrorists in order to intercept and avert their actions in a timely manner.[22] Its attention and priority level reflected the foreign policy priorities of the Bush administration, which was to win the GWOT at any cost.

Africa and the War on Terror

Cillier's three elements of globalization—global interconnections, the use of communications technology, and movements of individuals across borders— significantly impacts Africa's war on terror in three ways. The flow of human capital across its extensive unsecured borders made its boundaries impervious to terrorism from the Middle East, allowing the flow of terrorism to move freely within the continent and throughout the world. The poor information infrastructure and poor border security system undermined the ability of the vast majority of African states to authenticate travel documents, and its inability to amass data in a format that is readable and transportable to other states swiftly severely undermined its ability to win the war on terror. Third, coordinated institutionalized relations of cooperation between states throughout the region using communication systems that facilitated the speedy and efficient communication of information that would effectively hinder the spread of terrorism and that would assist in international investigations of terrorism were clearly unlikely given Africa's post-September 11 information infrastructure.

Africa's regional effort to address its security dilemma began in 1999 after the bombing of the US embassies in Kenya and Tanzania with the negotiation of the Organization of African Unity's *Convention on the Prevention and Combating of Terrorism*. A clear mandate was handed down to address the security concerns through the monitoring of customs and immigration check points; establishing databases for the collection and analysis of information and data on terrorism, and by creating a network of cooperation between domestic security agencies within the region.[23]

The bombing of the World Trade Center in New York on September 11th immediately signalled a shift in the global agenda. The Counter Terrorism Committee (CTC) was created as a result of the Security Council Resolution 1373 in response to the September 11 tragedy. Under the auspices of the UN Security Council, the CTC, the African Union (AU), and its member states agreed to cooperate in order to defeat terrorism wherever it exists throughout the globe. The CTC generated consensus among states that they would specifically maintain terrorism as a high priority on their political agenda; that they share data and best practices relevant to international cooperation; and that they liaise with international, regional and sub-regional institutions to assist in fulfilling the mandates of international counterterrorism.

The CTC was also established to provide technical assistance to states in need of such assistance. Such assistance included connecting resource-poor states with donor states. The CTC would also make available to states a donor database to assist resource-poor states to meet their obligation to combat terrorism. At the March 2003 meeting of the CTC, the AU expressed its commitment to working with the World Bank to eliminate terrorism on the African continent.[24]

The CTC priorities were fulfilled under the auspices of the AU. The importance of establishing a secure and safe continent that would prevent a safe haven for terrorists was established in the creation of the Peace and Security Council (PSC) of the AU. The PSC had the definitive mandate of promoting peace and security on the continent, an environment which was necessary for sustainable economic development to occur.[25] The PSC was given the mandate of coordinating and harmonizing African signatories with the purpose of implementing the OAU Convention on the Prevention and Combating of Terrorism.[26]

By October 2004, the AU's Declaration of the Second High Level Intergovernmental Meeting on the Prevention and Combating of Terrorism in Africa established Africa's strategic priorities in fighting and winning the GWOT. Theses instruments included establishing bilateral and multilateral agreements to strengthen intelligence and border surveillance; improving interregional cooperation that will facilitate more efficient exchange of information; the facilitation of consultations with regional economic communities to implement the AU Protocol; and employ ICT in a greater capacity in combating terrorism. The modalities for "information gathering, processing, dissemination ... and exchange" were formalized in Articles 4 and 5 of the Protocol to the OAU Convention on the Prevention and Combating of Terrorism.

Technological Innovation, ICT and Africa's Global War on Terror (GWOT)

A clear global, regional, and national agenda had been established after the events of September 11. For Africa the GWOT would require more than a military or security strategy but an economic development strategy as well. The new agenda would be predicated on a solid foundation of technological innovations and information technology if the GWOT were to be winnable. The technological innovation would consist of border control surveillance equipment, intelligence equipment including a modernized satellite surveillance system; airport border control equipment, computer-readable passports, and the appropriate machines to read them; and border control intelligence and computerized systems at all points of entry.

Nevertheless, Africa's ICT infrastructure endured many challenges that stood in its way to winning the war against terror. These challenges include reduced access to telephones, computers and the internet. In addition inadequate ICT human resource capabilities and the lack of coordination ICT policies and regulatory systems have also hindered progress in the region. These inadequacies have created a widening gap in the digital divide between Africa and the industrialized nations in the West, creating urgency for the region. It required the partnership and coordinated efforts with The New Partnership for African Development (NEPAD) and a variety of other key Regional Economic Commissions (RECs). These RECs included Common Market for Eastern and Southern Africa (COMESA), Eastern African Community (EAC), Economic Community for Central African States (ECCAS), Economic Community for West African States (ECOWAS), Intergovernmental Authority on Development (IGAD) and Southern Africa Development Community (SADC).[27]

NEPAD

In May of 2002 The New Partnership for African Development (NEPAD) produced a Short Term Action Plan (STAP) in which it outlined the regional priorities that would bridge the infrastructural gap between Africa. There are two aspects of the Plan that were of high priority and had tremendous significance for the GWOT. The first area is a set of NEPAD's Information and Communication Technology Infrastructural enhancement initiatives. The enhancement initiatives consisted of three programs: *ICT Infrastructure and Development and Roll-out Projects*; ICT Infrastructure and Development and Roll-out Facilitation Projects; and ICT Infrastructure Exploitation and Utilization Initiatives.[28]

Under *ICT Infrastructure and Development and Roll-out Projects*, five regional projects were initiated to enhance both regional and global connectivity. These high-priority projects were sponsored primarily through the RECs: COMESA's COMTEL project connecting its member states; ECOWAS' regional interconnection project; SADC's Regional Infrastructure Initiative (SRII); South, Central, West and East connectivity project; and RASCOM's global interconnectivity project.

Regional African Satellite Communications System (RASCOM) is an intergovernmental commercially operated satellite provider. RASCOM's mission is to establish regional connectivity between all African states and to support and enhance international interconnectivity and provide a range of services that include voice, internet, fax transmission, television, and video conferencing. It consists of 45 of the 53 African countries in partnership for regional telecommunications coverage. The RASCOM project began in March of 2003.

The *ICT Infrastructure and Development and Roll-out Facilitation* initiatives also consists of five projects to enhance the continent's ICT infrastructural development. The primary objective of this group of projects is to: harmonize regulatory systems throughout the continent; develop human resource capacity; and to facilitate African states with effective participation in the global ICT decision-making arenas. Facilitation projects are continental in scope and are initiated in conjunction with the ITU, the African Telecommunications Union, and RECs. They consist of the following: Strengthening of Africa Telecommunications and ICT Institutions Project; ICT Policy and Regulatory Framework Harmonization at the Regional Level;

Program to Enhance Africa's Participation in the Global ICT Policy and Decision Making Fora; the ICT Human Resource Capacity Development Initiative for Africa; and the Telecommunications Equipment Manufacturing in Africa Study.[29]

The *ICT Infrastructure Exploitation and Utilization Initiatives* are continent-wide endeavors that include: the Electronic Governance and Government Initiative for Africa; the African Continent Development Promotion Initiative; the African Regional Tele Education Initiative; the African Electronic and Trade Initiative; the African Regional Telemedicine Initiative; and the African SCAN-ICT and E-Readiness Initiative.[30]

The infrastructure and development programs are instrumental in Africa's participation in the GWOT as they enhance the information-sharing abilities of member states and their ability to communicate effectively within the region. The second aspect of the NEPAD STRAP initiative that would assist the region in the GWOT was the transportation goal of "safe, secure and efficient skies and airports."[31] This program would be accomplished through the implementation of a four initiatives: the Yamoussoukro Decision; the Upper Air Space Control Center (UACC) project; two Regional Global Navigation Satellite Systems (GNSS); and Cooperative Development of Operational Safety and Continuing Airworthiness Project (COSCAP).[32]

The first initiative involved the implementation of the 1999 Yamoussoukro Decision to liberalize the aviation market, to privatize the industry and to restructure and upgrade the sector. The second initiative concerned the implementation of a variety of initiatives designed to enhance the security sector. The first initiative undertook a feasibility study to ascertain the feasibility of implementing the Upper Air Space Control Center (UACC) project, a single air-space corridor above 24,000 feet. The second initiative involved the setting up of two regional Global Navigation Satellite Systems (GNSS) to enhance navigational safety, complying with all International Civil Aviation Organization (ICAO) standards, and establishing Joint Safety oversight units under ICAO's Cooperative Development of Operational Safety and Continuing Airworthiness Project (COSCAP).

Conclusion

Turjan argues that as a result of globalization, terrorism has emerged as a global and unmanageable phenomenon.[33] The GWOT has become the number-one priority in a globalized world to protect globalization from its very own instruments of success. Winning the war on terror therefore mandates a global approach, the success of which depends on the very instruments of globalization: information and communications technology. As a result, the very strategies for winning the GWOT require a greater level of commitment to ensure that states battling terrorism are endowed with ICT infrastructures that will enhance their ability to detect and hinder the activities of terrorists.

What is the participation of poor states in the GWOT? As developing states become intertwined in the GWOT, Turjan et al. argue that one can expect to encounter a strategic connection between development assistance with security considerations in the policy of major donors.[34] Turjan et al. assert that:

> As the war on terror becomes the number one global political priority, development cooperation is increasingly being influenced or captured by the global security agenda. Security considerations are being promoted as key in the granting of development aid, either in the selection of programs or partners or in the actual promotion of military or quasi-military assistance as development aid. Governance and the rule of law, promoted in development cooperation, are also being reinterpreted to encompass more effective anti-terrorism legislation and enforcement.[35]

Central to this global security agenda is to curtail the free movement of terrorists, much like the controls placed on the free movement of labor.

> Security considerations provide justification and opportunity for strengthening the boundaries between the global North and the global South. While globalization espouses economic integration and the free movement of capital, this has never included the free movement of people. The war on terror has, in fact, provided an excuse for pursuing vigorously the pre-September 11 agenda of increasing constraints on movement—and the human rights—of refugees and economic migrants.[36]

The rise of terrorism has signaled a significant threat to the existing system of global economic interdependence. As a result we have witnessed a variety of hegemonic responses to protect its interests and the system over which it presides. These responses include a variety of domestic policies to protect its 'homeland' and a variety of external bilateral, multilateral and regional initiatives that have been devised to address the security dilemma: all designed to bring stability to a system that stands at the brink of possible destruction.

However, the existing strategies for the GWOT address several key areas in the spread of global terrorism. The first involves the securing of borders to prevent infiltration of known terrorists and their sympathizers throughout the world. Second, great pains are also undertaken to infiltrate the communications network, which also includes engaging in financial transactions that will facilitate terrorist activities. Finally, some effort is also made to provide financial assistance to weak and unstable states to enhance stability within their borders as well as to enhance their financial wellbeing. What is missing from the existing strategy is an understanding of the ideological transfer of allegiance to a regional hegemon whose actions are deemed benevolent, and away from one whose actions are demonized and whose structures are perceived to be destructive.

There are three possible outcomes to the long-term stability of the international system. The first is that the GWOT is a roaring success and terrorism is utterly defeated and the system is restored to the former hegemonic order. A second outcome of the GWOT and its technological imperative would lead to a distortion of the development needs of many states that would lead to additional burdens on the development priorities of a continent seeking to make meaningful strides in meeting its development goals. A third possible outcome of the GWOT is the emergence of a new thinking in the international political economy which acknowledges that under the existing international order, a system of global inequality creates a growing international security dilemma as well as hinders the ability to address such problems, ultimately resulting in a genuine restructuring of the present international system.

Appendix

List of Charity Organizations Suspected of Ties to Terrorist Groups

Al Haramain Foundation
Alavi Foundation
Benevolence International Foundation (BIF)
Global Relief Foundation (GRF)
Help the Needy
Holy Land Foundation for Relief and Development (HLF)
Human Appeal International
Institute of Islamic and Arabic Science in America (IIASA)
International Islamic Relief Organization (IIRO) or Internal Relief Organization (IRO)
Islamic African Relief Agency and/or Islamic American Relief Agency
Islamic Assembly of North American
Islamic Association for Palestine
Islamic Circle of North America (ICNA)
Islamic Foundation of America
Islamic Society of North America
Kind Hearts
Muslim Arab Youth Association (MAYA)
Muslim Student Association
Muslim World League
Rabita Trust
SAAR Foundation and all members and related entities
Solidarity International and/or Solidarity USA
United Association for Studies and Research (USAR)
World Assembly of Muslim Youth

Source: See Saudi Commitment to Establishing Islamic Centers. An Assessment of Current Efforts to Combat Terrorism Financing. Hearing Before the Committee on Governmental Affairs, June 15th 2004. (US Government Printing Office). Appendix B, p. 107.

Notes

1   United States Institute of Peace, *Terrorism in the Horn of Africa: Special Report* 113, p. 2. See also Ron Suskind, *One Percent Doctrine: Deep Inside America's Pursuit of Its Enemies Since 9/11* (New York: Simon & Schuster, 2006).
2   Cyril Obi, "Oil, US Global Security and the Challenge of Development in West Africa," *CODESIA Bulletin*, Nos 3 and 4, 2005, p. 38. http://www.codesria.org/Links/

Publications/bulletin3_05/obi.pdf. The site was accessed on December 10, 2006.

3   Statement by Dr. Susan Rice, Former Assistant Secretary of State Testimony before US House of Representative the Subcommittee on Africa. November 15 2001.

4   Kamran Kahn, "Pakistan Holds Top Al Qaeda Suspect," *Washington Post*, Friday, July 30, 2004; p. A10. http://www.washingtonpost.com/wp-dyn/articles/A25194-2004Jul29. html. The site was accessed on January 2, 2007.

5   Thomas Dempsey, *Counterterrorism in African Failed States: Challenges and Potential Solutions*. (Carlisle, PA: Strategic Studies Institute, US Army War College Commandan).

6   Marc Sageman, *Understanding Terror Networks* (Philadelphia: University of Pennsylvania Press, 2004).

7   Jessica Stern, "The Protean Enemy (al Qaeda)," *Foreign Affairs*, Jul/Aug 2003, 82(4): 27–40.

8   Ibid.

9   Ali Mazrui, ed. *Islam: Between Globalization & Counterterrorism* (Oxford: James Curry Publishers, 2006), p. 81.

10   Ibid.

11   See Saudi Commitment to Establishing Islamic Centers. An Assessment of Current Efforts to Combat Terrorism Financing. Hearing Before the Committee on Governmental Affairs, June 15, 2004. (Washington, DC: The US Government Printing Office). Appendix B, p. 107.

12   Joe Strange, Center of Gravity and Critical Vulnerability, Second Edition (Quantico, VA: Marine Corps War College, 1996), p. ix.

13   Davis McCormack, *An African Vortex: Islamism In Sub-Sahara Africa.* Occasional Paper Series #4 (Washington, DC: Center for Security Policy, January 2005). http:// www.centerforsecuritypolicy.org/Af_Vortex.pdf. p.5. The site was accessed on January 2, 2007.

14   Ibid. p. 8.

15   US Senate Finance Committee, Senators Request Tax Information on Muslim Charities for Probe.

16   See the Introduction of the National Security Strategy of the United States. September 2002. http://www.whitehouse.gov/nsc/nss.html. The site was accessed: January 2, 2007.

17   See "Fighting Terrorism in Africa," Hearing Before the Subcommittee on Africa, April 2004 (Washington, DC: GPO), p. 14. The site was accessed on January 2, 2007.

18   Daniel Volman, "US Military Programs in Sub-Sahara Africa 2005–2007," (Washington, DC: Association of Concerned African Scholars). http://www.prairienet.org/acas/ military/military06.html. The site was accessed on January 2, 2007.

19   Jakkie Cilliers, "Terrorism and Africa," *African Security Review*, 12(4), 2003. http:// www.iss.co.za/pubs/ASR/12No4/Cilliers.pdf. The site was accessed on November 28, 2006.

20   See, Gary H. Anthes, "IT to Fight Terrorism," *Computerworld*, 36(48), November 25, 2002.

21   Ibid.

22   See the Report to Congress Regarding the Terrorism Information Awareness Program, May 20, 2003.

23   See Part II, Areas of Cooperation, Article 4 and Exchange of Information, Article 5 of the OAU Convention on the Prevention and Combating of Terrorism. See also the AU's Protocol to the OAU Convention on the Prevention and Combating of Terrorism.

24   See Article 3 a) and b) of the Protocol Relating to the Establishment of the Peace and Security Council of the African Union. Durban, South Africa, July 2002.

25   See Article 7: Powers, section 1(i) of the Protocol Relating to the Establishment of the Peace and Security Council of the African Union.

26   Ibid.

27   COMESA consists of 20 member states; EAC has 5 members; ECCAS has 11 member states; ECOWAS 15 members; IGAD 7 members; and SADC 14.

28   28   NEPAD, *Executive Summary: Short Term Action Plan (Infrastructure)*, May 2002,
     p. 8.
29   Ibid.
30   Ibid. p. 9.
31   Ibid, p. 7.
32   Ibid, p. 9.
33   Antonio Tujan, Audrey Gaughran, and Howard Mollett, "Development and the 'Global
     War on Terror,'" *Race and Class*, 46(1): 53–74, 2004, p. 55.
34   Ibid.
35   Ibid.
36   Ibid.

Chapter 5

North African Responses to Bush's War on Terror

Mohamed A. El-Khawas

Introduction

The September 11, 2001 terrorist attacks on the World Trade Center and the Pentagon forced President George W. Bush to shift his attention from domestic problems to international affairs. Because the hijackers were of Middle Eastern and North African origin, his administration also began to pay more attention to this region, seeking new strategies to protect the US from future terrorist attacks. What emerged were fundamentally altered US attitudes and policies toward the Arab and Muslim world.

President Bush launched a new strategy to defend the US against those who would inflict mass violence. The Bush doctrine allowed the US to launch preemptive strikes against any group deemed to pose a threat to America's national security or any nation harboring terrorists. As Bush told West Point cadets, "the military must be ready to strike at a moment's notice in any dark corner of the world. All nations that decide for aggression and terror will pay a price."[1] He called on other states to join the US-led war on terrorism. As he put it, "you are either with us or the terrorists."[2] He insisted that there was no place for neutrality in this war.

The US went to the United Nations and obtained Security Council approval to take military action against the perpetrators who were behind the 9/11 attacks. This meant that the US would take action against al Qaeda. Within a week after the attacks, Bush authorized the CIA "to kill, capture and detain members of al Qaeda anywhere in the world."[3] Having little experience in foreign affairs, he turned to Vice President Dick Cheney, Secretary of Defense Donald Rumsfeld, and his deputy Paul Wolfowitz for advice. Their objectives were to use the September attacks as a pretext to try to re-shape the Middle East and to ensure US hegemony and dominance over its energy resources. Their agenda, according to William Quandt, a Middle East expert and former member of the National Security staff, was based on two themes: that "Iraq is too dangerous for containment and that the entire region is ripe for fundamental transformation—not by nurturing indigenous movements, but by getting rid of the bad guys."[4] The Bush administration thus embarked on a dangerous new course, abandoning diplomacy in favor of direct military intervention. The administration had become unilateralist and unconstrained by international law or the UN Charter. Its policy was to be carried out by ultimatum and backed up by force rather than through collective decisions achieved by reaching consensus among traditional allies. Washington is ready to sacrifice the stability of other countries by meddling in their internal affairs for the sake of achieving its policy goals.

The Bush administration decided on a three-pronged approach to combat international terrorism. The first was to go after al Qaeda, which presented the most immediate threat to the US. Bush's top priority was to capture Osama bin Laden by waging a war in Afghanistan, where his movement had been given sanctuary. The Taliban regime would have to be overthrown because it had not complied with an American ultimatum to turn over al Qaeda leaders and fighters. Between October and December 2001, Washington waged a relentless military campaign that destroyed al Qaeda's training camps in Afghanistan, captured many of its fighters, and significantly disrupted its operation. The Taliban government was replaced by a secular, pro-US regime, led by Hamid Karzai, and supported by NATO forces. However, the failure to capture bin Laden alive or dead and the renewal of violence in Afghanistan led the White House to turn its attention to Iraq.

The second phase concerned the president's decision to extend the war on terror to Iraq to save the US and the region from President Saddam Hussein's weapons of mass destruction. The Iraqi president had been a thorn in the side of the Republican conservatives since the end of the Gulf War in 1991. As Bush told a group of friends in Texas, "this guy tried to kill my dad." It was a family matter that he intended to take care of and to end the criticism levied against his father for failing to march on Baghdad and remove Saddam Hussein from office in 1991. The administration mounted a systematic campaign to prepare the American public for military action against Iraq. It was no longer whether a war would be waged but only a matter of when and how. This decision to invade a sovereign nation and oust its government marked a dramatic shift in American foreign policy, causing a rift with traditional US allies in the region.

The third phase was non-military, aimed at overhauling political institutions in North Africa and the Middle East as a means to stamp out threats from militant Islamists. Administration neo-conservatives argued that democracy-building programs are needed throughout the region as the primary mechanism for the US to eliminate religious extremism. A lack of political freedom and a lack of economic opportunities in any of these countries, they believed, would prove harmful not only to the countries themselves but also to the US. The administration's remedy was to bring about greater citizen involvement in the political process so citizens within the region would not have to take their frustration out on Americans.

This chapter examines the challenges that the Bush administration faced in trying to convince North African governments to support the global war on terror, to take new steps toward democratization, and also to destroy the extremist organizations within their own countries. How have these governments responded to Washington's new agendas, even as they avoided the glare of world attention on these matters? This chapter analyzes the reaction of North African countries to the US-led war on terrorism. Each of the three phases in that campaign is analyzed in order to identify areas of agreement or conflict between North Africa and the US and to assess their impact.

Cooperation with the War on al Qaeda

The American people were angered by the September 11 attacks and felt vulnerable. They were horrified by the graphic scenes on television and shocked by the loss of thousands of innocent lives. American anger was shared by many nations across the world. Al-Azhar University, through its Rector Mohamed Sayed Tantawi, was "among the first ... religious institutions in the world to condemn the September 11th attacks,"[5] Undersecretary of State Karen Hughes has said. Libya's Mu'ammar Qaddafi, whose country had no diplomatic relations with the US at the time, joined other world leaders in condemning the attacks on New York and Washington. He sent his condolences and offered humanitarian assistance to the victims' families. He also allowed Libyan intelligence to meet their American and European counterparts and share information on al Qaeda and its regional affiliates. Qaddafi felt that the US had the right to strike against those who were behind these horrendous acts.[6]

The Bush administration especially sought the help of Arab countries as it planned its global war on terrorism. When the offensive against Afghanistan began in October 2001, Egypt's President Hosni Mubarak, who had fought radical Islamist groups trying to overthrow his own regime in the 1990s, came out in support of the war on al Qaeda but urged the US to avoid civilian Afghani casualties. As he explained, "We support all measures taken by the United States [to fight terrorism] because we suffered from terrorism before."[7]

For years, the Mubarak government had warned of the dangers posed by Islamic extremists and had criticized Europe, especially the United Kingdom, for giving political asylum to Egyptians who had committed terrorist acts in Egypt. The Egyptian leader also had warned the Bush administration of a possible terrorist attack a week before September 11.[8]

Egypt cooperated fully with Washington in supporting its overseas investigations and helped identify individuals with possible connections to al Qaeda. Mubarak later outlawed domestic groups within Egypt. The Egyptian regime allowed the agents of the US Federal Bureau of Investigation (FBI) to interview members of Islamic Jihad, which had merged with bin Laden to form al Qaeda, as well as the family and friends of Mohamed Atta, who had piloted one of the planes that hit the World Trade Center. Despite the US State Department's annual criticism of the Egyptian government's human rights record, the Bush administration, without any legal procedures, secretly transferred to Cairo for interrogation several people suspected of links to al Qaeda. The Egyptian intelligence services, which routinely uses torture to extract confessions, were used by the CIA to interrogate dozens of suspected terrorists arrested in other parts of the world during the post-September 11 roundup.[9] For example, the CIA apprehended Mamdouh Habib, an Egyptian-born Australian citizen, in Pakistan and transported him to Egypt. During interrogation, "he was burned by cigarettes, given electric shocks and beaten by Egyptian captors,"[10] he later reported. After six months of imprisonment in Egypt, he was transferred to Guantanamo prison camp, where he was kept until his release in 2005. Egyptian authorities also passed on sensitive intelligence about suspected terrorists regarding plans for future attacks in the US or its facilities abroad.

As for Sudan, President Omar El-Bashir condemned the September 11 terrorist attacks and wanted to join the war on terrorism. He wished to remove the stigma attached to his country as a haven to Islamist extremists, including bin Laden, who had resided there between 1991 and 1996. Khartoum traded intelligence on bin Laden and his group to improve relations with Washington.[11] Sudan provided the CIA access to files of suspected terrorists and handed several suspects over to the US.[12] Similarly, the government of Sudan offered the US military bases[13] to be used use to monitor the situation in East Africa, where al Qaeda members had bombed the American embassies in Kenya and Tanzania in 1998, and also to keep a watch on fractured Somalia, which could become a hiding place for terrorists. Because of the armed conflict in southern Sudan, the Bush administration opted instead to use Djibouti as a base of operations for American troops to enhance its counter-terrorism efforts in East Africa.

American and European intelligence agencies also paid special attention to the northwestern region of Africa (the Maghreb) because of its close proximity to southern Europe. These agencies worked closely with their North African counterparts and encouraged them to share information with each other in an effort to stop al Qaeda operatives from recruiting and using their citizens to carry out attacks in Europe. Millions of immigrants from Algeria, Morocco, and Tunisia live in Europe and many youth, who are alienated from the rest of European society, suffer from general prejudice against Muslims. They are disenfranchised, suffer from high rates of unemployment, and live in crowded housing in the slums of large urban areas. These conditions have made them susceptible to radical messages and offer a fertile ground for recruitment by terrorist groups, which are known to operate secretly in the Mediterranean region. European youth of North African origin have been implicated in plots to attack American embassies in Rome and Paris in 2001 as well as the truck explosion outside a synagogue in Djerba, Tunisia in April 2002.

Morocco participated in the war on terrorism and provided valuable services to the US. Following a visit to Rabat by George Tenet, then CIA Director, in February 2002, Moroccan intelligence agents went to interrogate some Moroccan nationals detained at Guantanamo Bay prison camp. They were gathering information on a top al Qaeda operative, Abu Zubair al-Haili, who was thought to be recruiting Moroccans for an attack. Upon receiving information from the CIA in May, Moroccan authorities arrested three Saudis at Casablanca airport as well as their Moroccan accomplices. They were accused of planning attacks on American and British ships in the Strait of Gibraltar in a manner similar to the 2000 suicide attack on the US destroyer Cole in Yemen. As a Western diplomat in Rabat put it, "The Moroccans worked hard to help nail these guys."[14] The Saudi suspects were secretly taken to a detention center in Temara, south of Rabat, run by the Direction de Surveillance du Territories (DST), which is Morocco's domestic intelligence service. They were interrogated in the presence of American agents because, as one American official put it, the Moroccans "can use more persuasive methods of questioning."[15] At the end of 2002, their trial in Casablanca was postponed because five witnesses, including the Saudi Ambassador, did not appear in court. Some observers began to wonder about the strength of the case because no explosives were ever found and confessions were extracted through torture.[16]

The DST has provided other services on behalf of the CIA. On 26 December 2002 the *Washington Post* reported that some detainees from Guantanamo Bay prison were handed over to Rabat for interrogation. Morocco has paid a high price for its support for the US campaign against al Qaeda, however. Casablanca was struck by several bombings in May 2003.

Algeria, which had gone through civil strife in the 1990s, has benefited from the US-led war on terrorism. It provided Algeria's military-backed governments with an opportunity "to capitalize on the international situation and to be recognized as a partner in the anti-terror campaign,"[17] Ikhlef Bouaichi, spokesman of the Berber-based Socialist Forces Front, said. In October 2001, the Algerian Ambassador to the US reminded the Congressional Black Caucus that his country, which lost tens of thousands of people to terrorism, received little support from the West at the time.[18] The situation changed after September 11. As the *Africa Research Bulletin* of January 2002 reported, "The military-backed rulers are riding high. They argue that their actions against Islamists 10 years ago have been vindicated."[19]

The global war on terror has given Algiers an excuse to kill and detain radical Islamists within its midst, especially Algerian veterans who had fought against the Soviets in Afghanistan in the 1980s. To justify its military campaign, the government claimed that there is a link between the Salafist Group and al Qaeda.[20] This accusation helped Algeria avoid open criticism for its repressive campaign against Islamist groups. The US and the European Union have shown no interest in finding a political solution to the power struggle in Algeria. As Ali Yahya Abdennour, head of Algeria's Human Rights League, pointed out, "The West has not understood that internal terrorism in our case is caused by dictatorship at the top."[21] The US and the European Union have turned deaf ears to internal criticism of the Algerian regime's violations of human rights. As a Western diplomat put it, "after September 11, they're on the good guys list."[22]

On the first anniversary of September 11, senior North African officials, along with other Africans, attended a conference in Algiers that was aimed at increasing cooperation among African agencies involved in the fight against terrorism. The Bush administration encouraged these governments to work together and to share intelligence in order to foil future terrorist attacks.

In brief, North African countries generally cooperated with the initial requests made by the US as part of its global war on terrorism. They had concerns about the next stage of the US war, however, when Bush named Iraq as a member of the "axis of evil." It was troublesome for North African governments when Bush expanded the war beyond al Qaeda to confront nations acquiring weapons of mass destruction, which he perceived as a threat to America's national security. It was especially problematic for them when, in early 2002, Bush ordered the CIA "to undertake a comprehensive, covert program to topple Saddam Hussein" and authorized the agency "to use lethal force to capture the Iraqi president."[23] To North African governments, it was one thing to fight an outlawed terrorist organization but it was another to use force to remove a government.

Divided Over Iraq

Immediately after the September 11 attacks, a concerted effort began at the highest level of the Bush administration to pin the terrorism problem on Saddam Hussein. Former General Wesley Clark told Tim Russet of *NBC*, "Bush administration officials had engaged in a campaign to implicate Saddam Hussein in the September 11 attacks—starting that very day." As he related, he got a call from the White House, asking him to link the Iraqi leader to the terrorist attacks. He had replied that he "was willing to say it, but What's your evidence? And I never got any evidence."[24] *CBS* has also reported that, five hours after the Pentagon was struck, Rumsfeld told his aides to prepare a plan for a strike against Iraq. His abbreviated instructions included: "Best info fast. Judge whether good enough [to] hit S.H."[25]

The administration scrambled to find evidence to support the decision to attack Iraq. The burden to come up with proof fell on Deputy Secretary Wolfowitz, the leading proponent of the war against Saddam Hussein. The Office of Special Plans was established in the Pentagon in the fall of 2001 to produce reports, to drum up public support, and to convince skeptical allies about the necessity of the war. This office turned to Israel and the Iraqi exile community, especially Ahmad Chalabi's Iraqi National Congress, for help even though these sources were biased and had their own self-interests in removing Saddam Hussein.[26] The administration neo-conservatives manipulated data on Iraq, exaggerated the threat from its weapons of mass destruction, and demonized its leader in an attempt to rally Americans behind the White House's hard-line policy toward Iraq.

North African governments disagreed with the Bush administration on how to proceed with Iraq. Although they did not like Saddam Hussein, they were suspicious of Bush's plan for the Arab world in general and Iraq in particular. They did not want the war on terror to be extended to their region. As events unfolded, they urged Saddam Hussein to cooperate with the UN inspectors to eliminate any weapons of mass destruction (WMD). Soon, however, it became clear to them that American neoconservatives would not be satisfied with the resumption of inspections and the disarmament of Iraq. Their worst fears were realized when Bush told British television in April 2002 that he had "made up [his] mind that Hussein must go."[27] It was a whole different ballgame when senior American officials started talking about war no matter what. It was necessary for North African leaders to decide individually on the course of action to be taken in the face of this US decision to go to war against an Arab country.

North African governments were caught between a rock and a hard place. First, the states were under increasing pressure from Washington to endorse its plan to wage war against Iraq. Second, it was difficult for them to side with the US against another Arab government, a member of the Arab League, when public opinion strongly opposed a US effort to oust Saddam Hussein. These regimes could not risk going against their citizens, who had been moved by the suffering of Iraqi civilians for twelve years under the UN's comprehensive sanctions, which had been enforced by the US and the United Kingdom.

Another reason for the general discontent was Bush's lack of concern for the suffering of the Palestinian people under Israeli occupation. North African populations were outraged about Israeli incursions into areas controlled by the Palestinian Authority. Al-Jazeera televised Israel's killing of Palestinians and demolishing of their homes to the living rooms and cafes across the region, inflaming public opinion. They blamed the US for its failure to intervene to end violence in the West Bank and Gaza and its failure to revive the peace process, which had been stalled since President Clinton had left office. In their view, Israel was a bigger threat to their national security than Iraq.

When American officials sought North African support for the Iraqi war, they were told to forget about Iraq and to focus on the Israeli–Palestinian problem. Many North Africans viewed the White House stance on Iraq as another example of a US double standard. While Bush was ready to go to war to force Iraq to get rid of its weapons of mass destruction, he had never advocated a similar action against Israel's nuclear arsenal.[28] They argued that it was hypocritical of Bush to insist on Baghdad's compliance with UN Security Council resolutions, while looking the other way on Israel's refusal to comply with UN resolutions. They also noted that, for Iraq, the US wanted to go to war but, for North Korea's nuclear crisis, the US policy was one of containment and diplomacy. Wamidh Nadhame, an Iraqi professor of political science, believed that the US invasion was "basically an angry response to the survival of Saddam Hussein, and it has something to do with oil interests in the area."[29]

A couple of weeks prior to the opening of the March 2002 Arab summit in Beirut, Vice President Cheney shuttled between Arab capitals but failed to convince their governments that Iraq's weapons of mass destruction were a threat to their national security as well as to the US. Arab leaders knew that Saddam Hussein could not inflict harm on his neighbors because his military was devastated during the 1991 Gulf War and he did not have the financial resources to rebuild his armed forces because of the UN sanctions. There was other evidence to support their conclusion. Scott Ritter, a former US Marine officer and a chief UN weapons inspector in Iraq, reported that nearly 95 percent of Iraq's weapons of mass destruction had been destroyed. In his view, Saddam Hussein posed no threat to the US.[30]

North African and Middle Eastern leaders who met with Cheney urged him to allow the talks between the Iraqis and the UN officials to continue. Mubarak informed the vice president that Saddam Hussein was going to allow weapons inspectors to return to Iraq.[31] Despite Cheney's urging, the Arab League summit unanimously called for an end to US threats of war against Iraq, which they considered "a threat to the national security of all the Arab states." They also told Iraq "to implement UN Security Council resolutions, particularly those concerning the monitoring of weapons of mass destruction." Their objective was "to deprive the US of any pretext for launching an offensive" against Iraq.[32]

North African governments strongly opposed having the US go to war without UN approval. They considered it a dangerous precedent for a superpower to unilaterally overthrow a government of a smaller and weaker nation just because Iraq was viewed as hostile to US interests. As Michael Elliott put it, "Outside the US, it is widely thought that, unless an attack on Iraq is authorized by the UN, it will encourage nations to overthrow regimes just because they don't like them."[33] In fact, the North African attitudes toward the war were no different from that of the British public, whose Prime Minister Tony Blair was the strongest supporter of Bush's war on Iraq. A poll taken in the fall of 2002 found that 70 percent of the British opposed military action against Iraq unless it was approved by the UN. Even the majority of Americans took a similar position. According to a *Gallup/CNN* poll in early January 2003, 52 percent of Americans would only support the war if UN weapons inspectors found evidence of weapons of mass destruction, while only 23 percent would support it if the Bush administration asserted that evidence existed.[34]

North African governments argued for caution because Iraq is not Afghanistan. Mubarak warned, "Striking Iraq is something that could have repercussions and post-strike developments. We fear chaos happening in the region."[35] They feared that a war against another Muslim country would inflame public opinion, adding another grievance to the long list of US misdeeds in the region. Radical religious groups would have new ammunition to increase anti-American sentiment. They warned that a military confrontation would create more problems for American allies in the region. During the Cold War, US presidents would have weighed these arguments heavily in order to avoid alienating their Arab allies, but September 11 changed everything. Bush had no interest in listening to the views of his friends in the region and did not care if they were destabilized to make America safe. As Abdal-Wahhab Badra Khan pointed out in *Al-Hayat* newspaper on March 14, 2002:

> Americans are not feigning any interest in taking the views of others, friends included, into account. The method employed is simply to inform those whom it may concern, in the region and the world that preparations are being made to attack Iraq. Never mind whether it is in the context of the war on terror or outside it, never mind whether Baghdad agrees to the return of arms inspectors or not, never mind if there are parties that in reality as well as verbally oppose an assault on Iraq.[36]

On January 23, 2003 foreign ministers of Egypt and five Middle Eastern countries met in Istanbul to try to stop the war [37] by convincing Saddam Hussein to go into exile. It was reported that Egypt offered him asylum. Other voices, including Arab writers and intellectuals, urged the Iraqi leader to step down to spare his country a destructive war. Their pleas fell on deaf ears, as Saddam Hussein had no plan to quit or to leave the country.[38]

Four days later, Hans Blix, the head of UN inspectors, reported to the Security Council that they found no concrete evidence that Baghdad hid weapons of mass destruction. He added that Iraq was cooperating with the inspection but there were some issues still under discussion.[39] American officials were not happy with the report and turned the heat on the inspectors to come up with reasons to assist Washington to start a war in the next few weeks.[40]

Despite increasing Arab and European opposition, Bush put the international community on notice that he was going to war with or without UN approval. In his State of the Union Address on January 28, 2003 Bush told the nation that "the course of this nation does not depend on the decision of others. Whatever action is necessary, I will defend the freedom and security of the American people."[41] A few days later, Secretary of State Colin Powell delivered a presentation to the Security Council and tried again to link Iraq to al Qaeda. Citing French sources, he alleged that Abu Mousab Zarqawi was providing training to Chechen fighters from Iraq.

French investigators were surprised to hear his statement because none of the terror suspects mentioned Zarqawi's name during their interrogations or even knew of him.[42] On the whole, Powell's evidence was flimsy and unconvincing because, as the *Economist* reported, the information came from al Qaeda "captives, who may be saying what they think their captors want to hear, or may even be hoping to provoke a war."[43] A declassified document released by Senator Carl M. Levin (D-Michigan) revealed that, a year before Powell's presentation to the Security Council, the Defense Intelligence Agency had doubts about the reliability of information extracted from Ibn al-Shaykh al-Libi, a top al Qaeda leader, on Baghdad's training of terrorists in biological and chemical weapons.[44]

Contrary to US claims, North African governments knew that there were no ties with al Qaeda, whose leaders considered Saddam Hussein an apostate and despised his suppression of Islamist groups in Iraq. There was no evidence that the terrorist organization received any funds from Iraq. In fact, Saddam Hussein had not been on good terms with al Qaeda, as evidenced by bin Laden's offer to raise a volunteer army to end Iraq's occupation of Kuwait in 1990. Moreover, the US report about a Prague meeting between an Iraqi intelligence officer and one of the September 11 hijackers (Atta) turned out to be false after the claim was investigated by American and Czech intelligence agencies. As the CIA reported, "The Iraqis have actually been consciously avoiding any actions against the United States or its facilities abroad." This was further corroborated by the State Department's annual report on Patterns of Global Terrorism, which "did not list any serious act of international terrorism by the government of Iraq."[45]

Having failed to link Iraq to al Qaeda, American officials brought up other charges, accusing Saddam Hussein of restarting his nuclear program. Cheney's office alleged that Saddam Hussein had tried to buy large quantities of uranium from Niger. After an investigation by former US Ambassador Joseph Wilson, the CIA notified the White House in March 2002 that there was no evidence to support the claim. The administration intentionally hid these CIA findings from Congress and used the bogus report of Iraq's nuclear threat to persuade both the House and the Senate to approve the use of force against Iraq. Furthermore, Bush made an explicit reference to the Iraq–Niger deal in his State of the Union Address at the end of January 2003.[46]

In February Secretary of State Powell sought the Security Council's authorization to wage war on Iraq. He presented "a mosaic of circumstantial material" based on testimony of Iraqi defectors and old satellite photographs to show that Iraq was in violation of the Security Council resolutions. However, Blix had reported that there was no significant evidence of forbidden weapons in Iraq. In the absence of a smoking gun, many Council members felt that they could not approve a war at this time. China, France, and Russia wanted to give UN weapons inspectors more time.[47] The US refused to wait until the final report was completed, fearing that it might deprive them of reasons to invade Iraq and unseat Saddam Hussein. Because of the persistent US refusal to share whatever evidence it had with UN inspectors to expedite the process, many diplomats and UN officials began to question Bush's assertion about Iraq's weapons programs.[48]

With war drums beating louder in Washington, the Arab League met in early March in Sharm El Sheikh, Egypt, to come up with a united stand on Iraq. During the meeting, Qaddafi criticized Saudi Arabia for allowing Americans to keep military bases in the kingdom after the Gulf War was over. Syria proposed to forbid Arab states from allowing the US or United Kingdom to use their territory for war against Iraq. However, Arab governments could not reach an agreement because Bahrain, Kuwait, and Qatar had already allowed American and British troops and weaponry into their countries—a situation leading Qaddafi to claim the entire Arabian Peninsula had become "an American protectorate." The summit finally settled on a compromise, calling on Saddam Hussein to increase cooperation with UN weapons inspectors and on the UN Security Council to give the inspectors more time to finish the job.[49]

When the US realized that it did not have enough votes in the Security Council to authorize the war, Bush decided to lead a "coalition of the willing" and launched an invasion of Iraq in March 2003. He ignored predictions from the CIA and the State Department that "postwar Iraq would be chaotic, violent and ungovernable, and that the Iraqis would greet the occupying armies with firearms, not flowers."[50]

North African Reaction to the Second Iraq War

There was a strong reaction to the war's outbreak across North Africa. Massive demonstrations took place in Egypt, Libya, Sudan, and Tunisia, where thousands protested the bombing of Baghdad. In Algeria, the government asked for nation-wide adherence to a minute of silence as an expression of solidarity with the Iraqi people.[51]

The Bush administration was not pleased with the Egyptian government's refusal to voice open support to the war. It demanded access to Egyptian facilities and to sharing of its intelligence because the US had no human intelligence on the ground in Iraq. President Mubarak was put on the spot with little room to maneuver. On the one hand, he had to respond to popular opposition to the war in order to keep the mass anger from turning against his regime. Conversely, Mubarak could not antagonize Washington, which provided Egypt with nearly $2 billion in aid annually. In the end, Mubarak walked a narrow path. He quietly allowed Americans to use Egyptian airspace to transport troops, aircraft and equipment to the Gulf and provided security for US warships crossing the Suez Canal. He also shared intelligence about the internal situation in Iraq and possible terrorist threats against the US. On the diplomatic front, Egypt was instrumental in preventing the Arab League from passing strong anti-American resolutions. It also urged Syria to close its borders to fighters and military hardware bound for Iraq—a step it took several days before the US publicly demanded such action.[52]

As the war concluded, North African governments were disappointed that Bush's pre-war promise to quickly turn over the country to the Iraqis was forgotten. They considered it highly regrettable that the intended liberation of Iraq had turned into an occupation backed by approximately 160,000 troops. The US took on the role of an occupier, putting an American administrator, retired General James Garner, and later L. Paul Bremer, in charge and empowering them with all executive, legislative, and judicial functions in Iraq. Deputy Defense Secretary Wolfowitz made it clear that they were in for a long haul. He told the Senate Foreign Relations Committee at the end of May 2003 that "it will be years before a fully functioning [Iraqi] national government is elected."[53] It is not surprising that an insurgency broke out four months after the invasion and was helped by masses of unemployed Iraqi military personnel and disgruntled Sunnis. On 6 January 2006 Bremer admitted on *NBC-TV*, "We really did not see the insurgency coming."[54]

North Africans didn't like Arab land occupied and abhorred Americans subjecting Iraqi civilians to searches at checkpoints, to arbitrary detainment, and to raids of private homes at night in search of weapons and contraband. They complained about the torture, interrogation, and punishment of Iraqi detainees in the US-run Abu Ghraib prison. They were critical of the US failure to restore water and electric services in Iraq or to maintain law and order across the country. Conditions for the majority of Iraqis were much worse than before the invasion. As Dhia Abbas, an Iraqi citizen, put it in December 2005, "Bush called for a war on terrorism, but he fought on our soil, not his. He protected his people but destroyed Iraq" he added, "Iraq is being destroyed day after day."[55]

North African governments were taken aback by the Bush administration's initial decision to exclude the UN from any involvement in Iraq's reconstruction. They were willing to work through the UN to make the transition smooth. It became clear to them, however, that the US was planning to stay in Iraq and control its oil. According to a 2003 public opinion survey by Zogby International conducted in Egypt, Morocco, and four Middle Eastern countries, nearly 95 percent of people interviewed believe that the Bush administration invaded Iraq to control its oil, not to make the region more democratic.[56] This view was confirmed by the fact that the first thing US forces did following the invasion was to secure control of the oilfields and to give American corporations unrestricted access to Iraq's oil resources. North African leaders were disappointed by Bush's decision to grant lucrative business contracts to the coalition members and to exclude Iraqis from participating in reconstruction projects. North Africans were also left out of any involvement in postwar Iraqi reconstruction. Nevertheless, the Bush administration pressured their governments to send diplomats back to Baghdad to lend legitimacy to the US occupation and to its plan for establishing a democratic form of government in Iraq.

Despite the fact that Iraq's democratization is proceeding slowly under adverse circumstances, many North African leaders are worried about the future of Iraq. The failure of the US and its allies to end the insurgency has led to widespread attacks and high casualties among civilians across the country. North African leaders have warned that this situation could evolve into a sectarian war that will tear the country apart, leading to the disintegration of Iraq. Currently, the country is divided into three zones: the Kurds in the semiautonomous north, the Shiite majority in the south, and the Sunni minority in the middle. This political configuration, reinforced by the coalition forces, has led to the emergence of a powerful Shiite-Kurd coalition that intends to control power and to weaken the Sunni minority, which had dominated the political scene in the past. During his visit to the White House in October 2005, Iraq's provisional president, Jalal Talabani, told the American people that the withdrawal of US troops from Iraq at this time would lead to the outbreak of a civil war and would leave the survival of Iraq as an integrated country in doubt.

Democratic Transformation: A Myth or Reality

Bush, who has turned Iraq into a battlefield where the war on terrorism is being fought, has other plans for the rest of North Africa and the Middle East. The president intends to bring democracy to every country in the region as part of an administration campaign to eliminate conditions that support the rise of radical ideologies. Although most North African nations have formal elements of being democratic (holding multiparty elections, for example), the democratization process is still far from complete. Over the years, reforms have been on and off because the incumbent presidents are in a position to decide how fast reforms should proceed. Generally, it is in their interest to slow the process as long as they can in order to prolong their stay in office.

The Bush administration argued that the lack of political freedom and widespread poverty have led to instability and created an environment conducive to religious fanaticism, and thus a threat to US security. Al Qaeda and other militant groups have found it easy to gain support in such settings and to promote their radical ideologies. Shibley Telhami, University of Maryland professor and a board member of the US Institute of Peace, stated his views: "It is not Islam that breeds militancy, but the lack of democracy, the lack of sufficient and appropriate mechanisms to handle dissent."[57] This thinking led Washington to conclude that the war on terrorism must include programs to install democratic governance, end economic stagnation, and expand educational opportunities, especially for women, in North Africa. In a speech at West Point in June 2002, President Bush asserted that: "The peoples of the Islamic nations want and deserve the same freedom and opportunities as people in every nation, and their governments should listen to their hopes."[58] Bush pledged to work with these governments to further democratic reforms, especially building a freer press and a more engaged civil society.

North African governments have increasingly been under external and internal pressure to reform. Within these countries, the Islamists are the only organized, well-resourced groups that offer options for change. Their messages have found receptive audiences among restless youth—rich and poor, educated and uneducated alike. If extremism is to be defeated, moderates must take the lead in forcing change. As Raghida Dergham, correspondent for the London-based *Al-Hayat*, put it, "The repeated failure of Arabs to do something about their affairs and shape their own future, along with continued frustration and desperation, will make [Arab countries] a ticking bomb not only for themselves but [also] for Washington."[59]

The US-sponsored democracy program has received a mixed reaction in North Africa. Many people are suspicious of Bush's motives because, at the outset of the war on terrorism, Bush blundered by speaking of a "crusade," an upsetting image for the people of North Africa, implying a clash of religions. Another reason was their distrust of the leadership behind the US program. The Christian right and conservatives have harshly criticized Islam and have urged the Bush administration to open the Muslim world to allow American missionaries to spread the Christian gospel. These groups wish to pursue a similar strategy to the one they used against the Soviet Union in the past, where the US supported Jewish dissidents and opposition groups. White House officials, including Bush, met with Natan Sharansky, an Israeli legislator and a former Soviet dissident, who has spoken widely about how to promote democracy in the Middle East; within the Arab world Sharansky's "writings are closely read in the administration."[60]

Bush has gone out of his way to assure the Muslim world that the US is not waging war on Islam, but only against terrorist groups whose actions are falsely carried out in the name of the religion. At the end of October 2001, Condoleezza Rice, then National Security Advisor, told African ministers attending the annual African Growth and Opportunity Act (AGOA) Economic Forum that "this is not a war of civilizations, [but] this is a war of civilization against those who would be uncivilized in their approach to us."[61] Nevertheless, many North Africans are suspicious of US intentions. They have grounds to believe that US actions will weaken their religion and destroy their culture under the guise of democratization. Many do not like some aspects of Western culture that are penetrating their societies and undermining Islamic values and traditions. They are especially critical of Western magazines, videos, and films that they believe corrupt the morals of young people. On the official front, US ambassadors have pressured Muslim governments to close religious schools, which the US considers to be breeding grounds for radical Islam. They have supported governmental crackdowns on private mosques and also have backed government efforts to weaken political Islam.

Every North African country, except Libya, has allowed opposition groups to form political parties. However, Egypt and Tunisia consistently have denied Islamist groups the right to organize political parties. Egypt's Muslim Brotherhood and Tunisia's Renaissance Party are only allowed to run independent candidates in legislative elections as long as they do not pose a threat to the ruling party. The government's insistence on the separation between religion and politics is in line with the thinking of the Bush administration, which wants to eliminate all manifestations of political Islam. It will be difficult over the long term to deny such political rights to moderate religious groups that have denounced violence and have agreed to abide by democratic rules.

If the neo-conservatives within the Bush administration thought that the Iraqi war would help bring democracy to North Africa, they have misjudged the overall situation. In fact, US influence was at its lowest point in the region in March 2003 and anti-Americanism was on the rise. The war has had the opposite effect on some democratic freedoms. Popular outrage over the war forced several North African regimes to use heavy-handed tactics to suppress dissent and to contain anti-war protests that called for expelling US ambassadors and halting oil sales to the US and the United Kingdom. They were blamed for not stopping the US from overthrowing an Arab government. In Egypt, for example, emergency laws were reactivated and the police used force to disperse some 40,000 demonstrators protesting the outbreak of the war. According to the *Economist*, "police dragged off and beat up several hundred, including two members of parliament."[62] In the Sudan, police clashed with protestors, killing some people.[63] Consequently, fundamental freedoms, a cornerstone of democracy, were curtailed and human rights were violated.

Bush's campaign to promote democracy in the region is, in part, a way to distract the American public from the widespread Iraqi insurgency and the mounting casualties among American troops in Iraq. North African leaders have been concerned about such US meddling in their internal affairs and have warned Washington against pushing its democracy campaign too hard out of fear that it might increase hostility to the US. Public opinion in North African countries was already incensed by the US occupation of Iraq and by its lack of concern for the welfare of Palestinians in the occupied territories. Government leaders worried that opening their political system at this time might bring to office Islamists who seek to establish theocratic states like the one in Iran. They consider such regimes a threat to democracy, human rights, and, above all, regional security and stability. For all these reasons, they would like the US to respect their sovereignty and allow them to do it their way.

In the face of such resistance, National Security Advisor Rice indicated that the US was willing to work with those governments that have already embarked on reform. Morocco attracted the administration's attention for two reasons. First, the young King Mohammed VI is more liberal than his father and seems to be interested in improving his country's record on human rights and advancing democratic reform. Second, the country had gone through a lengthy period of political liberalization ending in 2002. During that period, reforms were enacted to enforce the rule of law, expand the powers of parliament, and allow for the direct election of the lower house in parliament.[64]

In September 2002, Morocco held reasonably free legislative elections, in which twenty-two political parties participated and the opposition made a strong showing. For example, the Islamist Justice and Development Party (*Hizb Adl wa Tanmiya*), which called for serious political and constitutional changes, captured 42 seats, tripling the number of its seats in the lower house. King Mohammed VI appointed the former interior minister, Driss Jettou, an independent politician, as the new prime minister. Despite this progress, democracy still has a long way to go because the court clique (the *Makhzen*) is still said to "indulge in democracy more as a parlor game than a decision-making procedure."[65]

There is little democracy in Algeria. In 1992, the end of its experiment with democracy and the military's crackdown on Islamists led to the outbreak of civil war. Since then, the ruling elite or *pouvoir*—a group of generals, senior conservative politicians, and crony businessmen—have dominated the political scene. Although multiparty elections returned in 1995, this group has manipulated the electoral system and has used the constitutional court to stop strong candidates from running for the presidency.[66] To create a façade of democratic elections, they encouraged small parties to nominate candidates, even though they had no chance of winning.

In April 1999, all opposition candidates dropped out on the eve of Algeria's presidential election after accusing the *pouvoir* of fixing the elections in favor of their own candidate, Abdelaziz Bouteflika, and asked their followers to boycott the elections. As the *Economist* reported,

Most Algerians seem disillusioned with the entire political process. Even before the six pulled out, many young people were saying that they did not intend to vote since they did not believe that any of the candidates would improve their chances of finding a job, or better yet, of getting a visa to escape from the country altogether. [67]

This attitude helps explain the low turnout. Less than a quarter of eligible voters went to the polls and cast their votes in the 1999 presidential election.[68]

Voter apathy continued in the legislative elections in May 2002 when the majority of voters (54 percent) stayed home either out of frustration with the *pouvoir* or in response to boycott calls from opposition groups, including two Berber-based political parties. The boycott was total in the Berber region of Kabylia. As a businessman put it, "it is not really about identity any more. It is about justice and this feeling is everywhere in Algeria."[69]

In 2004 President Bouteflika was re-elected for another term by 83 percent of the votes in a competitive election that was judged to be fair by international observers.[70] This is a step in the right direction if it portends a new trend. It is doubtful, however, that serious reform will take place because of the ongoing struggles between the military and civilian contenders, between secularists and Islamists, between Algerian nationalists and ethnic Berbers. Factionalism is likely to continue to play into the hands of the military and intelligence, which are not only the power brokers but also the decision-makers behind the scene. Change will be hard to achieve because the ruling elite wishes to maintain the status quo and to hold on to power.

Nevertheless, reform-minded North Africans have been encouraged by US pressure for democratic reform. Civil society groups and politicians have spoken more openly about the need for change. In March 2004, a pan-Arab NGO conference on democratic reform, held at the Library of Alexandria in Egypt, issued the Alexandria Declaration. They called for all Arab governments to have an "elected legislative body, an independent judiciary, and a government that is subject to popular and constitutional oversight, in addition to political parties with different political ideologies." They also advocated "the freedom of all forms of expression, especially freedom of the press ... and the support of human rights in accordance with international charters, especially the rights of women, children, and minorities."[71]

By mid-2004, it was evident that the US campaign to promote democracy had made little progress in North Africa. To deal with the stonewalling by some North African regimes, Bush shifted strategy. He instead sought transatlantic cooperation to speed up political and economic reforms across North Africa. At the Group of Eight (G-8) summit at Sea Island in Georgia in June 2004, Bush proposed to establish a Forum for the Future to provide financial and technical assistance to North African and Middle Eastern governments and NGOs, which were working for democratic and economic reform. The G-8 endorsed the proposal but agreed only to play a supportive role because many European countries have their own assistance programs. A country like France would have no interest in funding a US initiative.[72] The G-8 endorsement was important to Washington. It sent a unified message and added to the pressure on North African and Middle Eastern governments for greater democratic and economic reform.

The first Forum of the Future was held in Rabat, Morocco, in December 2004, and was attended by the G-8 and North African and Middle Eastern governments. They primarily discussed American initiatives to support increased political participation and to accelerate economic development across the region. In their statements, Arab officials disagreed with the US that speeding up democratic reforms was a good way to uproot terrorism and restore stability in the region. In their view, "reforms must be gradual and come from within." They also pointed out that American support for Israel "made it harder for [them] to fight extremists and emphasized the need for finding a permanent solution to the Palestinian issue before any progress could be made."[73]

Of all North African countries, the Bush administration has paid special attention to Egypt, which has long been a close ally of the US. In the State of the Union Address in February 2005, Bush called on Egypt to "show the way toward democracy in the Middle East." He also made it clear that "the United States has no right, no desire, and no intention to impose our form of government on anyone else."[74] However, when Ayman Nour, a legislator and head of *Al-Ghad* (Tomorrow) party, was arrested, the State Department criticized the detention and the new Secretary of State Rice cancelled her trip to Egypt in protest.

Many Egyptians have complained about having limited political freedoms, a rubberstamp legislative assembly, and a weak opposition. They are frustrated because, for twenty-four years, Mubarak has used preserving security and stability as an excuse to control the political process and to list himself as the only candidate for the presidency. They are encouraged that US pressure has led the Egyptian government to eliminate some elements of the emergency laws and to allow an increased level of public debate and dissent. The summer of 2005 witnessed a surge in street demonstrations organized by different opposition groups such as *Kifaya* (Enough), *Al-Ghad*, and the Muslim Brotherhood. Despite the government's crackdown and the detention of thousands of opposition leaders and activists, the demonstrations continued, calling for more democratic reforms and for opening the political systems.

After decades of resistance, Egypt's constitution was amended and multiparty candidates were allowed to run for president in the fall of 2005. Although opposition parties boycotted the referendum on the new amendment, First Lady Laura Bush praised Mubarak's "very bold step" during her visit to Egypt in May. Her statement upset opposition groups, which "regard it as a sham"[75] because the amendment leaves the final decisions on the presidential candidates in the hands of the legislative assembly, which is controlled by the ruling party.

During her visit to Cairo in June 2005, Secretary of State Rice called on the Egyptian government "to end violent attacks on pro-democracy demonstrators, stop 'arbitrary justice' and lift emergency decrees."[76] She also met with the opposition groups, namely the registered political parties. Her decision left the leading opposition group—the Muslim Brotherhood—and the pro-democracy *Kifaya* (the coalition of human rights, professional, and legal organizations) out of the meeting.

Although the September presidential election, which Mubarak won easily, was relatively peaceful, parliamentary elections were not. Following the success of the Muslim Brotherhood in early November, stern measures were taken against its rank and file. During the next two rounds, its supporters were harassed; hundreds of candidates and activists were detained; its monitors were barred from entering some polling stations. Voters were also prevented from casting their votes in districts where opposition was strong. Despite these adverse measures, the Muslim Brotherhood captured 88 seats, compared with 15 seats in the outgoing Assembly.[77]

Meanwhile, international efforts were underway to further democratization in the region. In November 2005, the second annual Forum for the Future was held in Manama, Bahrain, and was attended by the G-8, North Africans, and Middle Easterners. It was the first time that both civil society organizations and government representatives met together to exchange views and to make recommendations on reforms they would like to see in their countries. During the deliberations, there was sharp disagreement on American initiatives to create a foundation to give grants directly to civil society groups trying to promote democratic practices and human rights in their countries. The NGOs were in favor of the new funding,[78] which will liberate them from regulatory government control and will give them direct access to badly needed funds to expand their activities, which often bring them in conflict with their governments.

On the other hand, some governments, led by Egypt, opposed the loss of regulatory control and the funneling of foreign money directly to civil society groups, a change which could give American officials undue influence on these groups. Egyptian officials are upset by the Bush administration's decision to give direct grants totaling $1.5 million to 5 out of the 15,000 Egyptian NGOs. As Leslie Campbell, director of Middle East Programs at the federally funded National Democratic Institute, put it, "we're not going to ask Egypt's permission to give [money] to a certain group."[79] This attitude led Egypt to insist at the Manama meeting on the need to prevent foreign interference in the country's political life through the work of the NGOs. Egypt's refusal to compromise led to the forum's failure to agree on the wording of a final declaration.[80]

It is important to note that the majority of Egyptian civil society groups do not support the US push for external funding because they consider American interference a hindrance to reform. Nader Fergany, director of a policy institute in Cairo, who declined to attend the Manama forum, explained, "Nobody seriously interested in the cause of reform would join the United States in this effort."[81] To these critics, it does not matter whether the Foundation for the Future is managed by people from the region. In their view, the US will be in control by providing most of the funds and by insisting on using foreign consultants to advise these groups. Receiving US funds will stigmatize these NGOs and reduce their credibility, resulting in accusations that they work for the CIA. This would make them unable to work with other groups and ineffective in promoting democracy and human rights.

The controversy over external funding is just an example of the difficulties that the Bush administration is encountering as it tries to change attitudes and practices to support democratic institutions. There is a limit to what the US can do to force changes in North African countries. In the end, with the US fighting insurgencies in Iraq and Afghanistan, it has no choice but to work with these governments.

Conclusion

Like the US, North African governments have made decisions on the war on terrorism based on what would further their own national interests. They have supported the US war whenever their interests coincided with that of the US and have parted company when there is a clash of interests. These governments have generally cooperated with the US on the first phase of the war. Although they did not join the battle in Afghanistan, they were supportive of the fight against al Qaeda. Additionally, North African governments have assisted in whatever ways they could to diminish the terror threat. The assistance comes in a number of forms, including sharing intelligence with Washington, interrogating suspected terrorists from other countries for the CIA, and taking actions to ensure that their countries are not used to launch attacks against the US. Nevertheless the terror attacks in Morocco, Tunisia, and Spain that have shown that it is premature for Bush to claim success in the war on terrorism. It is clear that al Qaeda has been able to attract new recruits, replenish its resources, and readjust its strategies to meet new challenges. Bin Laden's terror network is still capable of carrying out terrorist attacks, as seen in Egypt and the United Kingdom in 2005. In the end, this means more trouble ahead for pro-US regimes in North Africa, which are vulnerable to attacks by terrorist groups or individuals affiliated with al Qaeda.

As for the second phase of the war on terror, North African governments did not see eye to eye with Bush's plan to extend the war to Iraq. They had their own doubts about the evidence Powell presented to the Security Council in February 2003 about Baghdad's link to al Qaeda and its resumption of the nuclear weapons program. After leaving office, Powell came around to agree with North African assessment. In September 2005, he told Barbara Walters that "people in the intelligence community[,] who knew at the time that some of these sources were not good and shouldn't be relied upon ... didn't speak up. That devastated me."[82]

Unlike the Bush administration, North African governments accepted the 2003 IAEA report that Iraq did not restart its nuclear weapons program. Later on, FBI investigations confirmed that the document related to Iraq–Niger uranium deal, which Bush used to justify war against Iraq, was "fraudulent,"[83] as John Miller, the agency's spokesman, reported. A few weeks before the start of the war, the Arab League urged Bush to give UN inspectors more time to complete the mission and Saddam Hussein to cooperate with the UN. They also insisted that if there was going to be a war, it must be mandated by the UN Security Council. They therefore could not support the invasion of Iraq when Bush went to war without UN approval.

Although no weapons of mass destruction were found after the invasion, the US turned the liberation of Iraq into an occupation. North Africans did not like excluding Iraqis from any involvement in the Bremer administration or from participating in their country's reconstruction. Wolfowitz was wrong in predicting that American forces "would be welcomed as liberators"[84] and in never anticipating the outbreak of insurgency. Despite the heavy military presence, the US has not been able to contain a stubborn insurgency, which has killed tens of thousands of Iraqi civilians and over 2,500 American troops. North African governments also have criticized the US for its failure to provide safe water and electricity, ensure access to basic services, and reduce the high rate of unemployment (over 40 percent). Three years after the invasion, the situation there is still far from normal. At the end of 2005, David Ignatius described the situation in Iraq as follows:

> The most frightening symbol of dysfunctional government this year was Iraq. Despite a stirring election in January [2005], the new Iraqi government—burdened with a hated American occupation and vicious sectarian tension—failed to thrive. Indeed, over the past year, Iraq seemed to be becoming more of a mafia state, with each party, sect, and tribe fighting for its share of what's left of the ruined economy.[85]

North African leaders are worried about the future of such a highly polarized society. There is a de facto partition of the country along ethnic lines, which might continue to be a source of instability and might lead to the breaking up of Iraq. They also fear that the Bush administration plans to maintain a long-term military presence in Iraq; it is now building military bases across the country to protect American interests in Iraqi oil and to prevent Iran from gaining a foothold in Iraq. In an interview in December 2005, former Secretary of State Powell confirmed that "the United States will have a military presence in Iraq for years."[86]

As for the third phase of the war, North African governments have been reluctant to go along with Bush's democracy program. In fact, they view such a program as meddling in their internal affairs. They prefer to be left alone to implement reform gradually in order to prevent radical Islamic groups from coming to power and turning the clock back on democracy. It is true, however, that American demands for reform have encouraged opposition groups to speak publicly about the need for change and to challenge openly the power structures in several countries. Although domestic opposition remains divided and fragmented, some progress has been made. Governments are beginning to respond positively to internal and external pressures in order to weather the storm and stay in power. After resisting for twenty-four years, for example, Mubarak amended the Egyptian constitution in 2005 to allow other political parties to nominate candidates to compete for the presidency. Morocco's King Muhammad VI has been praised for his political reforms and for improving the status of women.

In view of these developments, the Bush administration should keep up its pressure for further democratization in the region. However, it is counterproductive for the US to use the stick rather than the carrot in pushing its democracy campaign in the region. The cooperation of North African governments is essential to US efforts to succeed. The US must work with them to overhaul their political institutions. It should support civil society organizations that share American values and goals to win the battle against religious extremism. According to Amy Hawthorne, who is involved in the Democracy and Rule of Law Project at the Carnegie Endowment for International Peace, "What is needed is a sustained policy of high-level engagement with Arab governments, along with support for openings that would bolster reformist groups, and a willingness to accept that genuine political change will be bumpy."[87]

To become effective in promoting democracy and in fighting terrorism, the Bush administration needs to lower its rhetoric and launch a campaign to improve its image in the region. The majority of citizens have reasons to suspect every move by Bush, who has occupied Arab land and has continued to side with Israel against Palestinians. Although the appointment of Karen Hughes as Undersecretary of State for Public Diplomacy is a step in the right direction, her first tour of Muslim countries proved that she is not yet ready to undertake this difficult mission. Token measures are not going to help Bush gain the trust of North African people who must see some real changes in his foreign policy. Finally, the White House must dispel its image as an empire builder, address some Arab concerns, and refocus on the war against the al Qaeda network. It also must remain actively engaged, working with North African governments to stabilize the region, promote democracy, and accelerate economic growth.

Notes

1   Jonathan Steele, "The Bush Doctrine Makes Nonsense of the UN Charter," *The Guardian*, June 7, 2002. http://www.guardian. co.uk/Print/0,3858,4428724,00.html. The site was accessed on August 5, 2006.
2   Stephen Zunes, "Seven Reasons to Oppose a US Invasion of Iraq," *FPIF Policy Report*, August 2002, p. 3. http://www.rider.edu/phanc/courses/350-web/mideast/iraq/7reasonsxUSattack.html. The site was accessed on August 5, 2006.
3   Dana Priest, "CIA Holds Terror Suspects in Secret Prison," *Washington Post*, November 2, 2005.
4   Jane Adas, "Bush Has Abandoned Long-Term Consensus on Mideast, Says William Quandt," *Washington Report on Middle East Affairs*, April 2003, p. 58.
5   Al Kamen, "Martyr Complex," *Washington Post*, September 30, 2005.
6   Mohamed A. EL-Khawas, "Qaddafi's Turnabout: From Defiance to Cooperation," *Journal of South Asian and Middle Eastern Studies*, 28(3), 2005, p. 77; Ronald Bruce St. John, Libya and the United States: Two Centuries of Strife (Philadelphia: University of Pennsylvania Press, 2002), p. 191.
7   Daniel Williams, "Mubarak Backs Strikes by US on Afghanistan," *Washington Post*, October 10, 2001.
8   "North Africa-Middle East: Al Qaeda Connections," *Africa Research Bulletin*, 39(6), June 2002, p. 14913.
9   "Egypt to Push Iraq on UN Sanctions," *Africa Research Bulletin*, 39(3), May 2002, p. 14797.
10 Dana Priest, "Wrongful Imprisonment: Anatomy of a CIA Mistake," *Washington Post*, December 4, 2005.
11 Stephen Ellis and David Killingray, "Africa After 11 September 2001," *African Affairs*, 101(402), January 2002, p. 6.
12 Ted Dagne, "Africa and the War on Terrorism," *CRS Report for Congress*, January 17, 2002, p. 1.
13 "Africa and America: Feeling America's Fly-Whisk," *Economist*, March 15, 2003, p. 44.
14 "North-Africa-Middle East: Al Qaeda Connections," *Africa Research Bulletin*, 39(6), June 2003, pp. 14913–14914.
15 Eileen Byrne, "Tangled Web," *Middle East International*, 678, June 28, 2002, p. 24.
16 Eileen Byrne, "Morocco: Disappearance," *Middle East International*, 691, January 10, 2003, p. 21.
17 "Algeria: Tenth Anniversary," *Africa Research Bulletin*, 39(1), January 1, 2002, p. 14711.
18 Dagne, CRS-4.
19 "Algeria: Tenth Anniversary," p. 14711.
20 Heba Saleh, "Algeria: Bouteflika & the Generals," *Middle East International*, 692,

January 24, 2003, p. 22.

21   "Algeria: Tenth Anniversary," p. 14711.

22   Ibid.

23   Adel Darwish and Ed Blanche, "Ousting Saddam Hussein," *The Middle East*, 325, July/August 2002, p. 6.

24   Fairness and Accuracy in Reporting, "Media Silent on Clark's 9/11 Comments: General Says White House Pushed Saddam Link Without Evidence," *FAIR*, June 20, 2003. http://www.fair.org/press-releases/clark-iraq.html. The site was accessed on August 9, 2006.

25   "Plans for Iraq Attack Began on 9/11," CBSNews.com, September 4, 2002. http://www.cbsnews.com/stories/2002/09/04?Sptember11/printable520830.shtml. The site was accessed on August 6, 2006.

26   Robert Dreyfuss, "More Missing Intelligence," *Nation*, June 19, 2003, pp. 1–2; Joe Klein, "What Is Your Government Not Telling You?" *Time*, June 2, 2003, p. 25.

27   Darwish and Blanche, p. 6.

28   Zunes, p. 6.

29   Anthony Shadid, "Tracing Iraq's Painful Arc, From the Past to the Future," *Washington Post*, December 12, 2005.

30   Zunes, p. 6.

31   Steve Negus, "Egypt Unconvinced," *Middle East International*, 671, March 22, 2002, p. 10.

32   Michael Jansen, "Arab Summit: Palestine and Iraq," *Middle East International*, 672, April 5, 2002, p. 8.

33   Michael Elliott, "Not as Lonely as He looks," *Time*, September 16, 2002, p. 35.

34   Ian Williams, "Iraq: A Battle Won?," *Middle East International*, 692, January 24, 2003, p. 9.

35   "Nations Comment on Use of Force," *USA Today*, September 3, 2002.

36   Abdal-Wahhab Badra Khan, "Opening the Iraq Bazar," *Al-Hayat*, March 14, 2003. Reprinted in the *Middle East International*, March 22, 2002, p. 30.

37   "Iraq, the UN and America: The Contradictions of a Crisis," *Economist*, January 25, 2003.

38   Sana Kamal, "Iraq: Preparing for War," *Middle East International*, 691, January 10, 2003, pp. 10–12.

39   Ian Williams, "Iraq, Israel and the US," *Middle East International*, 691, January 10, 2003, p. 8. For the complete text, see Hans Blix Report to the UN on January 27, 2003. http://www.moderntribune.com/hans_blix_report_to_united_nations. The site was accessed on August 6, 2006.

40   Williams, "Iraq: A Battle Won?," p. 12.

41   Michael Brown, "Bush Knows Best," *Middle East International*, February 7, 2003, p. 8.

42   Bruce Crumley, "Doubting Iraq's Ties to Al Qaeda," *Time*, March 3, 2003, p. 22.

43   "Iraq and Al Qaeda: Imaginary Friends?" *Economist*, February 8, 2003, p. 25.

44   Walter Pingus, "Newly released Data Undercut Prewar Claims," *Washington Post*, November 6, 2005.

45   Zunes, p. 4.

46   Nancy Gibbs, "The Rover Problem," *Time*, July 25, 2005, pp. 26–27.

47   "The Case Made Clearer," *Economist*, February 8, 2003, pp. 24–26.

48   Williams, "Iraq: A Battle Won?", p. 10.

49   Mohamed A. El-Khawas, "North Africa and the War on Terror," *Mediterranean Quarterly*, 14(4), Fall 2003, p. 182.

50   Robert Dreyfuss, "More Missing Intelligence," *Nation*, June 19, 2003, p. 1.

51   Nizar Wattad, "US Attack on Iraq Provokes Anger Across the Arab World," *The Washington Report on Middle East Affairs*, May 2003, p. 88.

52   El-Khawas, "North Africa," p. 183.

53   Joe Klein, "What Is Your Government Not Telling You?" *Time*, June 2, 2003, p. 25.

54   Reuters, "Bremer Says US Was Surprised by Insurgency," *Washington Post*, January 7, 2006.

55 Anthony Shadid, "A US and Talk of Iraq's Future," *Washington Post*, December 11, 2005.
56 Youssef M. Ibrahim, "A Post-War Arab World—Three Views," *The Washington Report on Middle East Affairs*, May 2003, p. 14.
57 "Advancing Human Rights and Peace in a Complex World," *Peace Watch* 7 and 8(6) and (1), 2001, p. 10. Published by United States Institute of Peace, Washington, DC.
58 Peter Slevin and Glenn Kessler, "US to Seek Middle East Reform," *Washington Post*, August 21, 2002.
59 Raghida Dergham, "Arab Doubts, Inside and Outside," *Washington Post*, April 27, 2003.
60 Slevin and Kessler, "US to Seek Middle East Reform."
61 Dagne, CRS-2.
62 "Arab Protest: Damning and Damned," *Economist*, March 29, 2003, p. 28.
63 Wattad.
64 Abdesalam M. Maghraoui, "Depoliticization in Morocco," *Journal of Democracy* 13(4), October 2002, pp. 29–30.
65 "Democracy in the Maghreb, Where Voting is a Parlour Game," *Economist*, June 2, 2002, p. 41.
66 Frederic Volpi, *Islam and Democracy: The Failure of Dialogue in Algeria* (London: Pluto Press, 2003), pp. 78–79.
67 "Algeria: A Farce, Again," *Economist*, April 17, 1999, p. 50.
68 William B. Quandt, "Algeria's Uneasy Peace," in Larry Diamond, ed., *Islam and Democracy in the Middle East* (Baltimore, MD: Johns Hopkins University Press, 2003), p. 60.
69 "Democracy in the Maghreb," p. 42.
70 Frederic Volpi, "Algeria 2004: Plus ça Change, Plus C'est le Meme Chose." Fride. comments@fride.org.
71 Jackson Diehl, "Listen to the Arab Reformers," *Washington Post*, March 29, 2004.
72 Steven R. Weisman, "US Offers New Bid on Democracy," *New York Times*, November 10, 2005.
73 Mazen Mahdi, "Aid for Reforms Focus of Forum for the Future," *Arab News*, November 12, 2005. http://www.arabnews.com. The site was accessed on August 9, 2006.
74 "State of the Union Address by President George W. Bush," February 2, 2005, p. 5. http://www.whitehouse.gov/news/releases/2005/02/print/20050202-11.html. The site was accessed on August 9, 2006.
75 Glenn Kessler, "Rice Criticizes Allies in Call for Democracy," *Washington Post*, June 21, 2005.
76 Ibid.
77 Daniel Williams, "Banned Islamic Movement Now the Main Opposition in Egypt," *Washington Post*, December 10, 2005; *News Services*, "The Middle East: Cairo," World in Brief/*Washington Post*, 1 and December 4, 2005; Associated Press, "Egyptian Police Fire on Voters Outside Polls," World in Brief/*Washington Post*, December 2, 2005.
78 Weisman.
79 Ibid.
80 "Talks Sour at Democracy Summit," *Los Angeles Times*, November 13, 2005.
81 Weisman.
82 William Rasberry, "We're Past Politics with Iraq," *Washington Post*, November 28, 2005.
83 Associated Press, "Greed Spurred Uranium Tale, FBI Concludes," *Washington Post*, November 5, 2005.
84 Dana Millbank, "Intelligence Design and the Architecture of War," *Washington Post*, December 8, 2005.
85 David Ignatius, "The Year in Bad News," *Washington Post*, December 30, 2005.
86 News Services, "Rendition not New to Europe, Powell Asserts," *Washington Post*, December 18, 2005.

87 Amy Hawthorne, "Can the United States Promote Democracy in the Middle East?" *Current History*, 102(660), 2003, p. 21.

Chapter 6

Political Terrorism in West Africa

Ambassador Ronald D. Palmer

Introduction

There is disagreement about the extent of local or externally generated politically motivated terrorist violence in West Africa. There is no disagreement that political violence exists now and has existed since the independence era of the 1960s. Sadly, however, West Africa has what it takes to become a terrorist breeding ground: it is resource rich and democracy poor; protection is lacking for civil society and human rights; regional, ethnic, and religious conflicts abound as does economic distress, lawlessness, and criminal activity. Corruption is rife.

In the cities of West Africa, rapidly growing populations of the young, unemployed or underemployed are easy targets for those who seek "to turn resentment and despair to their own purposes."[1] This study will focus on those who would seek to turn resentment and despair for their own purpose. Those include national elites jousting for political power as well as those who have been trained or educated elsewhere in the ways of organizations such as al Qaeda. Realism demands that though there has been significant activity by Wahhabist missionaries, the Palestinian, Iraq, and Afghanistan issues have generally had a negative impact on public opinion, including Muslim opinion, and have made recruiting of possible extremists easier.

Background

The West African region is considered by the Department of State to include fourteen countries. More or less north to south, they are: Mauritania, Senegal, the Gambia, Guinea-Bissau, Mali, Burkina Faso (formerly Upper Volta), Sierra Leone, Liberia, Ivory Coast, Ghana, Togo, Benin (formerly Dahomey), Niger, and Nigeria. Reflecting their colonial pasts, eight are francophone, five are anglophone and one (Guinea-Bissau) is lusophone.

Colonialism and the introduction of modern administrative and educational techniques and methods came late to Africa. As colonialism was ending, only thin modernized elites had been created in the subject peoples. When the wave of independence swept through West Africa in the former French, British, and Portuguese-administered territories the newly created entities lacked state capacity and were states in name only.

The concept of "failed states" is inaccurate. "Weak states" is a more appropriate designation. These entities were never states in the modern use of the term. Nevertheless, the "Failed States Index" developed by the Fund for Peace provides a useful prism to look at the problems shared by the West African polities. The following are the twelve indicators used in the study:

Mounting demographic pressure; (2) Massive movement of refugees and intruding persons; (3) Legacy of vengeance group grievances; (4) Chronic and sustained human flight; (5) Uneven economic development along group lines; (6) Sharp and/or severe economic decline; (7) Criminalization or delegitimation of the state; (8) Progressive deterioration of public services; and (9) Widespread violation of human rights; (10) Security apparatus as a "state within the state"; (11) Rise of factionalizing elites; and (12) Intervention of other states or external actors.[2]

Whatever the basic problems of the post-colonial administrative structures in West Africa, they were states in one important way: they had the capacity to raise and collect revenue. Elites quickly learned and mastered rent-seeking behaviors. A primary strategy was forming alliances with security forces in the police and military. It is useful to remember that colonial administrations ran what were essentially police states whose legitimacy rested on a monopoly of force. This lesson was not lost on local observers. The key to power was the gun, which brought the key to the treasury. The history of West Africa since independence has been fraught with contests for power and access to financial spoils.

Obtaining and maintaining power led to the formation of fragile coalitions of political forces reflecting urban–rural, ethnic, and other tensions. Inevitably with the presence of instability, military coups have been the classic means of transferring power in West Africa. The January 1963 Togo military coup led by Sergeant Gnassingbe Eyadema initiated the wave of seizures of power. Congo-Brazzaville followed in August, and Dahomey in October. In early 1964 there were mutinies in Kenya, Uganda, and Tanganyika. The Gabonese Army took power briefly in February before French troops restored order. In late 1965 there were coups in Congo-Leopoldville (later Zaire) and in Dahomey, and Dahomey again in December. Coups multiplied in 1966: the Central African Empire, Upper Volta, and Nigeria in January; Ghana in February; Nigeria again in July. Samuel DeCalo reports in his *Coups and Army Rule in Africa: Studies in Military Style* that "by 1975 twenty of the forty-one states were led by military or military-cliques."[3]

Without recounting the Africa-wide list of coups since 1975, it is worth noting that in West Africa, Senegal had one unsuccessful coup. The trend toward *coups d'état* in francophone West Africa was facilitated by the demobilization of African members of French forces who had served in Indochina and Algeria. Eyadema of Togo (1967–2005), Lamizana of Upper Volta (1980–1983), and Seyni Kountche (1974–1987) of Niger are examples. France played a powerful neo-colonial role in these states and an equally powerful but perhaps less visible role in its close association with President Leopold Senghor of Senegal and Ivory Coast President Felix Houphouet-Boigny. The latter appeared to play a fatherly role toward his sometimes impetuous associates in the French-sponsored Conseil d'Entente des État Afrique Occidental (Council of West African States, CEDEAO).

Unlike France which pursued neo-colonial goals in West Africa as part of its global policy of promoting "francophonie." Britain has paid relatively limited attention to its former colonial holdings, except for carefully looking after largely pre-independence economic interests. This is true of Gambia, Sierra Leone, and Ghana. However, Britain retains and seeks to expand its strategic involvement in Nigerian oil. The political instability that has characterized West Africa was inevitably accompanied by sporadic violence between competing groups. Once in power the victors used force, as necessary, to remain in power. Only a few leaders were able to hold power for prolonged periods. Senghor (19601990) and Houphouet-Boigny (1960–1993) practiced a restrained authoritarianism. Togo's Eyadema (1967–2005) did not.

Senegal

Senegal is a useful case study to observe democratic development in a modernizing and secular state. Muslims are 94 percent of the population but they have been guided to political and religious moderation by Sufi brotherhoods that have provided critical support to state goals.[4] This entente between religious leaders and the state goes back to the colonial period. The French set up a trading station at St. Louis as early as 1659 and slowly extended their control until the early 1800s when they began a series of military campaigns to bring the entire country under their control. By 1893 the last independent sultanate had been vanquished.

Senegal was officially declared a French colony in 1920 and Dakar became the capital of the vast French West African possessions. France deferred to religious leaders on matters within their competence, in exchange for their acceptance of the French secular administration. This arrangement has been continued by the post-colonial government of President Leopold Senghor (1960–1981) and his successors, Adbou Diouf (1983–2000) and Abdoulaye Wade (2000–present).

The four major Sufi brotherhoods are the Tidjaniyya, Murdiyya, Quadriya, and Layenne. They include three politically active reform groups: the Hizbut Tarquiyyah (Mouride), the Moustarchideine wai (Tijani), and the Moustarchidati (Tidjani). President Wade has declared himself a Mouride (Idem). The Brotherhoods have been the pillars of the secular state. They get out the vote and extend religious sanction to state activities and state leadership. The Sufi share the opposition of the radical Islamist minority to US policies in the Middle East and the secularization of the family code but are relatively moderate in their views. Only 40 percent of Senegal's Muslim leaders believe sharia law should be instituted. It seems clear that Sufi support of political pluralism and political and electoral reform has been instrumental in helping guide Senegal on a moderate political course while maintaining a strong and proud religious tradition.

Nevertheless, there is a small but radical minority, some of whom were inspired by the 1979 Iranian revolution. Some have been schooled in Arab countries and oppose Westernization, especially US influence.

Nigeria

Fifty percent of the Nigerian population is Muslim and they live overwhelmingly in the North. Islam was brought to the North by the so-called Sokoto Jihad that spread from the northern Sokoto Caliphate and increased to encompass much of northern Nigeria. Areas that successfully resisted the spread of Islam came under severe pressures of slave raids and other discriminatory practices perpetuated by the dominant Muslims.

Northern cultural minorities suffered similar religious pressure and had to adopt aggressive mechanisms for protecting their separate identities, which reinforced their alienation from dominant Muslims. Christianity was introduced in the southeastern and southwestern regions in the 1840s and produced a homogeneity that is similar to that of the Muslim north. The country was already divided culturally and geographically when the British began their colonial intervention in 1851.

Their actions resulted in the administrative clustering of three hundred or so linguistic groups. Three separate political administrative units were created and formed into a federation in 1914. The result was a near even balance between the traditionalist Muslim North and the modernist Christian South. British colonial policy favored the North under the rule of aristocratic emirs. The British supported the ruling class in exchange for their support of British colonial rule.

The policy of the Muslim leadership was to attempt to exclude modernization influences, including Christian missionary activities. Education suffered. By contrast, in the South Christian missionaries were active and gave vigorous support to education, including the teaching of English. Southerners, particularly the Yoruba and Igbo, responded eagerly especially to economic opportunities opened up by modernization.

Britain incorporated different groups with different languages, religions and cultures into its construct "Nigeria." The resulting entity was inherently unstable. Indeed, this colonial integrating system had an eventual disintegrative effect on the post-independence political system. There was no common political culture and thus no political community with shared political values. Another disintegrative factor in the Nigerian case is what has been termed "indigeneity." The practical implication of the principle was that only people who descended from the ancestor or founder of a town, village or settlement were and remain the only indigenous people or citizens of the locality. Newcomers must undergo extended periods of residency before they are permitted to play political or leadership roles.

This local identification exacerbates ethnic, religious, and cultural differences. Nigeria has had only three periods of democratic rule in the 45 years since 1960: the first republic, 1960–1966; the second republic, 1979–1983; and the third republic, 1999 to the present. Corrupt, typically short-lived and incompetent military governments often led by Muslim northerners ruled in the 1966–1979 and 1983–1999 periods.

Over these 45 years there has been a dislocating shift of political power from the Muslim North to the Christian South. Former General Olesegun Obasanjo, a "born-again" Christian elected in 1999, was re-elected in 2003. However, in reaction to growing Christian power Saudi-financed Wahhabi missionaries had already begun to make their presence felt in the early 1990s. Reportedly, activists from Saudi Arabia, Sudan, Libya, Syria, and Pakistan, among others, have been actively promoting a Wahhabist agenda. To encourage orthodoxy, Taliban-style justice has been demanding, instituting the following: chopping off of a hand for theft, stoning adulterers, caning for drinking alcohol, and death for apostasy. These demands have been specifically associated with a clamor for introduction of the sharia penal code. Indeed, 12 of the 36 Nigerian states have adopted sharia law. These are Sokoto, Zamfara, Kebi, Kano, Yobe, Borno, Katsina, Jigawa, Bauchi, Kaduna, Niger, and Gombe states. One reason for the introduction of sharia courts is that they are cheap, quick, and reasonably uncorrupt.

They contrast sharply with the slow, expensive, and often corrupt courts run by the central government. Since 1999, an estimated 10,000 have died in the unrest associated with the imposition of sharia law. Aside from Muslim unrest there have been outbursts of localized civil unrest and violence in the Niger Delta (Rivers, Bayelsa, Delta, and Anambra states), Central Nigeria (Taraba, Plateau, Adamawa), and Cross Rivers and Ebonyi border regions.

Al Qaeda is reportedly active in Nigeria. The extent of its organization is not known. I have seen no evidence regarding whether or if Nigerians participated as mujahideen in Afghanistan. However, it is not unreasonable to speculate that some did and came into contact with al Qaeda agents. Similarly, such possibilities may exist with regard to Nigerian jihadists participating in the Iraq war. What is known is that a student-led Islamic sect, Al Sunna Wal Jamma (Followers of the Prophet) of about 200 persons, launched an armed uprising in December 2003 with the apparent aim of setting up a local Taliban-like regime in northern Nigeria. The sect had moved into Kanamma, a small town in northeast Yobe State near the Niger border, sometime in 2002 and began preaching the need for attaining Islamic purity. However, they were arrogant and did not show respect for local customs, particularly property rights. Kanamma villagers complained to government officials.

Suddenly, in December the group resorted to violence. They attacked police stations in Kanamma and nearby Geidam and two policemen were murdered. Guns and ammunition were seized; the buildings were burned. The group retreated to a school house in Kanamma and defiantly hoisted the Afghanistan flag. Nigerian troops restored order but at least eight persons were killed in two weeks of fighting before the insurgents could be captured or dispersed. Subsequent investigations have revealed the insurgents had been recruited in Maidiguri, the capital of Borno State in the northeast and the capital city of Lagos in the southwest.[5]

The scale and scope of such activity is difficult to determine. It may be occurring alongside the widespread ethno-religious fighting and conflicts over resources. However, while the 23-page US Department of State Human Rights 2004 Report on Nigeria is replete with incidents of ethno-religious conflict, there are no references to al Qaeda-style activities.[6]

Nigeria is burdened by the reality and potential of internal political violence but al Qaeda appears to be only a minor actor to date. As noted above, however, the Al Sunna Wal Jamma incident in December 2004 demonstrates not only that al Qaeda is present in Nigeria but that serious questions must be raised about the source of that group's weapons and where its members got their arms training. Names of the insurgents have not been released but, ominously, they are said to be related to Nigerian notables.

There may be no direct connection between this incident and Osama bin Laden's February 2003 call for an uprising in a number of countries including Nigeria. It is noteworthy though that he gave his support for brothers in Nigeria during the

2004 Kanamma incident. Local newspapers describe an Osama bin Laden-like cult emerging in Nigeria. Osama, after bin Laden, is now one of the most popular names given to infants.

Meanwhile, a different brand of terrorism has grown in the southern Niger River Delta region where 65 percent of Nigerian federal reserves and 20 percent of Nigerian GDP are produced. The Movement for the Emancipation of the Niger Delta (MEND) has emerged and taken militancy to a new level and posed significant problems for the Nigerian security services.

MEND, like other militant groups in the Delta region such as the Federated Niger Delta Ijaw Communities (FNDIC), professes to be fighting for the rights of the Ijaw, the region's dominant tribe. Like other anti-government militant groups in the region, it traffics in oil stolen from the pipelines of the Western oil companies operating in the region. This provides militants with ample funds to purchase state of the art military equipment.

Militant groups operating in the Delta region have cut Nigerian oil production of 2.4 million barrels a day by one-fifth. MEND has warned the Chinese government against operating in the delta. China has signed an agreement with Nigeria to provide $4 billion in infrastructure aid in return for preferential access on four potential oil-producing areas in forthcoming auctions.

Taylor and Regional Terrorism: Liberia, Sierra Leone, Guinea, Burkina Faso

Liberia has been at the center of the West African vortex of political violence and terrorism since 1980 when the elitist and authoritarian Americo-Liberian government of President William Tolbert was overthrown in a non-commissioned officer's coup led by Sergeant Samuel K. Doe.

The seaside execution of Tolbert cabinet members was a fearful omen of things to come. President Doe ruled autocratically from 1979 to 1989 when a small rebel group of some 100 to 500 persons directed by Charles Taylor invaded the country from the Ivory Coast and precipitated civil war. It is useful to pause here and trace Taylor's background in some detail. He was born in 1948. His father was a member of an elite Americo-Liberian family. His mother was a native Gola tribeswoman.

He was rebellious as a youth and was expelled in his teens from a private preparatory school. He was a student of Liberian history, especially its ties with the United States. He began his studies in the US in 1972 in the Boston area and worked at various odd jobs while attending Chamberlayne Junior College in Newton. He transferred to Bentley College in Waltham where he obtained a B.A. in economics in 1977. While at Bentley he joined the Union of Liberian Associations. He rose through the ranks and became national chairman of the organization. He reportedly "won" a famous 1979 New York debate with visiting Liberian President Tolbert. Buoyed by this success, Taylor led a demonstration against Tolbert's policies outside the Liberian UN mission. He was arrested and jailed. However, Tolbert did not press charges and instead invited Taylor to return to Liberia, and he did so in the spring of 1980.

Meanwhile, as noted above, resentment of the Americo-Liberian elite political and economic control of the state had grown to revolutionary proportions and resulted in the April 12, 1980 coup that brought Samuel Doe to power as Head of State and Chairman of the "People's Redemption Council." Doe became a key figure in US geopolitical strategy in Africa but his regime was replete with election fraud and corruption. Taylor was one of "corruptibles." His crafty political skills and economics background commended him to Doe, who appointed him to head the General Services Administration, and thus to direct government purchasing.

Taylor took full financial advantage of the post. Taylor was fired from that position in May 1983 for allegedly diverting $900,000 in government funds to a private Citibank account. He fled to the US in October 1983. The Liberian Government sought to extradite him and he was arrested in May 1984. While his case was under review, Taylor was detained in the Plymouth, Massachusetts, House of Corrections. He escaped in September 1985.

Taylor's whereabouts for the next four years are shrouded in mystery. Part of the mystery is that he was reportedly in the employ of CIA. There are reports he was given political asylum and military training in Ghaddafi's Libya and reported to CIA. Taylor's Sierra Leone crony Foday Sankoh also reportedly underwent training in Libya during this period. There are also reports that Taylor's escape from imprisonment in the US was a result of collusion with the CIA, under whose direction he reportedly worked.[7] Whatever the case, on December 24, 1989, Taylor led about 150 anti-government guerrillas into Liberia from Ivory Coast. Fighting quickly took on an interethnic character. The Krahn and Mandingo supported the Doe Government. The Gio and Mano supported Taylor. A vicious civil war ensued in which Taylor employed child soldiers and used rape and other atrocities as military tactics. By August 24, 1990 a Nigerian-led ECOWAS peacekeeping force had intervened to mediate a cease-fire and prepare for elections.

President Doe was killed on September 10. A cease-fire was reached on November 28, 1990. Taylor's stronghold was at Gbarnga, about 100 miles northeast of Monrovia. The forces of his rival Prince Johnson occupied the Monrovia region. Despite the ceasefire, bitter civil war broke out in the 1990–1992 period when Taylor sought to gain control of the entire country. By 1993, ECOWAS and government troops succeeded in containing his forces. An interim government was formed representing the three factions including Taylor.

Elections were scheduled for November 1995 but warfare resumed and lasted until April 1996. Under Nigerian leadership, ECOWAS succeeded in brokering a July 1997 election which Taylor won in a landslide vote. Taylor's National Patriotic Front of Liberia (NPFL) had drawn increasing support from Liberians disillusioned with the Doe government's corruption and incompetence.

Taylor had consolidated his power. He expanded his power by adroit manipulation of the trade in "blood diamonds" mined in Sierra Leone. Hezbollah had traded in these diamonds since the 1980s. Taylor supported his Sierra Leonian accomplice Fodah Sandoh's murderous Revolutionary United Front's (RUF) 1991 violent intervention in Sierra Leone politics. The RUF targeted areas where the alluvial diamonds were found and used slave labor to mine them. The RUF controlled about half of Sierra Leone by 1999.

In doing so, the RUF "perfected" the brutal tactics that Charles Taylor had used in Liberia. These included the ruthless use of child soldiers, rape, murder, and unbridled violence. The RUF added the amputation of hands, arms, and other body parts to this "witches brew."

Charles Taylor supplied the RUF with weapons in exchange for diamonds. Thus, he was in the extraordinary marketing situation of monopolizing the supply of diamonds while controlling the price. If buyers wanted diamonds they had to come to him. The "anything goes" atmosphere that warlord Charles Taylor created in the area he controlled became a sanctuary for criminal elements from the Balkans, Russia, Israel, and other notorious arms dealers.[8]

After 1997 when he became president, Taylor expanded his remunerative criminal-abetting activities. Following the 1998 al Qaeda bombings of US embassies in Nairoi and Dar es Salaam, he gave sanctuary to persons who had participated in the bombings. His financial involvement in al Qaeda activities moved to a higher level after the US froze Taliban and al Qaeda assets. Ibrahim Bah, reportedly of Senegalese or Guinean origin, also Libyan-trained, had served with the mujahideen in Afghanistan in the 1980s where he became favorably known to and trusted by al Qaeda. Bah facilitated al Qaeda contacts with Taylor to gain access to the Sierra Leone diamonds.[9] Bah is a representative of an unknown number of Africans who had mujahideen experience in Afghanistan.

There are an estimated 400 or so foreign fighters opposing US and Iraqi government forces in Iraq. Twenty-five percent are believed to be from Africa, although most are probably from North Africa. Al Qaeda participated vigorously in the diamond trade after 1998. By 2000 Taylor was providing sanctuary for senior al Qaeda agents; some took up residence in Monrovia. Taylor also countenanced the operations in Liberia of Hezbollah agents as well as the notorious arms dealer Victor Bout who sold arms in Africa as well to both the Taliban and the Northern Alliance. Israeli drug and arms dealer Lee Minim also operated out of Monrovia as did Aziz Nass, a middleman for both al Qaeda and Hezbollah.[10]

Al Qaeda purchases of untraceable blood diamonds reportedly totaled $30–50 million prior to 11 September 2001. Al Qaeda purchases reportedly dried up the market for other would-be buyers. Meanwhile, President Taylor's forces did not have complete control of the countryside, where several competing warlords controlled various regions. A vicious civil war ensued in the 2001–2003 period in which the 15,000-man Nigerian-led ECOWAS contingent sought to establish order. By 2003 Charles Taylor was indicted by the Sierra Leone Special War Crimes Tribunal on 17 charges. Nigeria gave Charles Taylor asylum when he was forced to flee Liberia in 2003. The United States helped facilitate his flight and his asylum in Nigeria. During the 2003–2004 period, shaky stability and order was maintained in Liberia by ECOWAS troops. Taylor enjoyed a comfortable stay in Nigeria and was free to travel to Burkina Faso to visit with his friend President Blaise Compraore and to consult with members of his former Liberian regime.

The campaign for the 2005 national elections had begun in the turbulent aftermath of Taylor's departure. However, he was unable to stay in close touch with Liberian political events through his meetings with henchmen in Burkina Faso during his exile in Calabar. Taylor seemed poised to play a major role as a spoiler in the 2005 elections.

The US intervened strongly to stem Taylor's influence and put heavy pressure on Nigeria to turn Taylor over to the Sierra Leone Special Court. Nigeria countered by insisting it would do so only at the request of the Liberian government. Ellen Johnson Sirleaf won the December 2005 presidential election but the Taylor case was not a high priority in her plans. The US government applied unrelenting pressure on her and Nigerian President Obasano. Taylor became alarmed and sought to flee Nigeria, but was apprehended on April 4, 2006. President Sirleaf assented to his return and he was whisked through Liberia to Sierra Leone where he was imprisoned. He was transferred to The Hague on June 16 to face trial.

Conclusion

Political terrorism in West Africa existed before the threat of al Qaeda, and like groups and will continue to exist, whether or not Islamism prospers. In fact, Islamism is only one of the competing forces, and a lesser one at that, in the struggle for political power by rival elites. While there is great contemporary academic and policy interest in the phenomena of "failed" and "failing" states, virtually all West African polities could meet the less dramatic World Bank standards for "weak" states.

These criteria are suggestive of states that have only nominal military and police control over their territory and governments that are unable to enforce laws and regulations uniformly because of high crime rates, extreme political corruption, bureaucratic inefficiencies, judicial ineffectiveness, military interference in politics, and cultural, ethnic, and political differences. West Africa displays each of the aforementioned characteristics.

Nevertheless, virtually no mainstream analysts exhibit adequate awareness that the administrative structures erected by colonial powers were designed to exploit the technological and other European advances over the pre-modern African world, primarily to extract whatever wealth there was in the regions they controlled. The colonial powers were not benign social scientists intent on building tropical democracies. They were authoritarian imperialists motivated by racist values.

French, British, German, and Portuguese colonial administrators brought to Africa only shadows of the systems they had been able to create after the 1648 Treaty of Westphalia. The reciprocal relationships between the ruled and rulers that characterized European political development, even if fully, were not nurtured in the colonial police states, except in representations of feudal forms. Moreover, the pre-modern territories they administered were rural, with only scattered villages, poor communications, and poor infrastructure.

Colonies were formed with little regard for geographic, ethnic, or linguistic consideration. Traditional political authority was used or tolerated, if convenient, or destroyed if inconvenient. In short, the political, economic, and administrative structures colonial powers bequeathed to the emergent African polities were not states. They were the shadowy remains of colonial systems. Thus, in the unsettled conditions that have prevailed since independence, political systems have generally lacked legitimacy.

Consequently, transfers of power have often occurred by force of arms. Political terrorism is inevitable under such conditions, and where possible, Islamists will attempt to take advantage of such conditions. However, post-independence political terrorism is unlikely to end soon. A recent statement by Gambian President Yahya Jammeh is illustrative. President Jammah seized power in 1994 as a 29-year-old army lieutenant and recently vowed in an electoral campaign to rule for forty years. The future course of Gambian politics seems predictable.[11]

Notes

1   Matthew Levitt, "Terrorism in West Africa, Post-9/11." March 1, 2004, The Washington Institute for Near East Policy.
2   *Fund for Peace*, Promoting Sustainable Security. "The Failed States Index 2006." http://www.fundforpeace.org/programs/fsi/fsindex2006.php. The site was viewed on October 10, 2006.
3   Samuel Decalo, *Coups and Army Rule in Africa: Studies in Military Style* (New Haven, CT: Yale University Press: 1979), p. 6.
4   David Dickson, "Political Islam in Sub-Saharan Africa: The Need for New Research and Diplomatic Agenda," US Institute, Special Report, Washington DC, May 2005.
5   IRIN, "Nigeria: Muslim Fundamentalist Uprising Raises Fear of Terrorism," August 27, 2005.   http://www.irinnews.org/S_report.asp?ReportID=39110&SelectRegion=West_ Africa. The site was viewed on October 11, 2006.
6   US Department of State, Nigeria: Country Reports on Human Rights Practices 2004, February 28, 2005.
7   See the *BBC News*, June 4, 2003.
8   The Jewish Institute for National Security Affairs, "Washington Revisits Africa's Strategic Importance," May 14, 2004.
9   For more in this post, see "Tracking the Threat." The site is available at http:// tracking the threat.com/content/entities/ent1718.htm. The site was viewed on October 10, 2006.
10   Douglas Farah and Richard Shultz, "Al Qaeda's Growing Sanctuary," *Washington Post*, July 14, 2004, p. A19.
11   See *NY Times*, September 22, 2006.

Chapter 7

The Role of the African Union: Integration, Leadership, and Opportunity

Sam Moki

Introduction:

The Organization of African Unity (OAU) was created in 1963 to provide a collective voice for African states that had recently obtained independence from their European colonial masters. It was also charged with promoting African unity and collectively continued the struggle to liberate other African countries that were still languishing under the brutal system of colonialism. Unfortunately, the desire for solidarity and collectivism collided with the selfishness of each state. While these African states cherished the idea of a collective front, they became apprehensive that their respective sovereignty would suffer. They feared that the OAU would exert undue interference in the internal affairs of their respective states. Accordingly, the leaders of the various states decided to transfer only minimal powers to the new organization, which in turn limited its ability and leverage to make collective decisions for its members. Not long thereafter, individualism replaced collectivism and the OAU was essentially reduced to being a toothless bulldog that could bark but could not bite. In a notable example, the OAU failed to prevent genocide in any member state, nor could it compel member states to honor OAU decisions. In other words, it had no enforcement mechanism. Adherence to OAU agreements or decisions was left to the goodwill of member states.

These shortcomings ignited the need for a new approach, a new strategy to pursue Africa's interests within a new world order characterized by globalization. The efforts that led to the creation of the African Union (AU) intensified in the 1990s as it became increasingly clear that the OAU was ill-equipped to advance Africa's interests both within the continent and externally in a more sophisticated global economy. African leaders meeting in Libya issued the Sirte Declaration in September 1999 calling for the creation of an African Union. The Constitutive Act of the African Union was adopted in Togo in 2000 and its implementation agreed upon in Lusaka, Zambia in 2001. On 9 July 2002, the African Union was officially launched in Durban, South Africa.

Though the new organization faced many challenges, terrorism became a major item on its agenda just as it was on the world agenda. The destructiveness of terrorist attacks of 11 September 2001 against America's famous World Trade Center and the Pentagon dictated the pace of international relations during this period.

A Brief History of Global Terrorism

Though there are many definitions of terrorism, there is general agreement that terrorism is violence committed by non-state agents designed to create fear and intimidation, and to focus world attention on their cause.[1] Based on this guiding definition, it becomes evident that terrorism is not new. Several acts that fit this definition have been recorded as far back as several centuries. However, for purposes of this chapter, only prominent recent acts of terrorism will be discussed. In September of 1972, eight Palestinians took eleven Israeli athletes hostage in an Olympic village in Munich, West Germany.[2] In 1976, a French airliner with mostly Israelis on board was commandeered by members of the Baader-Meinhof Group and the Popular Front for the Liberation of Palestine (PFLP) to land in Uganda. This was part of the Palestinian–Israeli conflict, an act designed to draw world attention on their plight of not having an independent state of their own. In 1985 it was the Achille Lauro hijacking in which four Palestinians hijacked an Italian ship and murdered an American passenger before the situation was brought under control. During the final year of the Clinton administration, seventeen American sailors were killed in 2000 in Yemen when an al Qaeda terrorist cell attacked the USS Cole.

Though more recently terrorism seems to reflect the battle between Islamic and Western values, and between the Palestinians and Israelis, Africa has become an integral player in the fight against terrorism. Recently Africa has been the theater for dramatic terrorist acts not against African interests but against US interests located in Africa. In addition, like many regions of the world, Africa has become a breeding ground for terrorists.

Africa became the center stage in the battle against terrorism when two US embassies in Kenya and Tanzania were attacked in the late 1990s. As the United States, Britain, and France continued to fortify themselves against terrorist attacks, terrorists turned their attention to Western targets in less secure areas of the world. These attacks killed and injured several thousand individuals and unleashed another dimension in global terrorism: not only was it easier to attack Western targets in Africa but the continent was a fertile recruiting ground for terrorists. The carnage associated with these two attacks sent shock waves not just throughout the West but also affected Africans, who suffered far more in terms of human lives.

In the final analysis it became clear that, as a result of these attacks, Africa had become a battleground for future acts of terrorism. Worse still, states within Africa had become recruiting areas for terrorists, and ultimately safe havens. Collectively, these events emerged as a wake-up call for African states to adopt a more collective and comprehensive approach to dealing with the issue of terrorism. Terrorism was no longer a European, American, or Islamic concern: it became an African issue as well.

The Role of the African Union in Dealing with Continental Terror: The African Union's Plan of Action

The creation of the African Union transformed Africa's fight against continental and even global terrorism in substantive terms. In dealing with continental terror, the African Union (AU) has firmly aligned itself with the global fight against terrorism. It has taken several steps to put forth an effective strategic plan in dealing with terrorism. This plan, called the African Union's Plan of Action against terrorism, is the first comprehensive plan ever put forth by African states to confront the challenge of terrorism. The AU overall strategy represented an attempt to strengthen the capacity of African states through a more structured common approach in dealing with the terrorist threat. Through its Plan of Action of 2002, the AU's role in dealing with continental terror has been enormous. It acknowledged the destructive and manipulating nature of terrorism through a carefully drafted definition of terrorism. It called for the ratification and implementation of the Algiers Convention of 1999, provided for police and border control, harmonized legal and judicial measures, called for compliance with international agreements dealing with terrorism, adopted measures designed to curtail the financing of terrorism, called for a more open information exchange regime, and created the Peace and Security Council to implement The Plan.

The Destructive Nature of Terrorism

The first preoccupation of the AU Plan of Action was to define and acknowledge the destructive and destabilizing nature of terrorism. In its preamble, it defines terrorism as:

> a violent form of transnational crime that exploits the limits of territorial jurisdiction of States, differences in governance systems and judicial procedures, porous borders, and the existence of informal and illegal trade and financing networks.[3]

Not only did the African Union recognize the enormity of the problem, but in addition, the organization created a blueprint to prevent terrorist acts on the continent. Because of the nature of terrorism, one thing was certain: terrorists had become emboldened. The AU's plan implored member states that a concise legal framework, cooperation among member states, and between the African Union and the international community, are indispensable in a successful struggle against terrorism. These approaches are also captured in the preamble of the African Union's Plan of Action:

Eradicating terrorism requires a firm commitment by Member States to pursue common objectives. These include: exchange of information among Member States on the activities and movements of terrorist groups in Africa; mutual legal assistance; exchange of research and expertise; and the mobilization of technical assistance and cooperation, both within Africa and internationally, to upgrade the scientific, technical and operational capacity of Member States Joint action must be taken at the intergovernmental level. This includes:

coordinating border surveillance to stem illegal cross-border movement of goods and persons; developing and strengthening border control-points; and combating the illicit import, export and stockpiling of arms, ammunitions and explosives. These actions would assist in curbing terrorist networks' access to Africa. Informal and illegal channels for the transfer of funds and goods used to finance and support terrorism must be closed Few African governments are in a position, on their own, to marshal the requisite resources to combat this threat. Pooling resources, therefore, is essential to ensure the effectiveness of counter-terrorism measures.[4]

If such measures are implemented then the AU will have performed a valuable role in confronting continental terrorism.

Ratification and Implementation of the Algiers Convention of 1999

The ratification and implementation of the Algiers Convention on the Prevention and Combating of Terrorism (1999) became the first priority of the African Union. In the general provisions of The Plan, this intention is expressed in clear and concise terms when it calls on Member States to:

sign, ratify and fully implement the Algiers Convention on the Prevention and Combating of Terrorism and, where necessary, seek assistance of other Member States or the international community to amend national legislation so as to align such legislation with the provisions of this Convention.[5]

This Convention was crafted under the Organization of African Unity (OAU), the predecessor of the African Union (AU). It was a comprehensive document that addressed several issues pertinent to the fight against terrorism: its definition, obligations of Member States, cooperation modalities, state jurisdiction, and extradition. However, because of the lack of discipline and structured cooperation that reigned under the OAU, the pace of signing and ratifying the Convention was characteristically slow. Though it contained concrete approaches to deal with terrorism, and required only fifteen of over fifty members to ratify for it to go into effect, the OAU was having a difficult time getting the fifteen ratifications that were necessary to usher the Convention into force.[6] Member States for their respective reasons failed to sign on and ratify at a pace that would usher the Convention into force. Under the auspices of the African Union Commission, a Senior Officials' Meeting was called, the purpose of which was to secure the fifteen ratifications necessary to bring the Convention into force. The target was not only met at this meeting but it was exceeded. This was indeed a major accomplishment because the African Union had succeeded in bringing into force the Convention that provided the blueprint for the continental struggle against terrorism.

Police and Border Control

The African Union's Plan of Action has also made it difficult for terrorists to move freely from one state to another within the continent. The ability of terrorists to travel with ease from one country to another has on several occasions complicated the fight against terrorism. When individuals commit acts of terrorism, they usually escape to a neighboring state to evade capture or detection. In many cases they use forged passports and other travel documents to hide their identity. It is not uncommon for a terrorist to have more than one passport with different assorted names. These illegal strategies have made it more difficult to deal with terrorism. In some instances, these forgeries are perpetuated by officials within the government structures. Mindful that a successful fight against terrorism could not be achieved without limiting the ability of terrorists to move from one country to another, The Plan, among other things, employed Member States to undertake the following:

> Enhance border control and surveillance, as well as the necessary means to prevent the forgery and falsification of travel and identity documents; ensure identity documents contain advanced security features that protect them against forgery; keep a passport stop list containing information of individuals whose application would require special attention or who may not be issued with travel documents develop and upgrade the regulations governing border control and security procedures including land, sea and air exit and entry points so as to curb infiltration and promote cooperation among police agencies having due regard for relevant provisions of relevant regional and continental agreements on the free movement of persons and goods.[7]

In addition to these measures, The Plan also called for computerizing all points of entry to maintain a more accurate arrival and departure record, and to examine all passports for authenticity. It also called for a substantial investment in human resources through the training of immigration officers to detect forged travel documents and to be able to profile travelers.

In many instances, terrorists slip across the borders or through other entry points and immediately ask for political asylum. While a fear of persecution for political or religious beliefs are grounds for granting asylum, The Plan made it difficult for terrorists to use political asylum as a means to escape responsibility for acts of terrorism. It called for the refusal of political asylum to anyone who had been involved directly or indirectly with terrorist acts. A citizen of Kenya or Russia involved in terrorist acts cannot be granted political asylum in Cameroon even if his travel documents are legitimate. These African Union border and points of entry instruments if implemented properly go a long way in improving Africa's fight against continental and global terrorism. The Plan has instituted a stringent system of police and border patrols designed to complicate life for terrorists by limiting their ability to travel with ease and conceal their identity through forged travel documents.

The Harmonization of Legislative and Judicial Measures

The African Union's efforts have not been limited to measures designed to prevent terrorism. The AU has also focused on dealing with the aftermath of terrorism: bringing terrorists to justice. Even terrorists have rights to a fair trial. Accordingly, The Plan called for the creation of a common legal and judicial framework that would facilitate the prosecution of terrorists. Under the OAU, such a harmonized approach was far-fetched. Each state had its own legal and judicial regime that reflected its own interests. Some were stringent, others were weak. It offered terrorists opportunities for exploitation, preferring to engage countries with weak legal and judicial regimes. Under the African Union Plan, that luxury is extinguished. The prescribed legal and judicial regime for dealing with terrorists is not only more stringent than under the OAU but it is more uniform. The harmonization process signifies that terrorists can no longer shop for safe havens within the Member States of the African Union.

As part of the harmonization process, The Plan called on Member States to:

amend, where necessary, national laws relating to bail and other criminal and procedural issues so as to give effect to the requirements of expeditious investigation and prosecution of those involved directly or indirectly in the crime of terrorism. These measures should include issues such as the protection of witnesses, access to dockets and information, and special arrangements on detention and access to hearings; harmonize the standards and procedures regarding proof for terrorism-related crimes; promote specialized training and reinforce the capacities of the judiciary [and]; harmonize legal frameworks pertaining to the prevention and combating of terrorism.[8]

A very crucial aspect of the AU's legal and judicial harmonization measures is the institution of an extradition regime. Terrorists have been known to perpetuate their terrorist acts in "friendly" countries or tend to escape to "friendly" countries after committing acts of terrorism. In some instances, by so doing, they avoid prosecution for their terrorist activities. Take the case of Air France Flight 139 from Athens to Paris in 1976. In mid-air, hijackers from the Popular Front for the Liberation of Palestine (PFLP) and the Revolutionäre Zellen commandeered the plane with 248 passengers and 12 crew members first to Benghazi, Libya, for refueling and then, finally, to Entebbe Airport in Uganda. These terrorists were sympathizers to the Palestinian cause and therefore it was no accident that they decided to refuel the plane in Libya, which backed the Palestinians in their ongoing struggle with Israel. They finally ended in Uganda where President Idi Amin made no secret of his support of the Palestinians in their struggle against the Israelis. Indeed, when the plane landed in Uganda, the hijackers were joined by additional terrorists within the pro-Palestinian forces of President Amin. Though terrorism and hijacking were international crimes, Amin never attempted to bring the hijackers to justice. Instead, he used the incident for publicity and propaganda. He clearly had the influence and power to end the hijacking and hostage drama but elected not to do so. The terrorists counted on such a "soft landing" and they got it. From President Amin's sympathetic statements during the crisis, it is prudent to conclude that he would never have allowed these hijackers to be prosecuted. Indeed, he would never have turned these individuals over to France or Greece for prosecution.

The African Union has at least created a legal and judicial framework by which terrorists within the continent cannot shop for safe havens or count on their support. Article 12 of The Plan is loaded with numerous provisions addressing the issue of extradition. It calls for Member States to:

conclude extradition and mutual legal assistance agreements, where necessary, and adopt the legislation that would enable Member States to cooperate effectively; identity, if need be, the national authorities for processing extradition and mutual legal assistance requests and, where necessary, establish mechanism to ensure coordination between competent national authorities in this regard [and]; review existing extradition and mutual legal assistance legislation, and adapt such legislation with a view to ensuring effective and expeditious handling of extradition and mutual legal assistance requests.[9]

In addition, it calls for the simplification of the extradition process and a seamless transfer of criminal proceedings. To leave no room for complacency, it prohibits the use of political motivation as grounds for refusal to extradite a suspected terrorist. Even in worst case scenarios when a Member State refuses to extradite a suspected terrorist, The Plan makes it incumbent upon that State to prosecute the individual so accused. To ascertain that extradition agreements, and to withstand the legal and judicial muster, The Plan provides for all such agreements to be consistent with international law.

Coordinating Compliance with International Agreements

A major role that the African Union has played in the fight against continental terror is to coordinate African efforts with those of the international community. In this regard, the African Union has made it mandatory for its Member States to also honor and respect international agreements dealing with terrorism. Indeed, this requirement is not part of a separate instrument or document: it is enshrined in the African Union's Plan of Action on the Prevention and Combating of Terrorism in Africa. Thus, any Member State of the African Union automatically must adhere to all other international agreements designed to prevent and combat terrorism. Such an approach ensures that there is unity of purpose in defeating terrorism in the international environment. More specifically, The Plan calls on Member States to: "sign, ratify and fully implement all relevant international instruments concerning terrorism and, where necessary, seek assistance for amendments to national legislation so as to comply with the provisions of these instruments."[10]

This provision refers to two main international instruments in the fight against international terrorism: United Nations Security Council (UNSC) Resolution 1373 and the International Convention for the Suppression of the Financing of Terrorism in 1999. The provisions within Resolution 1373 are extensive in dealing with international terrorism. The Resolution:

Decides that all States shall: (a) Prevent and suppress the financing of terrorist acts; (b) Criminalize the willful provision or collection, by any means, directly or indirectly, of funds by their nationals or in their territories with the intention that the funds should be used, or in the knowledge that they are to be used, in order to carry out terrorist acts; (c) Freeze without delay funds and other financial assets or economic resources of persons who commit, or attempt to commit, terrorist acts or participate in or facilitate the commission of terrorist acts; of entities owned or controlled directly or indirectly by such persons; and of persons and entities acting on behalf of, or at the direction of such persons and entities, including funds derived or generated from property owned or controlled directly or indirectly by such persons and associated persons and entities; (d) Prohibit their nationals or any persons and entities within their territories from making any funds, financial assets or economic resources or financial or other related services available, directly or indirectly, for the benefit of persons who commit or attempt to commit or facilitate or participate in the commission of terrorist acts, of entities owned or controlled, directly or indirectly, by such persons and of persons and entities acting on behalf of or at the direction of such persons.[11]

These provisions are similar to those in the African Union's Plan of Action under Article 13. Like both international agreements above, Article 13 of the African Union's Plan of Action also calls on Member States to suppress the financing of terrorism. Among other things, it calls for the confiscation of assets intended for financing terrorism, the introduction of legislation to criminalize the financing of terrorism and money laundering, and the training of individuals in each Member State to prevent and combat money laundering.

Terrorism thrives because terrorists receive financing from different sources. In view of the fact that they have access to the purse strings from whatever sources, they continue to operate. One of the surest ways to prevent and combat terrorism is to cut off its financial life-line. Without money, terrorists cannot operate training camps and buy the weapons of terror they need. Suppressing terrorist financing, including money laundering, can be a very effective approach, though it is more complicated to achieve than it appears. By making this a prominent strategy in its fight against the proliferation of terrorism, the African Union has positioned itself on the right path.

Information Exchange

The African Union has also identified information exchange as a potent tool for fighting terrorism. In a new world order characterized by sophisticated technology, the war on terrorism cannot be won without the use of technology to detect and exchange information about terrorist planning. Currently there is terrorist planning in just about every region of the world. Without the sharing of information about possible terrorist activities and training, it is feasible for terrorist organizations to use some countries as safe havens from which to launch terrorist acts against other countries. For several years, al Qaeda used Afghanistan (from the end of the 1990s to the late part of 2001) as a safe haven. Afghanistan under the Taliban refused to share information about the activities of bin Laden's terrorist network.

Though the United States had some intelligence about al Qaeda, it was not as substantive as it would have been if Afghanistan had shared intelligence with the United States and the rest of the world. The end result was that the world and the United States were taken aback in 2001 by the al Qaeda-sponsored attacks on the World Trade Center, the Pentagon and an averted attack that could have targeted either the White House or the Capitol Building of the US Congress. The devastation was enormous and scars continue to linger in terms of family pains and the drastic changes in America's political landscape, as seen in the creation of the Department of Homeland Security. Similarly, many civil liberties that were formerly enjoyed have been eclipsed today because of the need for more security.

It is through planning by the African Union that required its membership to engage in information exchange regarding terrorist activities and planning that produced a plan of action requiring members to:

> enhance intelligence exchange, training and capacity-building (with the assistance from INTERPOL), including basic and improved specialized training for staff in charge of combating terrorism; identify individuals, groups and entities engaged in terrorist activities…; share lessons learnt and experiences gained on counterterrorist tactics; establish a common Terrorism Activity Reporting (TAR) schedule as data collection instrument on names of identified organizations, persons, places and resources by Member States. The TAR should then provide the source information to the content of an AU database that shall provide timely information.[12]

This approach to information sharing gives Member States the ability to monitor terrorist activities and planning. It empowers Member States with the ability to disrupt and prevent terrorist acts. It provides them with better opportunities to act proactively and to apprehend individuals within terrorist cells before they manifest their destructive acts of terrorism. Finally, it makes African states better prepared and more helpful in the global war against terrorism. It is worth noting that information sharing is not limited to member states of the AU. To that end information regarding terrorist activity is also shared with member states of the United Nations, most notably the Untied States.

The Creation of the Peace and Security Council

Mindful of a glaring short-coming of the League of Nations, the African Union decided to create a monitoring mechanism headed by a Commissioner to monitor the implementation of its Plan of Action against terrorism. The League of Nations was commonly referred to as a toothless organization because it could bark but could not bite. In other words, it had no mechanism to monitor and implement its decisions. Article 16 of The Plan cites Article 7 of the Protocol creating the Peace and Security Council as being responsible for the implementation of The Plan and other international, continental and regional conventions and instruments. Specifically, the Council among other things was required to "request all Member States, on an annual basis, to report on the steps taken to prevent and combat terrorism and, where appropriate, on the implementation of the Algiers Convention."[13]

The Creation of the African Center for the Study and Research of Terrorism

Finally, the African Union concluded that a research center would bolster the capabilities of African countries in dealing with terrorism. The center was created to research all aspects of terrorism: patterns of terrorist activities and a sociological and psychological study of individuals or groups engaged in terrorism. It currently serves to "centralize information, studies and analyses on terrorism and terrorist groups and develop training programs by organizing, with the assistance of international partners, training schedules, meetings, and symposia."[14] A center of this nature would research factors—both human and societal—that influence individuals to become terrorists. Such research empowers African states to minimize terrorism by making efforts to minimize factors that attract individuals towards terrorism.

The African Union and Continental Terror: Some Major Challenges

In its leadership role in preventing and combating terrorism in Africa, the African Union faces major challenges from two main sources: from the international community and the developed Western powers, and from Member States.

Major Challenges from the International Community

After devising several strategies for dealing with continental terror, the AU created the African Union Commission (with a commissioner and a secretariat to implement these strategies). A major challenge that the Commission has faced in implementing these instruments of the African Union is the dominance of the United Nations and the developed Western powers when it comes to the fight against terrorism. Efforts of the African Union, which are substantial, have been eclipsed by the actions of the United States, Britain, France, and the United Nations. The end of the Cold War has unfortunately taken the interest and attention away from Africa. While the international community is flooded with constant information on the Bush administration's efforts towards combating and preventing terrorism—wiretapping, the war on terrorism in Afghanistan, the war in Iraq, the Guantanamo prison in Cuba for suspected terrorists, new US flight rules, major changes in American Immigration Law—the efforts of the African Union have gone largely unreported. Yet, by every standard of measurement, the African Union has invested a lot into fighting continental terror, which is an integral part of the global war on terrorism.

Secondly, the African Union's plea for technical assistance in fully implementing its anti-terrorism instruments and those of the international community has not been satisfactorily answered by the developed Western countries that exert substantial control within the United Nations. The African Union through its implementing organ, the Commission, has championed the need for substantial technical assistance through its dealings with UN Counter-Terrorism Committee, the United Nations Office on Drugs and Crime (UNODC), the International Monetary Fund (IMF), and through numerous international forums. With poverty and the lack of technical expertise in Africa, it is no surprise that the region, in spite of its good intentions, is unable to finance its elaborate anti-terrorist agenda. Instead of substantial assistance to help Africa confront this malaise, the technical assistance that the African Union has received is "mainly advisory and capacity-building programs."[15] This is unacceptable. The West must consider Africa a true partner in the fight against global terrorism. Though the focus of the African Union is on continental terrorism, Africa remains an integral part in the global war on terrorism. Africa cannot be treated in isolation.

Indeed, Africa can make the case that it is fighting mostly a war not of its own making, and one led by the United States. The bulk of acts of terrorism that have occurred within the continent have targeted US interests, and not those involving African interests. In 1998 when terrorists struck Kenya and Tanzania, they struck two US embassies, killing 291 people and wounding over 5,000 in Kenya alone.[16] Of the hundreds that perished in these attacks, only 12 were American. In other words, Africa bore the brunt of the attacks in terms of human lives. In addition, Kenya's economy in particular suffered enormously as tourism, which was its most viable source of revenue, fell precipitously. Tourists stayed away for security reasons and it has taken several years for the tourist industry to recover.

Therefore, the West must appreciate the sacrifices of African countries and support them in substance rather than through token gestures. The African Union has issued a statement that the prevalence of poverty in the continent makes it an attractive recruiting ground for terrorists. In this respect, the deplorable economic situation of the continent is a crucial part of the equation to combat terrorism. The Bush administration and its NATO allies, along with the rest of the world, must take concrete steps to provide more economic and technical assistance to strengthen Africa's capacity to deal with the terrorist threat. While dealing with individual countries is still permissible, it is crucial, however, that the West and international organizations work more closely with the AU to develop impressive instruments to deal with continental terror.

The programs in the United States that target only specific countries for technical assistance is promising but a partnership with the African Union will go a long way in strengthening the organization. For example, the Bush administration's creation of the Pan Sahel Initiative (PSI) in 2002 was a good gesture designed to assist Mali, Niger, Chad, and Mauritania in securing their borders, combating terrorism, and tracking the movement of persons. It was also a program that brought both military and civilian officials of these countries together to encourage cooperation in counterterrorism and border issues. This certainly would have been a better program if it had been coordinated with the African Union. In the end the PSI could not achieve its full potential because of limited funding from the United States.

Major Challenges from African Union Member States

After several years of implementing its agenda to prevent and combat terrorism, the African Union continues to face many challenges from its Member States. The first set of challenges came in reference to measures taken to implement the 1999 OAU Convention on the Prevention and Combating of Terrorism. The goal was to get all Member States of the African Union to sign and ratify the Convention. That was not supposed to be a difficult task as there was general agreement that ratification was a prerequisite for effective coordination and harmonization in the fight against terrorism. However, because of the slower than expected pace of ratification, it became necessary for the Commission, which was charged with monitoring compliance, to organize a signing period from 3 December to 10 December 2003 to encourage signing and ratification of the Convention.[17] In addition, the Commission had to send out reminder letters, use informal and formal diplomatic channels, and even international forums, to plead to Member States to sign and ratify the Convention.[18]

In spite of these very proactive approaches, not all Member States of the African Union have signed or ratified the Convention. Since it was opened for signature and ratification in 1999, 46 out of 53 countries have signed, 34 have ratified, and 4 Member States have neither signed nor ratified the Convention.[19] Countries that have signed but have not ratified the Convention include: Botswana, Cameroon, Central African Republic, Chad, Ivory Coast, Congo Republic, Democratic Republic of Congo, Gabon, Gambia, Guinea Bissau, Liberia, Namibia, Niger, and Sierra Leone.[20] On the other hand, the four countries that have neither signed nor ratified the Convention are Somalia, Sao Tome and Principe, Zambia, and Zimbabwe.[21]

The second set of challenges that confronts the African Union involves its efforts to implement the Plan of Action on the Prevention and Combating of Terrorism. A major challenge in this area is the lack of funds and technical knowledge. The lack of adequate capacity by the Commission to fulfill its responsibilities as the implementing agent has slowed progress. Pleas for technical assistance from the West and the international donor community have not been forthcoming as they should. Because of these shortcomings, the Peace and Security Council only came into operation in 2004 and has since not really been able to sustain itself to carry out its responsibilities. Regarding their role, Member States have also complicated matters on this issue:

> Member States have not forwarded to the Commission, for appropriate coordination at the regional level, continental and international levels, the names and contact information of their contact points as provided in Section E Paragraph 15 of the Plan of Action.[22]

The main function of the African Union is to coordinate and develop a harmonious and integrated approach to preventing and combating terrorism throughout the continent. If Member States fail to meet their responsibilities then it complicates matters for the African Union. In order to coordinate African efforts to deal with terrorism, Member States are required to provide contact names with addresses and telephone numbers as points of contact for this coordinating strategy. In spite of the necessity of having this information to fulfill its responsibilities, some Member States, for whatever reasons, have failed to forward them to the African Union. This inaction seriously undermines the ability of the African Union to combat terrorism.

Conclusion

Though overlooked, the African Union has made substantive progress in developing an African regime to prevent and combat terrorism. All the instruments and mechanisms are in place to fight terrorism, however, the lack of adequate technical capacity and support from the West has been a tough mountain to climb. The West should understand that the prevalence of poverty in Africa and the lack of adequate institutional capacity illustrates why the continent is a fertile ground for recruiting terrorists. The West must also understand that preventing and defeating terrorism in Africa constitutes an integral part of their national security. The terrorists have decided that Africa remains the weak link through which they can attack Western interests. The attacks on American embassies in Kenya and Tanzania remain vivid reminders of the preceding assertion. To be more effective in its fight against terrorism, the African Union must continue to press for technical assistance from the international donor community. In the end, the AU must also continue to persuade its members to set aside their national interests in favor of continental interests.

Notes

1   Bruce Hoffman, *Inside Terrorism* (New York: Columbia University Press, 1988), p. 25.
2   At the time, Germany was still divided into East and West Germany so Munich at the time was under West Germany.
3   Plan of Action of the African Union for the Prevention and Combating of Terrorism, September 9, 2002, Preamble, Article 7.
4   Ibid., Preamble, Articles 3, 4, and 6.
5   Ibid., General Provisions, 10(a).
6   OAU Convention on the Prevention and Combating of Terrorism, 1999, Final Provisions, Article 20(1) and (2).
7   The Plan, Specific Provisions, Article 11(a) to (f).
8   Ibid., Specific Provisions, Article 12(a) to (d).
9   Ibid., Specific Provisions, Article 12(f), (g), and (h).
10   Ibid., General Provisions, Article 10(b).
11   See United Nations Resolution 1373 of September 21, 2001.
12   The Plan of Action, Article 14(b), (c), (d), and (e).
13   Ibid., Specific Provisions, Article 16(b).
14   Ibid., Specific Provisions, Article 20.
15   Report of the Chairperson of the AU Commission on the Implementation of the 1999 OAU Convention and the Plan of Action on the Prevention and Combating of Terrorism, Oct. 13–14, 2004, Article 22, p. 6.
16   See United States Department of State, Patterns of Global Terrorism, Africa Overview, April 30, 2003.
17   African Union, Report on the Chairperson of the AU Commission on the Implementation of the 1999 OAU Convention and the Plan of Action on the Prevention and Combating of Terrorism in Africa, 2004, p. 3.
18   Ibid.
19   Ibid.
20   Ibid., pp. 3–4.
21   Ibid., p. 4.
22   Ibid., p. 11.

PART 4
Clinton and Bush: Impact on Africa

Chapter 8

The Clinton Model: Sudan and the Failure to Capture bin Laden

John Davis

Introduction

For most observers the Clinton administration's signature response to terrorism in Africa commenced in the wake of al Qaeda's twin terrorist bombings that leveled two US embassies in Kenya and Tanzania. The historical record indicates that to those that accepted this perspective they would be incorrect. In fact the administration's decision to confront terrorism developed during the interregnum between the "transition period" and the conclusion of the "internal terrorism policy review" and thereafter terrorism quietly dominated the two terms of the Clinton administration. For many of the individuals that participated in this policy review (John Prendergast, Timothy Carney, a former Ambassador to Sudan, to name a few) the debate had a singular quality: a consensus that the time had come to confront Sudan's terrorist safe haven.

The evidence was clear. Of the numerous African countries, Sudan developed into the central hub of terrorist activity where a number of major terrorist groups—Hezbollah, Hamas, Islamic Jihad, a plethora of Palestinian groups, a host of lesser known transnational terrorist groups in Africa, and another that had yet to come into view: Al Qaeda—sought out and received sanctuary in Khartoum. In the view of those in the interagency working group that had been assembled to consider options against terrorism, the CIA, and those that worked as aides to the National Security Council Staff on Africa, and those within the Africa bureau at the State Department, Sudan posed a major threat to regional stability. Similarly, these same individuals reached a consensus on two issues: there was a perception that many of the aforementioned terror groups used the safe haven in Sudan to launch terror attacks against Israel, or launched them from within countries within the Middle East. The interagency working group came to a consensus over another point: the aforementioned attacks had another quality—they undermined the peace process. In the final analysis the interagency working group recommended (and it was later accepted) that the president focus on the threat of state-sponsored terrorism. In Africa that meant that the administration policy would target Sudan.

The subject of this study involves the examination of the Clinton administration's response to terrorism in Africa. The central focus of this study involves delineating the Clinton administration's counterterrorism policies against Sudan prior to the East Africa embassy bombings. Thereafter, the study examines the bureaucratic politics, the second-term policy review, the increase in sanctions, the use of anti-government forces within Sudan, and other means that the administration employed in its approach to end the terrorist sanctuary in Khartoum. Finally, the chapter closes with an assessment of the administration's post-embassy-attack policies, wherein in the Clinton administration launched a counterterrorist strike against Sudan (and another strike against an al Qaeda base camp in Afghanistan); and how thereafter the US government further supplemented the already bloated sanctions regime with the objective, as in the beginning, of ending the terrorist haven. At issue: how successful was the Clinton counterterrorist model against Sudan?

Pre-embassy Bombing Policy: Sanctions and al Qaeda

The Clinton administration, with regard to confronting terrorism in Sudan,[1] proved to be unusually active. Oddly, in 1993, irrespective of the February 26 attack on the World Trade Center, the administration focused greater attention and resources on terrorism in Sudan than it did with coming to grips with the nascent al Qaeda threat. With regard to Sudan, the subject of this study, the administration discretely targeted National Islamic Front (NIF) and made the North African country the centerpiece of its efforts to tackle terrorism. It fell under the purview of Assistant Secretary of State for African Affairs George E. Moose to articulate the administration policy. Consistent with the administration's policy in Africa, in testimony before the Senate Foreign Relations subcommittee on Africa on May 15, 1997, Moose formally outlined the president's policy toward Sudan:

> In 1993 the Clinton Administration placed Sudan on the list of state sponsors of terrorism, and we have unilateral sanctions consistent with that designation. Sudan was known to provide refuge, logistical support such as training facilities, travel documents, and weapons to a variety of radical terrorist organizations.[2]

Of interest is that the US Ambassador at that the time, Donald Petterson, had not been made aware of the decision to list Sudan as a state sponsor of terror, and in the final analysis he "expressed surprise" at the decision. The record, said Patterson, indicated that there was sufficient evidence to suggest collusion between the government of Sudan and various terrorist activities but he did not believe Khartoum was in the same league as Iran and North Korea, the more established state sponsors. It was for this reason the ambassador asserted "I did not think this evidence was sufficiently conclusive to put Sudan on the US government's list of state sponsors of terrorism."[3]

In keeping with the unspoken caveat, irrespective of these decisions, another set of orders had been given to the State Department: make sure foreign policy would not eclipse the administration's domestic agenda.

The administration's Sudan policy began to make waves in the Washington Beltway. Administration insiders had expressed early on that Sudan was "incapable of such terrorist influence" by itself; there had to be another connection. For administration officials, the source of Sudan's terrorist financing was clear:

US officials fear that Sudan, backed by money and expertise from Iran, is emerging as "a new Lebanon" from which terrorist groups can launch operations and export Islamic revolution across Africa. Sudan "is absolutely the place to watch," said one US anti-terrorism official in an interview yesterday. The official said the Iranians have spent between $10 million and $20 million to help establish a beachhead for Islamic radicalism in Khartoum.[4]

Following evidence that Sudan participated in a conspiracy to assassinate Egypt's President Hosni Mubarak in June of 1995, the administration intensified its effort to end Sudan's terrorist activities.

Since 1995, Sudan has failed to cooperate with the international community to help extradite to Ethiopia three suspects in the assassination attempt in Addis Ababa against Egyptian President Hosni Mubarak. After demands from the Organization of African Unity (OAU) that Sudan facilitate their extradition to Ethiopia went unheeded, the US played a leading role last year in the adoption of three UN Security Council resolutions. Resolution 1044 required that Sudan act "to extradite to Ethiopia for prosecution" the three suspects and that it "desist" from "activities of assisting, supporting, and facilitating terrorist activities and from giving shelter or sanctuary to terrorist elements." The United States emphasized at the time that we would consider Sudan responsible for extradition of the suspects even if they allowed them to leave the country, as may now have occurred.[5]

In spite of increasing US pressure, the administration was unable to alter Sudan's participation in terrorism. Indeed, in spite of the Clinton administration's efforts in the United Nations Security Council the Sudanese government did not comply with the terms of the resolution. Such action forced the administration to come up with creative ways to respond to what the administration dubbed "ideological arrogance" by the rogue state of Sudan. Thereafter the administration imposed its own sanctions: calling upon the Sudanese government to reduce its diplomatic presence in the United States; for those that remained in the country the administration restricted their travel; and finally, the administration "imposed a restrictive visa regime for government and military officials."[6]

The administration, while pressuring Sudan, received significant evidence that it was al Qaeda that was behind the conspiracy to kill Mubarak in June 1992. The administration briefly shifted its focus to al Qaeda but continued to increase the diplomatic and political pressure on Sudan.

Within the Clinton administration the influential Counterterrorism Security Group (CSG) held a number of meetings in the wake of the Mubarak conspiracy. The consensus of the group was fundamental: consider direct action against al Qaeda. The CSG recommended to the Principals' Committee (consisting of Clinton, Gore, Secretary of State Warren Christopher, the National Security Advisor Anthony Lake, CIA Director, the Joint Chiefs Chairman) that called for the Pentagon to consider the use of US Special Forces to attack bin Laden's (and Turabi's) facilities in and around Khartoum. According to Richard Clarke, "those facilities" included "a plan to blow up a bank in downtown Khartoum that was thought to house bin Laden's money."[7] The assault had been canceled because the Joint Staff in the Pentagon acknowledged "this isn't stealth. There is nothing quiet or covert about this. It's going to war with Sudan."[8]

Review of Policy: Bureaucratic Politics and the Elevation of Sanctions

During the second term of the Clinton administration, many African watchers anticipated "a new thinking" of US policy toward Sudan. Indeed, within the president's own party there was discontent about the "presence of sanctions fatigue." The policy, according to "the left," did not end the civil war in Sudan, nor did it impact the rampant human rights abuses. Republicans, had a similar view but went a step further, arguing that Sudan did not pose a national security threat to the United States and therefore the administration had invested far too much political capital.

Within the administration two debates unfolded. The first concerned the debate between Foreign Service Officers (FSOs) within the State Department, which questioned why the president made the decision to place two "political appointees"— Susan Rice (who would become the new assistant secretary of state for Africa) and John Prendergast, both Africanists that served in the White House National Security Staff—to head the Africa Bureau. According to the FSOs, they were not diplomats but political operatives and therefore were poor choices.[9] The president overruled the diplomats and made the appointment, but the decision did not end the wrangling over the administration's Sudan policy and did not end the perception that the administration's Africa policy was incoherent.

The second debate was far more substantial. This debate centered on whether the administration would "engage" Sudan "diplomatically" or if they would push the envelope and intensify the sanctions against the Islamic government in Khartoum. The debate remained within the State Department. This time many of the seasoned diplomats openly challenged Rice for control of US policy toward Sudan. Many of the administration's senior diplomats argued that the sanctions did little to alter the behavior of Sudan, and worse, the policy left the administration with few options. For her part, Rice and her allies argued that the use of sanctions represented a positive utility and that the administration should accelerate them.

The debate between the rival camps did not subside; indeed it intensified. The critical move came in the form of a challenge made by Thomas Pickering, the Under Secretary of State. As the following excerpt illustrates both camps became engaged in a bitter bureaucratic struggle:

> They [the diplomats] maintained that the threat posed by Sudan's regime is greatly exaggerated. They also maintained that the regime could be neither effectively undermined nor overthrown, so they encouraged Sudanese opposition groups to try to negotiate a settlement to the country's 15-year civil war. Pickering and his allies also actively searched for moderates within the Sudanese regime with whom they hoped to build relations. The rival camps fought a decisive battle last September. Though the United States has maintained relations with the regime in Sudan, in February 1996 the administration closed the embassy in Khartoum for security reasons and moved its staff to Nairobi. The security problems have since abated, but Rice's camp has nonetheless sought to keep the embassy shut in order to send a strong message of disapproval. Last September, while Rice was on maternity leave, Pickering and his allies made a move. Without White House authorization, Pickering told journalists—through an intermediary—that the administration would soon partly reopen the embassy in Khartoum. "It was an interesting squeeze play," says one official sympathetic to Pickering.[10]

It was Secretary of State Madeline Albright that intervened and forced Pickering to retract the statement, and the embassy remained closed. Thereafter, the debate over the course of the administration's Sudan policy shifted focus. This time regional players, Ethiopia and Uganda, concerned with the debate in Washington, openly requested that Clinton "stay the course." In late April two decisions were made that signaled a dramatic shift in administration policy. In the first decision, an interagency team shuttled to Egypt, Eritrea, Ethiopia, Kenya, and Uganda with the objective of seeking affirmation for the aforementioned countries to intensify the arming of anti-government forces in the southern Sudan. In the wake of this meeting, the administration provided $20 million in military assistance, the largest funding since the Cold War, to end terrorism in Sudan, with the ultimate objective of ending the el-Bashir regime.

In this new environment the administration increased sanctions against Sudan. The combined policy shift placed tremendous pressure on the regime in Sudan. In recognition of these twin threats, the Sudanese government increased its anti-American rhetoric and charged that the "local frontline states" were nothing more than "tools" of the Clinton administration.

Later in 1996 the administration again prepared to take on al Qaeda. This time, with bin Laden now in Afghanistan, the focus shifted to a senior operative in the organization, Abu Hafs al-Muratani. Intelligence sources within the administration and those from US allies indicated the al-Muratani had retained a hotel room in Khartoum; equally significant the operative had no guards and the CSG recommended "snatching him."[11] The use of this verbiage is significant because it illustrates that the Clinton administration was involved in "extraordinary renditions" long before the president signed an executive order authorizing their use after the East African embassy bombings in 1998.

After the failure of the administration to go to the source, the policy retained its original character: regardless of the terror groups that received safe haven, President Clinton asserted it was Sudan that was the subject of its displeasure and the administration's principal focus. In short, as former assistant secretary of state Moose observed in his earlier testimony before congress, "the US objectives are clear and unequivocal: to isolate Sudan and to contain its support for insurgents and terrorists and to oblige the Sudanese Government by exacting a price for unacceptable behavior, to change its domestic and international conduct."[12]

Sudan, bin Laden, and Clinton

Already reeling from the fallout from the events in Mogadishu in October of 1993 and Rwanda in 1994, the Clinton administration had another stigma attached to its Africa policy: the failure to capture Osama bin Laden during his remaining year in Sudan. In 1996 the Clinton administration, along with assistance from Saudi Arabia and Egypt, succeeded in pressuring the regime in Sudan to force bin Laden and the bulk of his "Afghan Arabs" to leave the country. Interestingly, the administration had the opportunity to capture bin Laden in 1996 (before his departure) along with key members of the al Qaeda (some of which would play critical roles in 11 September 2001) transnational network.

The historical record indicates the Sudanese government attempted on several occasions to hand over or to detain bin Laden. The regime offered the Clinton administration a quid pro quo: bin Laden (and senior al Qaeda operatives) in exchange for the reduction and eventual cancellation of US-led sanctions against Sudan. These things, according to Sudanese government, could pave the wave for normalization of relations between Sudan and the United States.

An example of the behind the scene horse trading is instructive. Mansoor Ijaz asserts that from 1996–1998 he was the pivotal link between the regime in Sudan and the Clinton White House in highly secretive discussions. In those discussions Ijaz explicates that there were definitive opportunities to detain bin Laden. The following statement symbolizing Ijaz's involvement:

> From 1996 to 1998, I opened unofficial channels between Sudan and the Clinton administration. I met with officials in both countries, including Clinton, US National Security Advisor Samuel R. "Sandy" Berger and Sudan's president and intelligence chief. President Omar Hassan Ahmed Bashir, who wanted terrorism sanctions against Sudan lifted, offered the arrest and extradition of Bin Laden and detailed intelligence data about the global networks constructed by Egypt's Islamic Jihad, Iran's Hezbollah and the Palestinian Hamas. Among those in the networks were the two hijackers who piloted commercial airliners into the World Trade Center. The silence of the Clinton administration in responding to these offers was deafening.[13]

Ijaz asserts that on several occasions, February 1996, August 1996, April 1997, and again in February 1998, the administration "listened to" but did not "act on" the opportunities to learn about and eventually capture al Qaeda officials. Ijaz noted he "persuaded Bashir to invite the FBI to come to Sudan and view the data." Thereafter he invited Sudan's intelligence chief, Gutbi al-Mahdi, to write directly to the FBI, by-passing senior officials that Ijaz believed were blocking efforts to complete the negotiations. Ijaz offered this comment on the reactions of the Clinton administration:

> When I returned to Washington, I told Berger and his specialist for East Africa, Susan Rice, about the data available. They said they'd get back to me. They never did. Neither did they respond when Bashir made the offer directly. I believe they never had any intention to engage Muslim countries—ally or not. Radical Islam, for the administration, was a convenient national security threat.[14]

Privately, despite Ijaz's statements, he continued to conduct private diplomatic missions on behalf of the Clinton administration until January of 2000.[15] The focus of the negotiations remained on bin Laden, but as one would suspect, Sudan and its involvement in terrorism remained a constant priority.[16]

In spite of the mounting evidence of the Clinton administration's back channel negotiations with the government of Sudan about bin Laden, al Qaeda, and the suspension of terrorist sanctions, the administration "spin machine" went into overdrive to deny the existence of such negotiations with the outlaw terrorist regime. In a vivid example, the administration's "terrorist czar" had this to say:

In recent years Sudanese intelligence officials and Americans friendly to the Sudan regime have invented a fable about Bin Laden's final days in Khartoum. In the fable the Sudanese government offers to arrest bin Laden and hand him over in chains to FBI agents, but Washington rejects the offer because the Clinton administration does not see bin Laden as important ... and cannot find anywhere to put him on trial. The only slivers of truth in this fable are that a) the Sudanese government was denying its support for terrorism in the wake of the UN sanctions, and b) the CSG had initiated informal inquiries with several nations about incarcerating bin Laden, or putting him on trial. There were no takers. Nevertheless, had we been able to put our hands on him then we would have gladly done.[17]

Clarke's statements denying the back channel negotiations, and those of other officials, surfaced after the "blame game" commenced in Washington following the 9/11 Commission's investigation into the nightmare al Qaeda attack that killed nearly 3,000 people. Clarke's clever words did little to impact the overwhelming evidence that indicated that a concerted campaign by Sudan had been underway in late 1995 to turn bin Laden over to the Clinton administration.[18] The episode about Clinton's refusal to "make a deal to capture bin Laden" emerged as a forgotten tragedy of the president's policies toward Sudan.

Irrespective of the Clinton administration's denials about the efforts to capture bin Laden, the president continued to increase the pressure on the government of Gen. Omar Ahmad al-Bashir. Once again the pressure came in the form of economic sanctions. In what was described as the "zenith of administration pressure," on 3 November 1997 President Clinton signed executive order 13067, authority granted under the International Emergency Economic Powers Act (50 USC 1703 et. seq.) and the National Emergencies Act (50 USC 1641), that imposed the most drastic of trade and economic sanctions against Sudan:

> The order declared "that the policies of Sudan constitute an extraordinary and unusual threat to the national security and foreign policy of the United States." On 1 July 1998, the Department of the Treasury's Office of Foreign Assets Control (OFAC) issued the Sudanese Sanctions Regulations (63 Fed. Reg. 35809, July 1, 1998). These regulations blocked all property and interests in property of the Sudanese government, its agencies, instrumentalities and controlled entities, including the Bank of Sudan, that were in the United States. The Clinton Administration has also brought pressure to bear on private banks and multilateral lending agencies not to lend to Sudan. They also prohibited: (1) the importation into the United States of any goods or services of Sudanese origin, with the exception of informational material; (2) the exportation or re-exportation of goods, technology, or services to Sudan or the Government of Sudan apart from informational materials or donations of humanitarian aid; (3) the involvement of any American person in the export or re-exportation of goods and services to or from Sudan; (4) the involvement of any American person in contracts relating to Sudan; (5) the grant or extension of credits or loans by any American person to the Sudanese government; and (6) transactions relating to the transportation of cargo.[19]

In spite of the ever-increasing enmity between the Sudan and the United States, the government of Sudan, in the face of the US-led "sanctions regime," attempted to negotiate with the Clinton administration. According to Ambassador Mahdi Ibrahim

Mohamed, Sudanese Ambassador to the United States, the administration repeatedly rebuffed his overtures:

> Toward March [1997], I delivered to the State Department a message from the president of Sudan to the president of the United States. The president, our president, requested in that letter that the two nations engage in open and cooperative dialogue aimed at resolving any differences that might have existed between our two governments. And namely, the message addressed the issue of peace, establishing peace in the Sudan; addressing the problems of neighborly relations and destabilization in the sub-region, the issue of terrorism and the general issue of human rights. It was communicated with the most sincere of intentions and meant to end an era of misinformation, disinformation, and open a time for cooperation and goodwill. President Clinton never afforded President Bashir with the courtesy of a response to that important letter.[20]

For the administration's part it rightly concluded that Sudan did little to end its support of terrorism and there was considerable evidence of the government's systematic human rights violations against Black Africans in the southern part of the country. Terrorist sanctions aside, the year 1998 dramatically altered the administration's counterterrorism policies both against al Qaeda and Sudan. This was the setting before the East African embassy bombings.

Post-embassy Bombing Policy

For the Clinton administration, 7 August 1998 was a watershed moment. On this date the US embassies in Kenya and Tanzania were destroyed by operatives of the al Qaeda transnational terror network. The administration made two significant decisions: first, it formally launched a war on terror against al Qaeda and, second, the administration's once private war with Sudan was no longer secret.

In announcing the war on terror, the president made two statements that signified his intensions to target al Qaeda, but it was also clear that Sudan would figure into the administration's post-embassy bombing strategy. The first occurred in a speech at Andrews Air Force Base on 13 August 1998, a location that served as a memorial celebration for those US citizens that were killed in the East Africa embassy attacks.

> No matter what it takes, we must find those responsible for these evil acts and see that justice is done. There may be more hard roads ahead, for terrorists target America f because we act and stand for peace and democracy, because the spirit of our country is the very spirit of freedom. It is the burden our history and the hope of the world's future…. America will not retreat from the world and all its promise, nor shrink from our responsibility to stand against terror and with the friends of freedom everywhere.[21]

This was the first of a series of administration pronouncements in the wake of the embassy attacks. The second presidential speech was far more specific, and served to launch the administration's war on terror. On 20 August 1998 the president announced the commencement of Operation Infinite Reach, the administration's response to the deadly attacks on August 7:

This morning, based on the unanimous recommendation of my national security team, I ordered our Armed Forces to take action to counter an immediate threat from the bin Laden network. Earlier today, the United States carried out simultaneous strikes against terrorist facilities and infrastructure in Afghanistan. Our forces targeted one of the most active terrorist bases in the world. It contained key elements of the bin Laden network's infrastructure and has served as a training camp for literally thousands of terrorists from around the globe. We have reason to believe that a gathering of key terrorist leaders was to take place there today, thus underscoring the urgency of our actions. Our forces also attacked a factory in Sudan associated with the bin Laden network. The factory was involved in the production of materials for chemical weapons. The United States does not take this action lightly. Afghanistan and Sudan have been warned for years to stop harboring and supporting these terrorist groups. But countries that persistently host terrorists have no right to be safe havens.[22]

In terms of objectives, the opening strike against bin Laden and his senior operatives failed for a number of reasons. The most notable concerned the fact that Pakistan's ISI, riddled with al Qaeda sympathizers, tipped off bin Laden about the pending attack. In the case of Sudan, the al Shifa plant was allegedly producing chemical weapons, but the administration's assertions proved to be false.

The reaction from Sudan was swift. President Omar el-Bashir warned that "Sudanese people will defend themselves against this criminal act." Similarly, the leader of Sudan noted his country "reserves the right to respond to the American attack using all necessary measures" and "We will retain the right to protest, and will ask the Security Council to investigate the truth ... about this factory."[23]

In the wake of the failed counterterrorist strike, the administration defended its decisions and pointedly noted that the twin cruise missile attacks were a complete success. In defense of the strike the administration did not respond to the defiant and critical statements of the Sudanese or Taliban governments. Instead the president's 22 August 1998 radio address was interpreted as one that divided the world between "good versus evil"; a rhetorical effort to shift the international community's attention away from the president's military response to one where Clinton attempted to remind the world about the "terrorists who struck American interests." Accordingly, Clinton lamented that "This is not just America's fight; it's a universal one, between those who want to build a world of peace and partnership and prosperity and those who would tear everything down through death and destruction.... A fight directed not any particular nation or any particular faith."[24]

Within Sudan anti-American protests engulfed the capital and in other areas of the country. The chants of "down, down USA" filled the streets and there was another chant that caught the attention of the local and international press: *Wag the Dog*, in reference to the film whose plot highlighted a fictitious president who invented a foreign policy event to shift focus away from a domestic scandal.

In the days that followed, the president's national security advisor, Tony Berger, attempted to address the controversy surrounding the strike on the al Shifa plant in Sudan: "Let me be very clear about this.... This was a plant that was producing chemical-warfare-related weapons, and we have physical evidence of that fact."[25]

Berger's remarks were undercut from a number of quarters, most notably from within his own administration. The FBI Director, Louis Freeh, whose personnel were involved in the investigation into the twin embassy bombings, had not been informed about the counterterrorist strike, and in the wake of the strike, the director openly opposed the decision. Elsewhere in the administration, Janet Reno, the Attorney General, also opposed the strike owing to the fact the evidence would not stand up to international scrutiny.[26]

Inside the Pentagon, the decision to strike Sudan caused considerable disappointment among senior military leaders. The issue concerned the exclusion of the senior military leaders and the overuse of cruise missiles:

> The four men who know more about the use of force than anyone in the White House—the three generals and one admiral on the Joint Chiefs of Staff, who run the nation's armed forces—were not briefed about the use of Tomahawk missiles until the day before the raids. The only member of the Joint Chiefs to participate fully in the planning was the chairman, General Shelton, who was instructed not to brief the other chiefs or to involve senior officers of the Defense Intelligence Agency.[27]

Elsewhere in the Pentagon, there was another matter that surfaced in the wake of the failed strike in Sudan: the misuse of force. According to a member of the Joint Staff,

> In the aftermath of the truck bombings in Kenya and Tanzania, the general said, "and with a wounded President, there are large pressures on the system. So who's in the room? Clearly not the uniformed military." The general concluded, "This is classic Sandy Berger." The general's point was that he and other senior officers believe that Berger and Madeleine Albright are too quick to advocate force as a solution to diplomatic problems. [The general concluded] "Madeleine is willing to fire a missile at anybody."[28]

This debate crystallized the internal fallout of the strike against the al Shifa plant in Sudan. In the end the final statement, this time by two members of the National Security Council staff was the most damaging of all. According to Daniel Benjamin and Steven Simon, the missile strike was "interpreted as the greatest foreign policy blunder of the Clinton presidency."[29]

In the final analysis, the counterterrorist strike did little to alter the course of Sudan and did even less to alter the behavior of al Qaeda. To illustrate the fallacy associated with the counterterrorist strike, consider a statement made by then Secretary of Defense Richard Cohen, who promised a long-term and concerted war on terror:

> The US strike against terrorist facilities in Afghanistan and Sudan should not be seen simply as a response to the Aug. 7 bombings in Kenya and Tanzania, but as the long-term, fundamental way in which the United States intends to combat the forces of terror. Just as those advocating terror have been relentless in their efforts, so shall we be relentless in ours.[30]

The great irony is that, politically, the administration's counterterrorist strike against Sudan precluded any future consideration of the use of force to contain or defeat terrorism.

In the closing period of the Clinton administration an oddity developed. On the one hand the administration re-instated the old sanctions-led policy—in the period after the presidential election of 2000, the Clinton-imposed sanctions prohibiting US companies from participation in any oil ventures in Sudan.[31] This sanction prohibited Sudapet, a joint venture between Sudan's National Oil Company and Chinese, Malaysian, and Canadian partners, from obtaining assess to US technology. Though there is little doubt this sanction impacted US businesses, in the short term the sanction clearly affected Sudan's oil industry and its export of oil.

In another oddity, the Clinton administration attempted to establish a dialogue with Sudan in late 2000. Interestingly, the very issue that surfaced from 1996–1998—sharing intelligence on al Qaeda—the Clinton administration was now amenable to discussions with Sudan. There was a dilemma afoot: the closure of the administration. Following the tragedy of 11 September 2001 the Bush administration would benefit from the "late talks" between the Clinton administration and Sudan.[32] As is now well known, Sudan provided the very intelligence on al Qaeda that the Clinton administration sought; there was one additional reality: the Bush administration dramatically scaled back, but did not completely end, the Clinton administration's sanctions against Khartoum.

Conclusion

The research obtained in this study offered a most interesting fascination: Clinton's war on terror did not commence with the counterterrorist strike against Afghanistan and Sudan after the East Africa embassy bombings in August of 1998. Rather, the war on terror targeted Sudan during the first and second terms of the Clinton presidency. The administration went to great lengths—from sanctions, to the use of frontline states, to the arming of anti-government forces within Sudan—to pressure the Bashir regime to end its support for terrorism and to force a host of terrorist entities, from al Qaeda, Hezbollah, Hamas, and Islamic Jihad, to leave the country. In spite of the administration's comprehensive policies, they were unable to dramatically force or alter the behavior of Sudan. The changes the Clinton administration sought emerged in the wake of the events of 11 September 2001 and under another president, George W. Bush.

There were several other important verities that emerged during the course of this research effort. One of the most interesting aspects of the research concerned the year 1996. During this year, the administration commenced a "not so private" review of its policy toward Sudan. In the midst of the review, the administration was at war with itself over the course and direction of its Sudan policy. Additionally, as the decision to augment the "old policy" had been made, the administration enlisted states within the region to further its war with Sudan. When that was not enough, the administration armed anti-government forces in the southern part of the country to assist in Clinton's policy to end terrorism in Sudan.

When these efforts appeared to offer no decisive victory, the administration enlisted the services of Saudi Arabia and Egypt to end what it called a "gathering threat" in the form of Osama bin Laden. In the midst of this threat, the Sudanese offered to detain bin Laden in exchange for the reduction of US-led sanctions that were crippling the economy. While the administration listened it refused to accept and eventually claimed there never was a "quid pro quo" diplomatic process with the government in Sudan, despite contrary evidence. As the year 1996 closed, the administration decided to increase the sanctions once again.

In the wake of the East Africa embassy bombings, US–Sudanese relations moved to a new level. Following the counterterrorist strike that destroyed a pharmaceutical plant in al Shifa, a facility the administration asserted was constructing chemical weapons, and in the wake of the attack, Clinton found himself embroiled in an international controversy that ultimately ended the president's vaunted war on terror during its infancy. Quietly the administration increased the sanctions regime one last time; this time during the period of increasing enmity between Washington and Khartoum.

Finally, the ultimate irony occurred during the final years of the Clinton administration, during their focus on al Qaeda. It was during this period that Sudan commenced its most prominent transition of the Clinton era. In late 2000 the regime in Sudan quietly signed all eleven of the twelve international conventions for combating terrorism. In a telling testimony to these events, Clinton remained silent in recognition that in spite of the tremendous pressure and in the face of the sanctions regime, the administration's policies against Sudan failed to meet its designated objectives. To validate this statement, the administration refused to remove Sudan from the list of state sponsors of terrorism and the administration still considered Sudan a haven for terrorism. As the administration era ended, despite a wealth of political capital employed against Sudan, the Clinton approach to confront terrorism yielded few notable successes.

Notes

1   In August of 1993 Saddam Hussein attempted to assassinate former President George H.W. Bush. In response to the conspiracy, the Clinton administration launched what would become the its signature counterterrorist weapon: cruise missiles. The administration launched a counterstrike that destroyed one of Iraq's three Intelligence facilities.

2   George E. Moose, Assistant Secretary for African Affairs, Statement before the Subcommittee on Africa. Senate Foreign Relations Committee, Washington, DC, May 15, 1997, US Department of State, Washington, DC.

3   David Hoile, *Farce Majure: The Clinton Administration's Sudan Policy 1993–2000* (The European Sudanese Public Affairs Council, 2000). http://www.espac.org/usa_sudan_pages/farce_majeure.asp#3. The site was viewed on December 3, 2006.

4   "The Sudan: A New Haven for Terrorists and Extremists in Africa?" http://www.fas.org/irp/congress/1992_cr/h920205-terror.htm. The site was viewed on December 3, 2006.

5   George E. Moose, Assistant Secretary for African Affairs, Statement before the Subcommittee on Africa. Senate Foreign Relations Committee.

6   Ibid.

7   Richard Clarke, *Against All Enemies: Inside America's War on Terror* (New York: Free Press, 2004), pp. 140–141.

8   Ibid., p. 141.

9   Frank Smyth, "A New Game: The Clinton Administration on Africa," *Washington Quarterly*, Summer 1998. http://www.franksmyth.com/A5584C/clients/franksmyth/frankS2.nsf/96fc0d81ccef8e1e85256b6c00561196/d6fa5c605a6992f385256b7b007906

62?OpenDocument. The site was accessed December 11, 2006.

10   Ibid.

11   Clarke, p. 143.

12   Moose, Assistant Secretary for African Affairs, Statement Before the Sub-Committee on Africa Senate Foreign Relations Committee.

13   Mansoor Ijaz, "Clinton Let Bin Laden Slip Away and Metastasize," *Los Angeles Times*, December 2005.
      http://www.infowars.com/saved%20pages/Prior_Knowledge/Clinton_let_bin_laden. htm. The site was accessed on December 12, 2006.

14   Ibid.

15   Richard Miniter, *Losing Bin Laden: How Bill Clinton's Failures Unleashed Global Terror* (Washington, DC: Regnery, 2003), pp. 132–133.

16   Robert A. Harris, *US Terrorism Policy Towards Sudan: Blinded by Islamic Fundamentalism?* (California: Naval Post-Graduate School, 1999), p. 29.

17   Clarke, *Against All Enemies*, p. 142.

18   One of the best examples of the evidence to support Sudan's case that it approached the Clinton administration is found in David Rose, "The Secret Bin Laden Files: The Al Qaeda Intelligence the US Ignored," *Vanity Affair*, January 2002, pp. 49–52.

19   Hoile, *Farce Majure: The Clinton Administration's Sudan Policy 1993–2000.*

20   Ibid.

21   The President's Statement at the Memorial Service at Andrews Air Force Base on August 13, 1998. *Public Papers of the Presidents of the United States, Administration of William J. Clinton* (Washington, DC: US Government Printing), p. 1428.

22   The White House, Office of the Press Secretary. For Immediate Release August 20, 1998. Address to the Nation by the President. The Oval Office. http://www.oldamericancentury. org/downloads/1998-08-20-clinton.htm. The site was accessed on December 8, 2006.

23   "Muslims, Yeltsin Denounce Attack."
      http://www.cnn.com/WORLD/africa/9808/21/strikes.world.reax.02/. The site was accessed on December 8, 2006.

24   The President's Radio Address, August 22, 1998. *Public Papers of the President of United States, Administration of William J. Clinton*, (Washington, DC: US Government Printing), p. 1465.

25   Seymour Hersh, "The Missiles of August," *New Yorker*, October 12, 1998. http://www. newyorker.com/archive/content/articles/020114fr_archive02?020114fr_archive02. The site was accessed on December 9, 2006.

26   Ibid.

27   Ibid.

28   Ibid.

29   Barton Gellman, "Broad Efforts Launched After '98 Attacks," *Washington Post*, December 19, 1998, p. A1.

30   William S. Cohen, Secretary of Defense, "We are Ready to Act Again," *Washington Post*, August 23, 1998, p. C1.

31   Joseph Kahn, "US Imposes Sanctions on Oil Venture in Sudan," *New York Times*, February 17, 2000, p. A11.

32   J. Stephen Morrison, "Somalia's and Sudan's Race to the Fore in Africa," *Washington Quarterly*, Spring 2002, p. 199.

Chapter 9

The Bush Model: US Special Forces, Africa, and the War on Terror

John Davis

Introduction

In the wake of the tragic events of 11 September 2001, the Bush model for encouraging African involvement in the war on terror would be far different and certainly far more successful than the Clinton model. As the previous chapter demonstrated, the Clinton approach was symbolized by rhetoric, inaction, and a misguided counterterrorist strike that in the final analysis undermined what few benefits may have existed following the East Africa embassy bombings that destroyed US interests in Kenya and Tanzania.

Much like Clinton, President George W. Bush recognized that Africa would serve as an important strategic venue as the president's war cabinet commenced calculations on when and in what areas the United States would launch the post-9/11 counter attack. In this context, African states emerged as an important strategic asset.[1] From another perspective, the administration recognized another verity: a host of weak and collapsed African states were potential safe havens. According to the administration, there were other calculations to consider:

> That [in the administration's view] weak states ... can pose as great a danger to our national interests as strong states. Poverty does not make poor people into terrorists and murderers. Yet poverty, weak institutions, and corruption can make weak states vulnerable to terrorist networks.[2]

To preclude this reality, as the planning for military operations moved forward, the administration began discussions with states in East Africa. At the conclusion of those discussions, many of those states (Djibouti, Ethiopia, and Kenya) eventually morphed into what came to be referred to as the "frontline states." Thus long before the administration's anticipated response to 9/11, select African states were set to play a critical role in what eventually developed into the war on terror.

The strategy involving African states in the aforementioned war continued to unfold as US warships, reconnaissance aircraft, Special Operations Forces, and supplies were quietly positioned in preparation for another verity: after commencing Operation Enduring Freedom the administration's contingency planning called upon the deployment of select NATO countries (Britain and France) to provide supplemental forces to assist the US and its new African partners in confronting fleeing al Qaeda forces that were seeking another sanctuary after their pivotal base of operations in Afghanistan had come under attack, forcing permanent displacement. From this point forward much of the African continent, for better or worse, found itself embroiled in another international conflict.

The objective of this chapter involves the examination of the Bush model, essentially its principal components: the Combined Joint Task Force in the Horn of Africa (CJTF-HOA), the Pan Sahel Initiative (PSI), and the Trans Sahara Counterterrorism Initiative (TSCTI). The second task involves the assessment of the impact of these counterterrorism initiatives.

The Combined Joint Task Force

The events of 11 September 2001 ushered in "The Age of Sacred Terror."[3] In the post-9/11 world, according to Greg Mills, after years of irrelevance one can now point to "Africa's New Strategic significance."[4] According to a senior intelligence official there was one certainty in the wake of 9/11: "States within Africa were not consider vital during the pre-9/11 period, but after the devastating attacks on 9/11 the strategic climate change."[5] In a follow-up statement the official observed, "We awoke to the need to prevent another Afghanistan and to preclude bin Laden's jihadists from setting up shop in Africa."[6]

In the interregnum before the opening phase of the war on terror, the administration made a significant decision: the Horn of Africa would be a critical component of the war on terror. The region consists of Djibouti, Eritrea, Ethiopia, Sudan, Kenya, Somalia, and Yemen. Another significant decision made by Central Command (CENTCOM) was to locate the headquarters of the CJTF-HOA in the tiny but highly significant country of Djibouti. The principal decision to headquarter the CJTF-HOA in Djibouti is based on its location on the Bab al-Mandeb Strait, what is viewed as the "second busiest shipping lane in the world and a potential conduit for terrorist activity."[7]

The objectives of the CJTF-HOA involved a host of interconnected objectives. In the words of Rear Adm. Richard Hunt, for example, in a statement before participants in the Joint Civilian Orientation Conference (JCOC), observed "The conditions out there to support terrorism are ripe" and "Our job is to diffuse that situation."[8] The conditions that the admiral spoke of are the daily struggle with disease, illicit drug trafficking, and human trafficking, along with internal religious extremism; all hallmarks of much of the region. From another perspective, with planning underway for the war in Iraq in 2002, the administration surmised that another contingency was required: to preclude the "opening of third front in East Africa" and to prevent an unwanted intrusion by al Qaeda into the region. Thus the mission objective of the CJTF-HOA called upon states in the region to seize the initiative and "to identify and capture, and to help host" countries "control their ungoverned spaces, especially borders and coastlines."[9]

With the use of "Airmen, Marines, Soldiers, Sailors, and Civilians" and host states within the region, the CJTF-HOA has one additional objective: they are "Dedicated to seeking out and destroying the terrorist social infrastructure by taking away terrorists' safe havens and driving them out of the region."[10]

In what is ideally an example of complex interagency cooperation, the principal focus of this section, however, is the role of Special Operations Forces (SOFs) and their activities as the center of gravity of the CJTF-HOA.

Below we examine the activities of US SOFs in the Horn. The following information is by no means exhaustive, but offers a clear sense of the training, assistance and operations of the SOFs in the Horn of Africa as part of its deployment with the CJTF-HOA.

Djibouti

In the wake of the strategic planning associated with the war on terror, Djibouti emerged as a centerpiece in the post-9/11 strategic calculus of the Bush administration. Secretary of Defense Donald Rumsfeld observed that Djibouti is and will be a significant piece of the war on terror. According to the Secretary, with radical Islam's burgeoning growth in the Horn of Africa "We need to be where the action is" and "There's no question but that this part of the world is an area where there's action.... There are a number of terrorists, for example, just across the water in Yemen and in the southern part of Saudi Arabia. These are serious problems."[11]

With war underway in Afghanistan, the decision was made: Djibouti would serve as the locus of activity in the administration's efforts to stem the tide of indigenous terrorist activity in the region and to preclude al Qaeda from establishing additional bases in the wake of the opening phase of the war on terror. Headquartered in Camp Lemonier, the CJTF-HOA in Djibouti illustrated the East African country's growing significance to CENTCOM. As the "center of gravity" in the war on terror, CENTCOM deployed 800 elite Special Operations Forces (presumably Delta Force, Green Berets, and perhaps Navy SEALS) to Djibouti with one objective: pursue al Qaeda forces in Yemen and Somalia.[12] In the early months of 2002, additional US forces, in the form of Army Rangers, and the elite SOAR that would ferry SOFs to operations in neighboring countries, were transported to the region. Additionally, to supplement US forces in Djibouti, the administration planned for two additional realities. First, the administration wanted to ensure the SOFs were given adequate protection in the event of any attack in Djibouti. In due course CENTCOM deployed the *USS Belleau Wood* amphibious assault ship replete with Marines, helicopters and Harrier Jump jets that would be utilized to preclude any assault on the SOF base in Camp Lemonier.

The second reality involved the contingency for war. The contingency discussed herein involved two scenarios, Somalia and Yemen. In the case of Somalia, the Special Forces in Djibouti were given the task of intelligence and "snatch," the notion that critical al Qaeda operatives in Somalia would be kidnapped, and if necessary, killed by these deadly operators. In the case of Yemen, the author reported in *The Global War on Terrorism: Assessing the American Response*, Djibouti was poised to play a pivotal role in an emerging conflict with Yemen. In short order CENTCOM "gave the go orders" for US SOFs to begin preparations for involvement in an operation to kill al Qaeda forces that established operational bases in the ungoverned territory in Yemen. In the end, however, "US Special Operations Forces continued their preparations for a showdown that has been predicted, but has not yet occurred."[13]

The contingences for the war that never developed included additional ships to include the amphibious assault ship *USS Iwo Jima*, the amphibious transport ship *USS Nashville*, and the dock landing ship *USS Carter Hall*, along with other ships and additional army personnel that were sent to the region; the administration recognized that Djibouti's signature position as a forward base may one day serve as a platform for the expansion of the war on terror.[14]

Finally, following the changing of the guard (Brigadier General Mastin Robeson supplanted Major General John F. Sattler as the commander of the Combined Joint Task Force and subsequently took command of CJTF-HOA is a floating headquarters aboard the flagship *USS Mount Whitney* in the Horn of Africa that served another purpose) the military facility in Djibouti became more active. In a highly secret mission, it has been established that US SOFs were training for another mission: Iraq. The climate and environment in Djibouti was consistent with Iraq. In the final analysis, for nearly six months SOFs were training for missions to seize the critical military facilities in the Western part of the country (other units were dispatched to Northern Iraq to train assorted Kurdish militias). This event and other still-classified assaults are indicative of the changing role given to Djibouti as an expression of Africa's increasing strategic value.

Ethiopia

As a neighbor of Somalia one can readily understand Ethiopia's significance to the regional task force. To facilitate its importance, CENTCOM dispatched SOFs to train Ethiopian troops in anti-terrorism and counterterrorist tactics. On the counterterrorist front, Ethiopia has expressed nominal concern about ongoing border incursions from al Qaeda and al Ittihad Islamists. As with all training and activities by the SOFs, such training originated from the central headquarters in Djibouti. Of interest and of great concern to regional experts is the increasing tempo of SOF operations in Ethiopia. The involvement of US Special Forces in Somalia, for example, has been in support of the Baidoa government (additional support is also given to the Rahaweyn Resistance Army (RRA)) and the separatist government in Puntland, entities that are supported by the Ethiopian government. Both Somali entities are locked in a struggle against the Union of Islamic Courts (UIC), which has seized control of Mogadishu. The SOF missions are in support of Ethiopian border protection but there are reports the SOFs have engaged in intelligence missions deep inside Somalia.

The SOF operations have been successful but there are issues on the horizon that may produce instability within the task force. The dilemma confronting the administration involves the increasing tensions between Ethiopia and Eritrea over the future of Somalia. The instability within CJTF-HOA partners has produced a sharp rebuke by the administration and the United Nations:

> [However] The US government and UN Secretary-General Kofi Annan both have warned Eritrea and Ethiopia they should stay out of the war in Somalia, as evidence accumulates the two foes are heading towards a proxy war in that country. Eritrea supports the Somali Jihadists with arms and troops, while Ethiopia supports the transitional government.[15]

The warnings fell on deaf ears. In Ethiopia Prime Minister Meles Zenawi has stated he will continue preparations for a conflict with the Islamists that control much of southern Somalia. Zenawi has argued such a deterrent is required because diplomatic negotiations with UIC have not produced a breakthrough.[16] The instability among task force partners and a potential showdown between Ethiopian and UIC forces has taken on new dimensions. That is, the administration recently dispatched a National Guard unit from Guam to increase the training of Ethiopian troops to ensure that UIC forces or their jihadists allies will not slip into Ethiopia and mount terrorist attacks. What remains unknown is the mission for the SOFs beyond the training of Ethiopian forces.

At the time of this writing, Ethiopian forces have invaded, along with troops from the Transitional government, have occupied Mogadishu.[17] To date the bulk of UIC forces have been slaughtered and the remaining forces have melted away into the city, while others have rejoined their traditional clans or sub-clans. Reports have been increasing about the not-so-secret role of US SOFs during the invasion. In particular, experts within the region assert that Ethiopian Special Forces, with assistance from there US trainers, called in the air strikes that helped to induce fear among UIC forces. Lastly, US SOFs are active in assisting Ethiopian forces with intelligence, tracking and detaining suspected al Qaeda forces in the south.

Kenya

One of the central roles of the SOFs requires that they interact with and train the military forces of all task force members. Kenya is no exception. Unlike most members of the CJTF-HOA, the Kenyan military has maintained a well established relationship with the US military, and specifically with US Special Forces. Long before the establishment of the CJTF-HOA, US Special Forces have interacted with Kenyan military forces, a process that began under the Clinton administration. The following excerpt is instructive.

> Compared to conventional units, special operations forces routinely deploy quickly in small units to remote locations with austere or nonexistent support bases. In July 1996, 5th Special Forces Group (Airborne), Fort Campbell, KY, deployed and established a Combined/Joint Special Operations Task Force Headquarters (CJSOTF) in Kenya to participate in a Joint Chiefs of Staff Exercise. The exercise's purpose was to foster the working relationship between the United States and the Kenyan military. Participating US units were elements from three services and two components: a special forces company from 5th Special Forces Group (Airborne), A-Teams from the US Army Reserve, 19th Special Forces Group (Airborne), US Navy SEAL Team 3 and elements of the US Air Force 16th Special Operations Wing. Training alongside the US military were a joint Kenyan staff, their 20th Parachute Infantry Battalion and Navy Clearance Dive Unit.[18]

In the wake of the events of 7 August 1998 (the embassy bombings in Kenya and Tanzania), US SOFs reentered the theater to renew their acquaintance with Kenyan forces. After the tragic events of 9/11, the SOF–Kenya relationship returned to previous levels. However, the numbers (SOF soldiers) eventually surpassed the levels that existed during the year 1996 or pre-East Africa embassy–bombing period.

There were additional characteristics that symbolized the changing characteristics of the military-to-military contact between Kenyan forces and their trainers, the US SOFs. The first is transparency. Previously post-Cold War–era US SOF operations were below the radar. In the post-9/11 world the missions of the SOFs remained secret because of the administration's announced objective to send a message to al Qaeda and its East African regional affiliates: "the region is off limits" or "no new safe havens will be permitted in the region." Thus the SOFs were rarely visible but al Qaeda and its allies in the region were keenly aware of their presence.

To provide policy to support the administration's rhetoric, the East Africa Counter-Terrorism Initiative (EACTI), which includes Djibouti, Eritrea, Ethiopia, Kenya, Tanzania, and Uganda, was launched and received over $100 million in funding. Though all member states of the EACTI reaped the benefits, there is little doubt that Kenya profited the most from the program.

The success of the EACTI aside, the second indices of the Kenya–US SOF relationship concerned the tempo of the training, the rapidity of the operations, and the danger associated with the missions. Dealing with the latter, SOFs accompanied Kenyan forces along the Somali–Kenyan border and in some instances SOFs and Kenyan forces ventured deep inside Somali territory in what was described as "probes." It remains unclear if there were encounters with the UIC or al Qaeda and if there were any casualties.

The tempo of the operations moved to a new level as the US–Kenyan forces participated in a host of operations designed to test the burgeoning growth of the Kenyan military's ability to demonstrate its ability to absorb the training administered by the US SOFs. Much of this training occurred on the huge Manda Bay naval complex near Lamu. This base supported joint exercises, one of which was dubbed Operation Edged Mallet.[19] In the view of Kenyan military authorities the exercises demonstrated that, should it become necessary, Kenyan forces are now capable of handling reconnaissance and patrols without their US military minders.[20]

During this and subsequent exercises a normally secretive US Special Forces Unit began to shoulder the load of training Kenyan forces as Army Special Forces rotated to other CJTF-HOA countries, Iraq, and even Afghanistan. The new US SOF unit came in form of US Marine Corps Forces Special Operations Command (MARSOC). These units aare very much like their Army counterparts: small, elite, and professional. Within the MARSOC is another unit referred to as Foreign Military Training Units (FMTUs) that were also deployed to Kenya[21] to speed the development of counterterrorist training in the wake of transiting US Army SOFs.

Finally, as events in Somalia continue to unfold, Kenyan forces may be asked to intercede in the ungovernable territories of its war-torn neighbor. In the event that Kenyan forces are deployed into Somalia, an interesting set of questions awaits: will they enter alone or with US SOFs? Will they enter on the side of Eritrea or Ethiopia, or will they act as a buffer between task force partners or focus their energies on the UIC? To date the Kenyan government has remained neutral, even after Ethiopian forces entered and then occupied Mogadishu. In the final analysis, in the near future the Kenyan military may yet find itself embroiled with its partners of the CJTF-

HOA; it will prove interesting to see how the US or allied partners confront this scenario.

Somalia

In the days immediately after 9/11 Somalia emerged as the critical piece in the post-September 11 strategic calculus of the US military. In this collapsed state, with no national government and indigenous jihadists who had established ties with al Qaeda (which maintains a safe haven within southern Somalia), there were troubling signs for the task force.

After the conclusion of the Afghan phase of the war on terror, the administration calculated that al Qaeda would seek a base of operations in Somalia. US SOFs have been operating in and around Somalia since late 2001 from bases in Ethiopia and from Kenya. The missions of the SOFs remain classified, but to date the SOFs have not been engaged in any direct action missions;[22] however, the SOFs—believed to be a combination of SEALs, Delta or Green Berets—have operated with impunity in the ungoverned lands of Somalia. The activities of the Special Forces operators are believed to be missions to gather intelligence on the movements of suspected al Qaeda jihadists.[23]

Recently the activities in Somalia, in the eyes of experts, have set the stage for possible war. A report by the think-tank the International Crisis Group observed, "In the rubble-strewn streets of the ruined capital of this state without a government ... Al Qaeda operatives, jihadi extremists, Ethiopian security services and Western-backed counter-terrorism networks are engaged in a shadowy and complex contest waged by intimidation, abduction and assassination."[24]

At another level a war of words has developed that has further exacerbated the tensions. Sheikh Sharif Sheikh Ahmed, the leader of the Union of Islamic Courts, made the following explosive statement: "If US forces intervene directly against us in Mogadishu ... we are ready to teach them a lesson they will never forget and repeat their defeat in 1993."[25]

In and around Somalia, US SOFs continue their intelligence operations. The tempo of those operations is currently at a level consistent to support "wider operations" that set the stage for intervention. The intervention may not be a US-led operation but an American-supported operation that will permit the Intergovernmental Authority on Development (IGAD)—a seven-state regional entity consisting of Djibouti, Eritrea, Kenya, Somalia, Sudan, Uganda, and Ethiopia—to provide peacekeepers to stem the flow of illegal arms in Mogadishu and to contain the movement of the Union of Islamic Courts.

Speculation about the reality of intervention provoked a sharp warning from European Union African experts. According to *Reuters*, "The warning given to envoys of the 25 EU states [was that] a peacekeeping operation without the consent of all sides would be seen as 'an invading force' and exacerbate the risk of conflict and of jihadist attacks."[26] The statement by the EU Commission drew a counter response by the US State Department. The view in Washington asserted "the whole premise that the United States wants to forcibly impose an outside peacekeeping mission on that situation in Somalia is 100 percent false."[27]

The debate on the intervention in Somalia ended after the Ethiopian government made the decision to intervene, with US backing, to end the threat posed by the UIC once and for all. For many experts in the region, the invasion by Ethiopia was not a surprise. They point to the SOFs' accelerated training of Ethiopian forces and the increase number of US trainers as a sign that some form of intervention in Somalia was a foregone conclusion.

Recently, the exiled Prime Minister Ali Mohamed Gedi returned to the capital promising peace and told the people of Mogadishu "that we are here to start our work."[28] The statement was a reference to talks with the warlords to prevent renewed clan violence and to ensure discussions where the militias respect the authority of the transitional government.

In the final analysis, the CJTF-HOA is a monumental regional success. The military capabilities of the regional partners have improved dramatically. The work of the task force has infused the importance of counterterrorism to all participant countries. In the end one thing is certain: the overall threat of terrorism is down. There are two dangers on the horizon. The presence of US troops, even if the administration has worked to reduce the SOF signature, will invariably fuel both anti-Americanism and provide a propaganda tool for the recruitment of jihadists dedicated to preventing "an infidel military establishment" in the region. Second, events in Somalia forced task force members to consider war as an option with the UIC, or with member states that were supporting the UIC or warlords in other parts of the war-torn country. Consistent with the aforementioned problem, another dilemma looms on the horizon: the task force may implode from within. That is, the corruption, anti-democratic practices, and human rights abuses, in Djibouti for example, will inevitably lead to groups that question the necessity of the task force. Thus the administration can claim a short-term success for the task force, but the future is replete with hurdles that will dictate the future of the CJTF-HOA.

The Pan Sahel Initiative

The Sahel is a vast desert region in West Africa and impacts nine Sahelian countries to include Burkina Faso, Cape Verde, Chad, Gambia, Guinea-Bissau, Mali, Mauritania, Niger, and Senegal. These countries are recognized as some of the poorest and "least food secure in the world." There are additional indices that have made this region attractive for terrorist penetration: weak states and ineffectual governance strategies have produced a decade-plus period of economic instability within the region. The problems are magnified when one adds the sprawling desert and uninhabited region (and since the US-led attack on Afghanistan) that could easily serve as a potential long-term safe haven for al Qaeda. The administration moved quickly to prevent Osama bin Laden's transnational terror network from the establishing a "beach head in the region", a move that could produce far more instability in the region and simultaneously effectuate US interests within the region.

The first hint of an administration response to this challenge developed after the release of the *2002 National Strategy of the United States*. Regarding Africa, the administration acknowledged the strategic requirement to assist Africa's "fragile states" and to "help build indigenous capability to secure porous borders, and help build up the law enforcement and intelligence infrastructure to deny havens for terrorists."[29]

The document provided another telling statement: the administration recognized that some states within the vast African continent were not able to tackle the issue of terrorism alone. To that end, the administration asserted "we will match their willpower and their resources with whatever help we and our allies can provide."[30]

The administration's rhetoric aside, the Sahel countries were not considered a high priority in the US post-9/11 strategic calculus. Put another way, in the *Pentagon's New Map*,[31] the countries of the Sahel region did not command the same focus as the vital Horn of Africa. Thus, while the post-9/11 spotlight focused on the Horn, the problems within the Sahel continued to fester.

By the close of 2002, events within the Bush administration would radically shift to a new focus and certainly an unexpected shift in US policy. In the midst of the debate over US–Iraq policy, the hawks, or the renowned neo-conservatives within the Bush administration, lost a critical debate. There was an intense debate over whether the administration should expend further military resources in Africa. In the view of then-Secretary of State Colin Powell, Africa, first in the Horn, and now the Sahel, were critical nodes in the war on terror. In the counter attack the neo-conservatives renewed their objections to further military engagement in the region. Following a period of six months, it was decided the Sahel would receive funding. For Powell this was a major victory, but another debate loomed on the horizon: which bureaucratic entity would manage US policy, the State Department or the Defense Department? Following another tense round of bureaucratic politics, Powell emerged victorious: the State Department would be tasked with implementing administration policy.[32]

In November of 2002 the program was finally given the green light. The new State Department–led counterterrorism program—a program that received $7 million in funding—was given the title of the Pan Sahel Initiative (PSI).[33] The program's target consisted of efforts to assist four weak North African countries—Mali, Niger, Chad, and Mauritania—in confronting terrorism. According to State Department officials the ultimate objective of the PSI concerned the need to prevent terrorists from using the vast expanse of unpopulated areas within the Sahel to foment instability and to take advantage of the porous borders in an effort to turn the region into a safe haven for terrorists. According to the Office of Counterterrorism, the PSI had additional objectives that consisted of the following:

Detecting and responding to suspicious movement of people and goods across and within their borders through training, equipment and cooperation. Its goals support two U.S. national security interests in Africa: waging the war on terrorism and enhancing regional peace and security. Technical assessments taking place in each country starting this month will help focus training and other capacity building resources over the coming months. PSI will assist participating countries to counter known terrorist operations and border incursions, as well as trafficking of people, illicit materials, and other goods. Accompanying the training and material support will be a program to bring military and civilian officials from the four countries together to encourage greater cooperation and information exchange within and among the governments of the region on counterterrorism and border security issues.[34]

The PSI had an extensive diplomatic arm to commence the program. Indeed, State Department personnel consisting of civilian components in Washington, DC and US embassy personnel within the host countries required majored planning with the targeted countries. Having engaged the Sahel countries in the dangers of regional terrorism, the administration, through the State Department, warned of the need to prevent the spread of transnational terrorism in the form of al Qaeda.

In order to implement the objectives of the PSI the US military would perform the critical function of training host countries in counterterrorism, border patrol, equipping the targeted states with weapons, leadership training, and intelligence to permit the Sahel countries to confront the increasing specter of terrorism.[35]

As the military operations commenced in the Sahel countries, a noticeable difference between the State and Defense Departments emerged. As one would expect, the language of US diplomats involved an effort to contain expectations and to preserve local sovereignty. The military communications and spin machine provided a more vivid and alarmist picture of the situation of the regional dynamics. The military noted that its objective was to prevent Africa, whether in the Horn, the Pan-Sahel region, or elsewhere, from "becoming the next front in the war on terror." In a series of interviews, Craig Smith quoted US military officials' assessment of the response to the threat this way: "American campaign against terrorism ... in a region that military officials fear could become the next base for al Qaeda—the largely ungoverned swath of territory stretching from the Horn of Africa to the Western Sahara's Atlantic coast."[36]

In spite of its bravado the US European Command (EUCOM) was quick to recognize the prevailing realities on the ground. A major recognition, according to EUCOM, is the requirement of secrecy of the missions of the Special Forces. This issue forced senior military leaders to tone down their statements. Additionally, within the EUCOM debates two additional decisions were made: turn training of Sahel military units over to Special Operations Command (SOCEUR), and permit the Special Forces community to act as the lead component of the operation. Consistent with this decision and in a clear recognition of the first two phases of the war on terror (Afghanistan and Iraq), EUCOM pledged to reduce the US "footprint." According to Lt. Colonel Powl Smith, chief of the counterterrorism branch, EUCOM deployment of the SOFs had a singular purpose: so "We don't become a lightning rod for popular anger that radicals can capitalize on."[37]

To that end the principal component that would be charged to implement the military phase of the PSI consisted of the introduction of Special Operations Forces. The 10th Special Forces Group (Airborne) had been tasked by EUCOM to train the militaries of the aforementioned countries. Headquartered in Timbuktu, Mali, the initial task of the unit called for equipping the militaries of the four Sahel countries (Chad, Mali, Mauritania, and Niger). To assist in the training of the Sahel troops at the company level, EUCOM transported 40-plus Toyota troop transport pickups, along with high-tech communications and navigation gear and desert camouflage uniforms with body armor to the each of the target countries.[38]

In addition to equipment, the US military provided a unique opportunity for the respective countries. In what was billed as a major regional conference, for the first time military leaders of the four countries met to assess and learn about the necessity of cooperation in assisting each country in dealing with a series of problems, including patrolling borders, containing terrorist penetration, increasing intelligence sharing, and setting the stage for joint military exercises.

By all accounts the training of indigenous military personnel proved motivating. In one example, Malian Army Lt. Col. Unisa Barizamega, the commander of the 5th Military Region, based in Timbuktu, explained, "We're fighting against terrorists, so this training is very important for us." Additionally, he observed "This training is helping us improve our combat skills and is teaching us new ones."[39]

During the second year of the program, the PSI had to confront a significant test, one that served as a barometer of the progress, or the lack thereof, of the program. That test involved a regional terrorist organization. An Algerian terrorist group, Salafist Group for Preaching and Combat (GSPC), led by the former Special Forces Paratrooper (Algerian Army) Ammari Saifi (a.k.a. Abderrezak al-Para), was the biggest threat to regional security. The GSPC, which had formally allied itself with al Qaeda and maintained close ties with a Moroccan Islamic Combatant Group, emerged as the central target of the PSI.[40]

This terror groups' profile is dissimilar to other Algerian terrorists in one critical aspect: most Algerian terror groups operated in Europe, whereas the GSPC is far more concerned with Africa. According to European terror experts on the GSPC, the organization, which consists of approximately 300–500 operatives, made an ominous move: the leadership of the "GSPC [approached] Al Qaeda leaders with a proposal that it be assigned a mission in North Africa that mirrors [Abu Musab] Zarqawi's role in Iraq."[41]

The GPSC assumed prominence following the organization's kidnapping of 32 European tourists in the Algerian desert in 2003. The shadowy terror group increased its stature after the GSPC claimed responsibility for a terrorist attack on a remote Mauritanian Army facility that resulted in the deaths of 15 of that country's soldiers.[42]

US intelligence sources assert that the German government secretly paid the GSPC $6 million for the release of the hostages. Elements of the US Defense Intelligence Agency (DIA) observed that the US and Algerian intelligence monitored the leader "with growing alarm."[43] Similarly Algerian military forces "intercepted a convoy carrying weapons north of Mali. Algerian officials say the cargo contained mortar launchers, rocket-propelled grenade launchers and surface-to-air missiles."[44]

This incident, and the kidnapping of European tourists, offered a window into the failures of the PSI. A series of events that followed were indicative of the weaknesses of the PSI:

> The United States European Command sent a Navy P-3 Orion surveillance aircraft to sweep the area, relaying Mr. Saifi's position to forces in the region. Mali pushed him out of the country to Niger, which in turn chased him into Chad, where, United States Special Forces support of an airlift of fuel and other supplies, 43 of his men were killed or captured. Mr. Saifi himself got away, American's say. With his money and experience and broader network, GSPC remains the most dangerous group in North Africa.[45]

In the weeks after the firefight between Chadian military forces, with the forces of the GSPC defeated, the US government sent in two Air Force C-130 cargo planes that delivered "19 tons of medical supplies, blankets and food to Chad."[46] The jester illustrated that the US did not abandon a Sahel country in a time of need. However, the incident to detain and eventually capture the GSPC proved problematic for US officials. Indeed in many quarters it became the central measure of the PSI. First, it was clear the PSI had been under funded; this invariably translated into insufficient training of the Pan Sahel countries. Second, the inability of member states to share intelligence and to effectively communicate with each other permitted the GSPC to cross a number of boundaries before the leadership of the terrorist group eventually escaped. Third, the US was forced to shoulder far more responsibility than had been anticipated or desired. The goal was to reduce the US signature in the region; rather the opposite was true: the presence of US forces or its aircraft were patently visible during the crisis.

These dilemmas overshadowed the successes of the PSI. The very fact, for example, that many of the poorest countries received training and the prevailing guidance and US assistance will serve to assist the Pan Sahel states in thinking about counterterrorism as a high-priority national interest. Additionally, Chad, Mali, Mauritania, and Niger were in agreement on one significant reality: Islamic missionaries from Saudi Arabia and Pakistan were undermining their fragile societies. Here again the PSI assisted allied states in locating the problem, but it will take the countries and their full abilities to construct effective governance strategies to confront this issue.

In the final analysis, the imperfections—lack of funding and limited training, and still uncorrected corruption within many of the Pan Sahel states—set the stage for a new initiative that would be far more robust and would include additional countries ignored in the PSI.

Trans Sahara Counterterrorism Initiative

The 2005 Trans Sahara Counterterrorism Initiative (TSCTI) was the successor to the PSI and was more adequately funded. The initial funding for the TSCTI was reported at $100 million a year for five years or $500 million to cover the life of the program. The TSCTI builds on the modestly successful Pan Sahel Initiative, which was launched after the 11 September 2001 terrorist attacks to prevent terrorists from setting up safe havens in Africa. The PSI program targeted four Sahel countries (Chad, Niger, Mali and Mauritania). The TSCTI, by contrast, targets nine countries—Algeria, Chad, Mali, Mauritania, Morocco, Niger, Nigeria, Senegal, and Tunisia—with the objective of building indigenous capacity and facilitating cooperation among host governments within the region in partnership to preclude Islamic extremism in the Sahel region.[47] In broader terms the objectives include "engaging with participating" countries:

> To assist in protecting their borders and exploiting opportunities to detect and deter terrorists by providing basic training and equipment and train additional forces. The TSCTI also envisions engagement with more countries than PSI with a greater emphasis on helping to foster better information sharing and operational planning between regional states. EUCOM would fully coordinate TSCTI efforts with US Country Teams to

ensure that the total US effort. TSCTI would help strengthen regional counterterrorism capabilities, enhance and institutionalize cooperation among the region's security forces, promote democratic governance, and ultimately benefit our bilateral relationships with each of these states. Key aspects of the TSCTI training would include basic marksmanship, planning, communications, land navigation, patrolling and medical care.[48]

In recognition of previously launched PSI program, the State Department recognized the deficiencies of the program and referred to it as "a little bit of a Band-Aid approach" to the "security crisis in the region." According to Theresa Whelan, Deputy Assistant Secretary of Defense for African Affairs, the PSI was a "stepping stone" and the bridge to the TSCTI.[49] The Deputy Assistant explicated that antiquated Cold War and Post–Cold War approaches would do nothing to preclude the development of safe havens in the vastly unpopulated areas in the region. Thus, said Whelan, "If we revert to bilateral, stovepipe programs, we simply won't be as effective" and it is therefore imperative that "we can maintain a multilateral effort."[50]

Much like the PSI, the State Department was charged with running the overall interagency initiative; however, the Department of Defense continued to focus on military operations. Previously, under the PSI, US SOFs were involved in training "a company" at time, a policy limited by the inconsequential funds made available to the program. The TSCTI's substantial funding now permits US SOFs to train at the battalion level, a decision that as the initiative dissipates, will ensure that targeted militaries will truly benefit from the program.

The principal SOF unit for the TSCTI previously served under the PSI. That unit was the 10th Special Forces Group and would be joined by the National Guard's 20th Special Forces Group.[51] It is important to note that the SOF group that had regional responsibility for Africa, the 3rd Special Forces Group, was assigned to Iraq. This is an important admission since the 3rd SOF group had the cultural and language prerequisites that the 10th and the 20th SOFs groups lacked. In short, these SOFs trainers were forced into a mission that they, like the targeted countries, were learning on the job. The first test of the TSCTI came during Flintlock 2005, an exercise that formerly "kicked off" the Saharan counterterrorism initiative.

Operation Flintlock, which began on June 6 and ended on 26 June 2005, was designated by the Bush administration as the largest American military exercise in Africa since World War II. In this SOF-led operation, in which there were over 700 Special Forces participants, supported by an additional 2,100 troops from the nine North and West African states, the opening phase provided a terrorist scenario in order to train 3,000 ill-equipped Saharan troops in counterterrorist techniques designed to share intelligence, prevent terrorist interdiction, and protect/patrol the borders.

The exercise received major attention outside of the United States, but within America itself there was little mention of its significance. Even the Pentagon attempted to downgrade its import:

> Flintlock is a series of military exercises conducted with America's theater security cooperation partners in Africa. European and NATO partner nations also participate, either directly or in an advisory role. The principal purpose of the training is to ensure all

nations continue developing their partnerships and further enhance their capabilities to halt the flow of illicit weapons, goods and human trafficking in the region.[52]

In subsequent phases, US SOFs led individual training in Algeria, Senegal, Mauritania, Mali, Niger, and Chad. The training permitted the soldiers from the aforementioned countries to learn skills in a variety of areas—airborne operations, small-unit tactics, security operations, land navigation, marksmanship, medical skills, human rights training, and land warfare—designed to sharpen their understanding of counterterrorist and other tactical techniques.[53]

As Flintlock 2005 concluded, the administration and participant countries have hailed the exercises as a complete success. On the surface the administration had much to celebrate. Member states received and were receptive to the training; the US military obtained additional forward bases, and al Qaeda and its affiliates were contained.

In the period since Flintlock, detractors of the administration's "new front" in the war on terror have been skeptical of the existence of the terror threat and have been concerned that the administration has allied itself with some of the most corrupt authoritarian governments in the region, with the government of Chad standing out as the most salient example.

The brunt of the criticism is two fold: an exaggerated terrorist threat and that the presence of US troops will act as "magnet for Islamic extremists." On the former, the International Crisis Group (ICG) noted that there has yet to be an independent confirmation to support the Bush administration's claim of terrorism in the region. In an example of the latter, Jeremy Keenan, a self-described Saharan specialist from the University of East Anglia, observed: "If anything the [TSCTI] will generate terrorism, by which I mean resistance to the overall US presence and strategy."[54] In another example, Moussa Ould Ham, editor of *Le Calame*, offered a similar perspective. He asserts that a new strand of the GSPC has developed, but he added this disclaimer, "Wherever the Americans are, whether it's Iraq or wherever, an Islamic resistance rises up, and perhaps it's this Islamic resistance that we are seeing appearing in Mauritania today."[55]

The administration's response to the disparagement of its claim of terrorism in the region and to the TSCTI has been anything but muted. The administration admitted that there is indeed a terrorist threat, albeit a singular one from the GSPC. The evidence of the threat, according to Defense and State Department officials, is overwhelming. For starters, the GSPC itself announced an offensive against what it describes as "infidels and their supports," an assumed reference to the presence of the US SOFs and their TSCTI supporters.

In support of its claims, the administration reminded its critics that thirteen Algerian soldiers were killed and another seven wounded after the GSPC placed a large explosive device under a vehicle ferrying a troop convoy on 8 June 2005. Prior to this attack the same Salafist Group ambushed twelve troops on May 17. On June 4, 2005 the Mauritanian government reported that fifteen of its soldiers were killed and an additional seventeen were wounded as the GSPC "attacked a remote outpost."[56] In a press conference in the capital of Nouakchott, the Mauritanian Defense Minister

Baba Ould Sidi said, "They killed in cold blood the soldiers they had taken prisoner before fleeing."[57]

Second, the administration acknowledged that there is substantial evidence of a nascent threat, and that the objective of TSCTI was to ensure that no "Wahhabist ideological entrepreneurships" will set up shop in the region. The administration's argument was subsequently supported, not by TSCTI member states, but rather by the GSPC, which offered this statement: the terrorist offensive was intended as a "message that implies that our activity is not restricted to fighting the internal enemy but the enemies of the religion wherever they are."[58]

Third, the administration asserts that the history in Iraq indicates the initiative is designed to preclude another Ansar Al-Islam from emerging. Prior to the US invasion of Iraq, the Zarqawi-led terrorist organization established an enclave in Northern Iraq that killed Kurdish leaders and attacked Shiites, and later coalition forces in Iraq. The GSPC was by no means dormant before the arrival of US SOFs and its activities have increased; interestingly they have not targeted US military personnel but instead directed the "on-going offensive" in the direction of its regional partners.

Fourth, the administration is equally concerned about another development: Islamists from North Africa have received training in various terrorist enclaves throughout Iraq where they have been captured or killed. EUCOM officials have presented evidence that "25 percent of [the] suicide bombers in Iraq are Saharan African."[59] Equally troubling for both EUCOM and CENTCOM is that the "fighters are being trained in Iraq and then sent back to Africa with the ability to teach [these] techniques"[60] to others in the region. This, according to EUCOM officials, could translate into increased attacks against US military forces that are attached to the TSCTI or perhaps those involved in the CJTF-HOA. It is for this reason that the administration is adopting a "drain the swamp" approach with the ultimate objective of precluding a terrorist enclave in region.

Conclusion

As noted above, the Bush model has vastly outpaced the Clinton approach to confronting terrorism in Africa. Indeed the administration has to date managed the singular problem that could undermine its strategy in the Horn or in the Sahel: confronting the dual dilemma: regional priorities versus the administration's strategic objectives. Within the two regions there are several commonalities: the need for external, long-term investment; poor development strategies; curbing internal mismanagement and corruption; and high unemployment rates.

Examining the various strategies, the CJTF-HOA and TSCTI, the administration has witnessed overwhelming success. However, as the following assessments will indicate, each strategy (the CJTF-HOA and TSCTI—the PSI no longer exists) is not without its problems.

The CJTF-HOA has offered member states the opportunity to participate in several military exercises; these same countries, with few exceptions, have had the occasion to engage in bilateral training, and each country, again with a few exceptions offered military facilities to entice the administration's money and the presence of US SOFs in the region.

Second, a problem that started out as a potential nightmare has instead emerged as an interesting issue for the Bush administration and participants in the task force. Following the commencement of the CJTF-HOA, anti-Americanism quickly ensued. In Kano, Nigeria, a Muslim area of the country, well over one hundred people were killed as a result of anti-American rioting. In coastal Kenya, local Muslim clerics whipped up the local populace into anti-American frenzy, and even in Khartoum the local media blasted the entry of US SOFs to the region. However, according to J. Stephen Morrison, collectively no widespread anti-Americanism was "transmuted" to the extent that it threatened the initiative.[61]

Third, it appears the task force will survive long after the war on terror concludes. Indeed, the administration is considering another contingency: to preposition military supplies to deal with a future Horn contingency or, if necessary, one that may call for intervention in Yemen. Consistent with these contingencies, the SOFs are gaining valuable experience in working with member states and offering the trainers invaluable cultural and linguistic skills. If there is an attendant problem, states beyond the Horn will begin to protest the presence of SOFs that train in the region. The fact that some of these units have rotated elsewhere (Iraq) and are alleged to have killed Muslims is problematic in that it will invariably increase anti-Americanism in those areas where US troops reside.

The first major problem concerns the uneven benefits of intelligence sharing. The Bush administration has called upon member states to share intelligence. In this venue administration strategy has greatly succeeded. However, a major source of controversy is the failure of US SOFs and "other intelligence gathering assets" to share intelligence with host countries. The issue of reciprocity is so prevalent among Horn countries that senior military officials of CENTCOM were called in for consultations on the matter. It remains unclear if the administration is now sharing more intelligence with host countries.

A second problem associated with the task force is the uneven training. Eritrea's military, for example, does not receive the same training, nor does it have the same access to US SOFs, as do other members of the task force. CENTCOM correctly argues that each country offers dissimilar benefits to meet US strategic objectives; however, what has emerged is enmity on the part of Eritrea and to a degree the forces of Ethiopia that remain unhinged about the US–Kenyan military relationship.

Third, a major dilemma that haunts the continued strategy of the training of host military forces is that the local police units (this very issue is endemic with the TSCTI) have not had similar training. According to CENTCOM (and EUCOM that has jurisdiction in the Sahel and Maghreb) the reason for not training the local police is that the vetting process is impossible to replicate at the local level. The fear for the US military planners is the local police are far more involved in human rights abuses then is the case with local military forces. The US strategy is understandable but it remains problematic. That is, it is the local police that will likely engage prospective terrorists within the cities, follow them to their homes, monitor their gatherings, and associate with local clerics. The inability of the US military to offer this training will tax the military and local intelligence agencies, activities that may result in an unintended consequence: the abuse of civil liberties.

Irrespective of a few dilemmas there is little doubt that the task force is an overwhelming success. From the American perspective the US has gained forward bases throughout the region, and the host Horn countries have obtained a unique balance. On the one hand, they have gained invaluable military training that will permit member states to quell any internal terrorist threat. From another perspective the combined or joint training allows member states to assist each other, without the presence or with the presence of US SOFs if necessary, to prevent any participant task force country from being overwhelmed by any internal terrorist group or external (al Qaeda) terrorist threat.

The TSCTI has succeeded where the PSI had failed. That is, the PSI was criticized from its conception for its exclusivity; that it did not include the more significant Sahel and Maghreb countries (Nigeria, Algeria and Morocco, to name a few). Similarly, the PSI was woefully underfunded, but the planners in Washington learned a valuable lesson and dramatically increased the support to the TSCTI program.

There were other significant indices of success. First, for the first time all participant members of the initiative have shared intelligence, witnessed a significant upgrade in military equipment (especially in the case of Chad, Mali, Mauritania, and Niger), and most significantly, all partners within TSCTI have upgraded their counterterrorism capabilities. Second, due in part to the length of the initiative all member states will benefit from having more troops trained in military tactics to ensure that safe havens will not emerge within their borders. Third, thinking in terms of domestic policy, all member states have made terrorism and counterterrorism priorities within their respective countries high priorities. Finally, there is another advantage that will have untold positive consequences for years, perhaps decades, to come: the notion that these countries have the opportunity to work with and adjust to US tactics will bode well in the event that such countries are called upon to work with the US in joint operations, but more importantly, should a crisis arise in the region member states will be positioned to jointly participate in peacekeeping or peace enforcement activities.

While there are many successes the TSCTI is not without its problems or potential dangers. The most significant problems are internal. African scholars continue to point to the fact that member states, as exemplified in the case of Mauritania, suppress democratic movements and therefore use the war on terror to stifle viable opposition; additionally, as a result of President Maayoya Sid'Ahmed Ould Taya's human rights abuses, he was deposed in a military coup. Since that time a small and burgeoning vocal minority continues to call for ending Mauritania's participation in the TSCTI.

Similarly, all member states must work to reduce corruption and foster an environment where governance extends to the whole of society as opposed to tribal or clan loyalties. There is no doubt the member participants of the TSCTI have benefited from US assistance, both military and economic; however, as soon as the armed forces of the region, to borrow the words of Bush in Iraq, are able to "stand up" then the SOF presence should dissipate, allowing African countries to deal with terrorism without the presence of Western forces. This will reduce, contain, and perhaps end any extremist revivalism in the region, but equally important it will force the reduction of anti-Americanism.

The major danger concerns US SOFs themselves. It is one thing to train the troops of the TSCTI in the region, but a whole new dangerous proposition could develop if the Special Forces repeat the unfathomable error that was made in Chad. In Chad the battalions that are being trained are those loyal to President Idriss Deby. Worse, the SOFs are training his "small but powerful" Zagawa tribe, which has a dominating presence throughout the government. Within Chad the administration is seen as taking sides and turning a blind eye to overt human rights abuses in order to retain the participation of the Deby government. Regionally, the failure of the administration to end this policy will, in the end, undermine the TSCTI and dramatically increase anti-Americanism and the use of terrorism as a utility to drive US military forces from the region.

Recently the TSCTI has received additional funding that will add two additional years and $250 million to the counterterrorism program. The TSCTI to date has greatly exceeded the expectations of the administration. It will take years to measure the long-term effects of the program of the nine member states of the initiative. It is equally certain that critics will continue to assert the initiative is nothing more than neo-imperialist impulse to protect another national security commodity of the United States: oil. Thus there is a growing perception that when one examines the participant states a major commonality emerges: several members of the TSCTI are oil-producing states, including Nigeria, Algeria, and Mauritania.

Finally, while there are dangers associated with the Bush model, one cannot deny the success of the multi-pronged strategy, whether in the CJTF-HOA, PSI, or the TSCTI. In the final analysis a significant irony has developed. The administration has succeeded in Africa but that success has been eclipsed by the cataclysmic decision to invade and then occupy Iraq. Perhaps equally astonishing, if one where to examine the war on terror with a neutral eye, an obvious conclusion will be reached: Africa will serve as the singular regional example of the administration's success, if not legacy, in the war on terror. The results of the administration's post-11 September counterterrorist efforts may even surprise Bush himself. This, after all, was the same presidential candidate that once remarked, "While Africa may be important, it doesn't fit into the national strategic interests" of the United States. One would be correct to ask what President Bush thinks of Africa's strategic significance now.

Notes

1   Adekeye Adebajo, "Africa and America in an Age of Terror," *Journal of Asian and African Studies*, March 2003, p. 182.
2   September 2002 National Security Strategy of the United States of America. http://www. whitehouse.gov/nsc/nss4.html. The information was accessed on October 24, 2006.
3   Daniel Benjamin and Steven Simon, *The Age of Sacred Terror: Radical Islam's War against America* (New York: Random House, 2003).
4   See the opening chapter by Greg Mills, "Africa's New Strategic Significance."
5   Interview with senior intelligence official, October 4, 2006, Washington, DC.
6   Ibid.

7   Deborah L. West, *Combating Terrorism in the Horn of Africa and Yemen*. World Peace Foundation Reports (Cambridge, Massachusetts, 2005), p. 6.

8   The Joint Civilian Orientation Conference (JCOC). http://www.navy.mil/search/display. asp?story_id=26198. The information was accessed on October 3, 2006:

9   West, *Combating Terrorism in the Horn of Africa and Yemen*, p. 6.

10   Maj. Ann Peru Knabe, 379th Air Expeditionary Wing, Public Affairs, "Combined Joint Task Force Horn of Africa: The Mission." http://www.willowgrove.afrc.af.mil/news/ story.asp?id=123019054. The information was accessed on October 3, 2006.

11   Robert Schlesinger, "In Djibouti, US Special Forces Develop Base Amid Secrecy," *Boston Globe*, December 12, 2002, p. A1.

12   William D. Hartung, Frida Berigan, and Michelle Ciarrocca, "Growing US Military Presence Since 9/11/01," http://www.commondreams.org/views02/1004-05.htm. The information was accessed on November 10, 2006.

13   See John Davis, editor, *The Global War On Terrorism: Assessing the American Response* (New York: Nova, 2004), p. 203.

14   "Added Forces Strengthen Horn of Africa Task Force." http://www.defenselink.mil/Utility/PrintItem.aspx?print=http://www.defenselink.mil/ news/Jun2003/n06132003_200306132.html. The site was accessed on November 16, 2006.

15   "US Warns Eritrea, Ethiopia on Somali War." October 31, 2006. http://www.afrol.com/ articles/22280. The article was accessed on December 11, 2006.

16   "Ethiopia Ready for Islamist War," *BBC News*. http://news.bbc.co.uk/2/hi/africa/6175976. stm. The article was accessed on November 24, 2006.

17   "Ethiopian Jets Blasts Somalia Airports as War Escalates," *Associated Press*, December 26, 2006.

18   CPT Todd H. Guggisberg, "'HAKUNA MATATA'—Supporting Special Operations in Kenya." http://www.quartermaster.army.mil/OQMG/professional_bulletin/1997/ Summer/hakuna.html. The site was viewed on November 13, 2006.

19   "Idyllic Hub of War on Terror," Guardian Unlimited. January 6, 2004. http://www. guardian.co.uk/elsewhere/journalist/story/0,7792,1117126,00.html.   Accessed   on November 12, 2006.

20   Andrea Leahy and Chris Davis, "U.S.-Kenyan EOD Experts Trade Skills in Edged Mallet Exercise - Around the Fleet - Explosive Ordnance Disposal," *All Hands*, March 2004. http://www.findarticles.com/p/articles/mi_m0IBQ/is_1043/ai_116525449. The site was accessed on November 14, 2006.

21   Kevin Maurer, "Scribbler Six." http://www.fayobserver.com/blog/comments?bid=10&e id=2947.

22   Jeffrey F. Addicott, "The Role of Special Operations Forces in the War on Terror," in *The Global War on Terrorism: Assessing the American Response* (New York: Nova, 2003), p. 172.

23   Ibid.

24   Joseph Winter, "Is Somalia Next for War on Terror?" *BBC News*, June 6, 2006. http://news.bbc.co.uk/go/pr/fr/-/2/hi/africa/4841170.stm. The site was accessed on November 14, 2006.

25   Ibid.

26   Paul Taylor, "EU experts fear US could Spark Horn of Africa War," *Reuters*, November 22, 2006. http://harowo.com/2006/11/22/eu-experts-fear-us-could-spark-horn-of-africa-war/. The site was accessed on November 24, 2006.

27   Ibid.

28   Stephanie McCrummen, "Somali Prime Minister Promises Peace Soon," *Washington Post*, December 30, 2006, p. A12.

29   September 2002 *National Security Strategy of the United States of America*. http://www. whitehouse.gov/nsc/nss4.html. The site was accessed on November 24, 2006.

30   Ibid.

31   Thomas P.M. Barnett, *The Pentagon's New Map: War and Peace in the Twenty-First Century* (New York, Penguin Books, 2005).

32   Interview with a State Department Official within the Bureau of African Affairs. November 13, 2006.

33   The US Agency for International Development (USAID), an agency within the State Department, provided support to the Sahelian countries via separate bilateral and regional assistance programs.

34   "The Pan Sahel Initiative." Office of Counterterrorism, Department of State, Washington, DC, November 7, 2002. http://www.state.gov/s/ct/rls/other/14987.htm.

35   Pan Sahel Initiative (PSI). http://www.globalsecurity.org/military/ops/pan-sahel.htm.

36   Craig Smith, "US Training African Forces to Uproot Terrorists," *New York Times*, May 11, 2004, pp. A1 and A8,

37   Smith, "US Training African Forces to Uproot Terrorists," p. A8.

38   Edward Harris, "U.S. Takes Anti-Terror Training to Africa," *Associated Press*, March 22, 2004.

39   Drew Brown, "U.S. Stepping up Anti-terrorism Efforts in Africa," *Knight Ridder*, May 12, 2004.

40   Kevin Whitelaw, "The Mutating Threat," *US News & World Report*, December 26, 2005, p. 33.

41   Ibid., p. 34.

42   Ibid., p. 35.

43   Smith, "US Training African Forces to Uproot Terrorists,"

44   Ibid.

45   Ibid.

46   Harris, "U.S. Takes Anti-Terror Training to Africa,"

47   House Report 109-168-Foreign Relations Authorization Act, Fiscal Years 2006 and 2007, SEC. 1001. Trans-Sahara Counter-Terrorism Initiative. http://thomas.loc.gov/cgibin/cpquery/?&sid=cp109ys1ns&refer=&r_n=hr168.109&db_id=109&item=&sel=TOC_314651&.

48   Trans-Sahara Counterterrorism Initiative (TSCTI). Global Security.org. http://www.globalsecurity.org/military/ops/tscti.htm. The site was viewed on December 4, 2006.

49   Donna Miles, "New Counterterrorism Initiative to Focus on Saharan Africa," *American Forces Press Service*. May 17, 2005. http://usinfo.state.gov/af/Archive/2005/May/19-888364.html. The site was viewed on December 4, 2006.

50   Ibid.

51   Ann Scott Tyson, "U.S. Pushes Anti-Terrorism in Africa-Under Long-Term Program, Pentagon to Train Soldiers of 9 Nations," *Washington Post*, July 26, 2005, pp. A1 and A21.

52   United States European Command, 2005 Exercises. http://www.eucom.mil/english/Exercises/main.asp?Yr=2005. The site was accessed on December 4, 2006.

53   "Exercise Flintlock 05 Under Way in Africa." http://www.eucom.mil/english/FullStory.asp?art=565. The site was viewed on December 4, 2006.

54   Jason Motlagh, "The Trans Sahara Counterterrorism Initiative: U.S. takes Terror Fight to Africa's 'Wild West'," *San Francisco Chronicle*, December 30, 2005.

55   Catherine Fellows, "US Targets Sahara 'Terrorist Haven'," *BBC News*, August 8, 2005. http://news.bbc.co.uk/2/hi/africa/4749357.stm. The site was accessed on December 4, 2006.

56   Motlagh, "The Trans Sahara Counterterrorism Initiative,"

57   "Al Qaeda 'behind' Mauritania Raid," *BBC News*. http://news.bbc.co.uk/2/hi/africa/4613107.stm. The site was accessed on December, 2006.

58   Motlagh, "The Trans Sahara Counterterrorism Initiative,"

59   Ibid.

60   Ibid.

61   J. Stephenson Morrison, "Somalia's and Sudan's Race to the Fore in Africa," *Washington Quarterly*, Spring 2002, p. 201.

Conclusion

Africa and the War on Terrorism: An Assessment

John Davis

Overview

Regardless of the commentator, the overwhelming question regarding the war on terror is the extent to which the United States has been successful. However, there is an equally important, and for some, a far greater series of questions to consider: What is Africa's role in the war on terror and what are the benefits and dilemmas associated with participant countries? Answering these questions requires an assessment, not just of the Bush administration's policies but also of the role played by individual states and an appraisal of the Combined Joint Task Force in the Horn of Africa (CJTF-HOA) and the Trans-Sahara Counterterrorism Initiative (TSCTI).

In a glimpse of Africa's role in the war on terror, the contributors to this book examined a host of variables, including: the role of states in the Combined Joint Task Force (Djibouti and Kenya), a host of regional dynamics, opportunities afforded to the African Union, the impact of globalization, political terrorism in West Africa, and the contributions of North African states, and the role of two US presidential administrations and their strategies in two disparate wars on terror.

At present no comprehensive assessment of Africa's role in the war on terror currently exists. It is therefore the purpose of this conclusion to illuminate some of the more essential aspects of Africa's participation the war on terror. The study commences with the benefits associated with a strategic partnership for those African states that elected to partner with the United States in the war on terror. Then this conclusion explores the dilemmas that, left unchecked, could undermine the long-term success of the war on terror in Africa; and finally, the study closes with a few recommendations that, if implemented, could ensure success for African states during and following the conclusion of the war on terror.

The Strategic Benefits of Partnership with the United States

The opening section of this conclusion examines the strategic benefits of partnership with the United States. In examining the twin partnerships, the CJTF-HOA and the TSCTI, the study will demonstrate that participant African states have received a host of benefits from partnership with the United States. Second, the study explores the threat (and efforts to end the safe haven) posed by Islamic fundamentalism (both internal and external) in Somalia. Third, this section concludes with an examination of Africa's role in the containment of al Qaeda in the region.

Combined Joint Task Force

Quietly the CJTF-HOA has emerged as America's most productive post-9/11 alliance. Structurally, participant members have received significant training from US Special Operations Forces (SOFs) and, equally significant, the armed forces of Kenya, Ethiopia, Eritrea (whose training is problematic), Djibouti, and Yemen have all benefited from the joint bilateral and multilateral exercises with US forces, both ground and naval.

Of the countries participating in the CJTF-HOA, Djibouti has received significant attention due in part to the fact the headquarters of the task force is located in the sprawling Camp Lemonier military facility. The activities on the base itself, and the considerable amount of economic and military assistance the country receives, are additional measures of the benefits that have accrued to this tiny African country. Additionally, because the US has stationed a large Special Operations contingent on the base, replete with support from 1,200 elite Army Rangers, commentators within and outside the region continue to speculate about the activities on the base and constant shuffling of forces between American, French, British, and those among the contingent of task force participants.

Of the task force participants, the military forces of Kenya are by far the best trained and equipped. Equally significant the relationship between US and Kenyan armed forces predates the CJTF-HOA. Almost without much media attention, commentators have rarely mentioned the American use of the army and naval facilities in Kenya. Recently, American military commentators have speculated about the need to deploy Kenyan forces in Somalia to provide stability in the Somalian capital. Another reason for the speculation regarding the need for this deployment is to replace the forces of Ethiopia which has spawned division within the task force. For its part the Kenyan government has maintained its neutrality, refusing to become embroiled in Somali internal politics.

Of the participants in the task force, few would have thought that Ethiopia would perform a significant role. In the case of Djibouti the large military base at Camp Lemonier serves as the central hub of the task force. That said, the military facility known as Camp United near Dire Dawa, Ethiopia, remains a best-kept secret among task force participants.[1] This facility has been and remains a hotbed of military activity as a significant number of joint exercises take place within the confines of the facility. Additionally, a number of major US military units including the 10th Mountain Division, which has participated in Iraq, Afghanistan, Uzbekistan, and other countries associated with the war on terror, have trained at or have had stopovers at Camp United. Similarly, US SOFs have had the largest presence in Ethiopia. By now it is no longer a secret that US SOFs have increased the training of Ethiopian forces (much of this training commenced at Camp United). Though Ethiopian border troops have received the bulk of the anti-terrorist and counterterrorist training, the 12th Army has received its share of training in the past year. It is suggested but not yet confirmed that this very force played an essential role in the invasion of Somalia.

The invasion of Somalia by Ethiopia came as a surprise to most but, as suggested in Chapter 9, the tempo of the training and the increased presence of US SOF and other American assets indicated something was afoot: what was believed herein was the planning of the intervention and subsequent occupation of Mogadishu. As a result of the intervention, Ethiopia has had to confront the domestic, regional, and international fallout of its occupation. Similarly, its assistance to warlords in Northern Somalia has exacerbated the tensions within the task force. Ethiopia's leader, Meles Zenawi, has pledged to remove his troops in the near future owing to the growing financial and political repercussions of the invasion and occupation. As will be discussed in the "dilemmas section," the situation in Somalia, and presence of Ethiopian troops, in the short and long term, may affect the unity of the task force. Unknown at this point is the extent to which the harmony of the CJTF-HOA will be disrupted.

On another level, in spite of the aforementioned successes, the task force cannot be viewed as means to resolve all the problems that affect Horn countries (as the situation in Somalia has demonstrated). Indeed the US effort in the task force has itself come under scrutiny.

US efforts alone are insufficient to deal with the ongoing threats of al Qaeda and homegrown terrorism. Seamless regional and international responses are also necessary. The United States must promote good governance throughout the region by strengthening diplomatic understanding of the area of and increasing support to those countries that already play a key role in counterterrorism operations, but that suffer from poor employment, education, and social services. At the same time, the United States can proactively support internal democracy in areas where the suppression of liberties is common.[2]

Though the US presence is essential for the stability of the Horn it is necessary that the actions of the Horn states themselves resolve the regional threats—particularly the al Qaeda terrorist threat—that are essential to providing confidence among Horn states. As this process unfolds, the US presence will decline. It is the latter that will go along way in defining the success of the task force. As the confidence builds the long-term objective is for the Horn states to come to the fore and lead in regional politico-diplomatic security discussions.

Trans-Sahara Counterterrorism Initiative (TSCTI)

Much like the CJTF-HOA the Trans-Sahara Counterterrorism Initiative, or "TSCTI," has exceeded the expectations of the participant countries and those of American military planners. Replacing the modestly successful Pan Sahel Initiative (PSI), the TSCTI was a far more substantial partnership, encompassing nine states. To measure the viability of the initiative, consider the following quote:

> [The TSCTI] help strengthen regional counterterrorism capabilities, enhance and institutionalize cooperation among the region's security forces, promote democratic governance, and ultimately benefit our bilateral relationships with each of these states. Key aspects of the TSCTI training would include basic marksmanship, planning, communications, land navigation, patrolling and medical care.[3]

The first, and central, index of the success of the TSCTI is the transformation of the armed forces of participant countries. Indeed, one of the failings of the PSI was the inability of the US to sustain and then to expand the training of participant countries. With respect to the TSCTI the Bush administration has supplemented the original $500 million program by adding funding to extend the life of the initiative two years beyond its intended date.

A second measure of the success of the TSCTI concerns the lessons learned from the previous initiative (the PSI). Besides that mentioned above, consider that many commentators argued the predecessor of the TSCTI was ill-conceived, lacked purpose, and did not take into consideration the importance of the contributions that could be made to regional security in the Sahel and Maghreb areas of Africa.

Third, another significant barometer of the success of the program involves the equipping of participant forces. In this area, based on the needs and quality of the troops, the Bush administration provided a significant amount of equipment in the form of uniforms, communications gear, transportation, and ammunition.

Fourth, the joint training of participant forces along side those of the United States proved beneficial. Member states noted the improvement in communications between member states, the experience gained in counterterrorist training in bilateral (with US forces or with an individual partner within the TSCTI) or multilateral settings that involved three or more countries. Similarly, another important indicator involves the numerous conferences between senior military officers of participant states. Such gatherings have increased confidence among states, improved the training practices, improved "joint tactics" to confront indigenous terror groups or those outside the region, and assisted in the synchronization of communication.

Fifth, border security has increased throughout both regions. The Sahel countries (Chad, Niger, Mali, and Mauritania) in particular have dramatically increased the presence of troops along their borders, helping to prevent the emergence of safe havens in the expansive desert areas within the region. If there is a weakness among these states, it is that the Malian armed forces remain too small and thus would require assistance from other states to protect its borders. Among the states in the Maghreb region, the armed forces are much larger and therefore the capabilities of the states are greater. That said, many states—Tunisia and those in Senegal—will require far more training to bring them up to speed with the forces of other members of the region. There is another problem that rarely receives attention: the dilemma associated with Nigerian troops. By far the most capable of all troops within the TSCTI initiative belong to Nigeria, but many of its soldiers have been inflicted with HIV/AIDS (the number or percentage is unclear) and during participation in peacekeeping operations Nigerian troops have been involved in a host of human rights abuses. These dilemmas involving the aforementioned states indicate that the TSCTI has been highly successful but it is by no means perfect.

These dilemmas aside, the TSCTI has institutional cooperation among participant states. It is this institutionalization that is the centerpiece or legacy of the TSCTI. The manifestation of both may be viewed this way:

Counterterrorism (CT) programs to create a new regional focus for trans-Saharan cooperation, including use of established regional organizations like the African Union and its new Center for the Study and Research on Terrorism in Algiers. These programs include training to improve border and aviation security and overall CT readiness; Continued specialized Counterterrorism Assistance Training and Terrorist Interdiction Program (TIP) activities in the trans-Sahara region and possible regional expansion of those programs; Public diplomacy programs that expand outreach efforts in the Sahel and Maghreb regions, Nigeria, and Senegal and seek to develop regional programming embracing this vast and diverse region. Emphasis is on preserving the traditional tolerance and moderation displayed in most African Muslim communities and countering the development of extremism, particularly in youth and rural populations; Military programs intended to expand military-to-military cooperation, to ensure adequate resources are available to train, advise and assist regional forces and to establish institutions promoting better regional cooperation, communication, and intelligence.[4]

These elements and the administration's consistent statements regarding the importance of democratic governance represent another aspect of the legacy of the TSCTI. This point is fundamental because it is clear that the success of the TSCTI in the short term and long term will depend on the ability of member states to adopt and to implement democratic principles.

Somalia: A Safe Haven No More?

With respect to Somalia, the track record of the government of the United States can be viewed two ways: one of embarrassment and failure under Clinton and moderate success under Bush.[5] During the administration of Bill Clinton, on October 3, 1993 the firefight that will live in infamy symbolized the ineptness of the president's policies in Africa and, worse, the president made a promise in the wake of the events in Mogadishu that "no more American combat troops" would die on his watch. Thereafter, the US Air Force and Naval and Marine aircrafts (along with a dramatic increase in the use of cruise missiles) became the weapons of choice.

The George W. Bush administration (after 9/11) periodically used spy planes and Special Forces to provide intelligence in Somalia. Thus from late 2001 until the spring of 2006 the administration's policy proved highly successful. During the summer of 2006 many Africa watchers asserted the administration had made a fatal decision: the United States has incessantly taken sides in Somalia. In the first example, the Clinton administration sided with moderate clans and then launched a "not-so covert war" to "snatch General Mohamed Farah Aidid." This decision increased the intensity of the anti-Americanism among ordinary Somalis. In July of 2006 the Bush administration supported the warlords with the hope they could preclude an Islamic takeover by the Union of Islamic Courts (UIC). The decision proved counterproductive. The bulk of the residents of the capital and elsewhere in Somalia supported the UIC. This fallout proved interesting. Envisaging certain defeat, the specter of increasing anti-Americanism, and a potential disaster if Eritrea and Ethiopia—each of which supported dissimilar groups and interests in Somalia— the administration could have been forgiven if it had decided to remove itself from Somali politics.

Instead, the administration confronted these dynamics and adjusted its strategy; thereafter, again in the face of anti-Americanism, refocused US policy on Somalia. On the Kenyan–Somalia border, for example, US Special Operation Forces (SOFs) increased their activities, launching a series of intelligence missions into Somalia. On the other side of the Somali–Ethiopian border, long before the invasion of Somalia, US National Guard forces from Guam had intensified the training of Ethiopian border forces and the SOFs had upped the tempo of its activities and training with Ethiopian forces, suggesting to many that invasion had long been an active consideration of the US. To supplement this perception, the administration, through CENTCOM, provided "assistance" to the Ethiopian-led invasion of Somalia. To further demonstrate the aggressiveness of its policy in East Africa, the administration coordinated the timing of the forces of the transitional government with those from Ethiopia in a strategy to rapidly secure the capital.

To date the administration's offensive shifted to an overt strategy, and is no longer dependent on "the hidden hands" of US power or, as some African commentators have suggested, the US acted as "puppeteers" pulling the strings and having the Ethiopian forces do its bidding. And when the requirement for direct action was needed, the administration conspicuously opted to use force. On 7 January 2007 (and again on January 23), utilizing the AC-130 Spectra Gunship, aircraft usually attached to SOF missions, launched devastating attacks against fleeing al Qaeda operatives long believed to be responsible for the bombings of the US embassies in Kenya and Tanzania in 1998. The administration has long suggested key al Qaeda operatives were the "central nodes" of the UIC. The air strikes were described this way:

> According to Abdul Rashid Hidig, a member of Somalia's transitional parliament who represents the border area, the American air strikes in the area wiped out a long convoy of vehicles carrying Islamist leaders trying to flee deeper in the bush. "Their trucks got stuck in the mud, and they were easy targets," he said. Mr. Hidig said two civilians were also killed. But representatives of the Islamist forces said that the number of civilian deaths was much higher. Mohammed Dakhani, the Islamists' health director, said that dozens of nomadic herdsmen and their families were grazing their animals in the same wet valley where the Islamist convoy was struggling to move across country. "Their donkeys, their camels, their cows, they've all been destroyed," he said. "And many children were killed."[6]

In the wake of the air strikes, one of the masterminds of the East Africa embassy bombings, Fazul Abdullah Mohammed, escaped. Additional air strikes and the use of helicopter gun ships unfolded in Badmado, Ras Kamboni, and in Afmadow, all areas in southern Somalia. The administration's strategy became more assertive following the dispatch of the aircraft carrier *USS Eisenhower*, along with other ships, off the Somali coast to prevent al Qaeda and UIC forces from using the coastal waters for escape. The combined air strikes purportedly killed over 50 UIC and al Qaeda operatives (it is unknown how many civilians were killed in these strikes). The Bush administration has made a number of post-attack comments. According to White House spokesman Tony Snow, "This administration continues to go after al Qaeda. We are interested in going after those who have perpetrated acts of violence against Americans, including bombings of embassies in Kenya and Tanzania."[7]

Ethiopian and Somali government forces continue to battle UIC and its supporters in southern Somalia. In terms of the war on terror, at least in the short term, this is clearly a victory in the struggle against terrorism. A number of critical issues remain on the horizon. For starters, the Ethiopian government had made it clear its occupation will not be one of long duration. Second, the Bush administration, at the time of this writing, launched a diplomatic offensive to enlist the African Union to commit member states to a African peacekeeping mission in Somalia. That initiative failed. Unless and until "other troops" are dispatched to supplant those from Ethiopia, it is only a matter of time before the Somali people revolt against Ethiopian forces (in various areas of the capital, and elsewhere in the southern part of the country, Somalis have attacked and killed several Ethiopian troops). Another issue is very much connected with the first. The transitional government now operating in Somalia is too weak to affect change among the warlords and assorted militia scattered all over the country. This issue is exacerbated by the fact that the militias themselves have become restive. Until the national government exerts control over the country, the tenuous existence between the ruling government and the warlords will rapidly dissipate, increasing the chances of instability. Third, if the relationship between the new government and the warlords collapses, and if Ethiopian forces vacate the capital before peacekeeping forces enter the country, there are two scenarios that may unfold, neither of which is good.

The first is that US "boots on the ground" could be inserted to stabilize the capital and perhaps the country. Few would doubt the ability of US forces to achieve this objective, but there is little doubt the Somalis would not wish to see Americans perform this role. Moreover, with events in Iraq, with potential for war in Iran still a contingency, it is clear CENTCOM is unlikely to entertain this question. There is a corollary issue that links both: the Somali people and American military commanders understand the legacy of "Black Hawk Down" (the downing of two American helicopters that unleashed a vicious firefight that culminated in the deaths of 18 US soldiers and over 1,000 Somali lives). The second involves an increased role by the United Nations. However, the UN missions failed and there is little respect among the Somali people for the UN.

In the final analysis, at least in regard to the defeat of the UIC, the Bush administration and its regional partners have achieved a significant short-term victory, but to sustain that success countries within the Horn, the AU, the UN, and the United States must confront the real issues in Somalia: stability, national unity, ending the influence of the warlords, nation building, and most certainly rebuilding the ravaged Somali economy—all are critical to preventing terrorism in Somalia. The verities of not doing so are apparent: if the international community is unwilling to confront the aforementioned issues that continue to fester within Somalia, then the world will be forced to incessantly intervene in the hopes of preventing an outside force from filling a vacuum or dealing with an internal one (like the UIC)—something the Taliban accomplished in Afghanistan—which will turn the country into a Sudan covering the years 1990–1995 or Afghanistan from 1996 to September 2001. This is what awaits the proponents of the war on terror in Africa if Somalia remains a terror haven or a collapsed state.

Containing the al Qaeda Threat

In the days after 9/11 the Bush administration moved swiftly to include African states in its plans to confront the increasing threat of bin Laden's transnational terror network. Long before finalizing its contingencies to use states within the region, the Bush administration received support from a host of African states that openly condemned the terrorist attacks that occurred on 11 September 2001.

In recognition of this support, the administration quietly began to develop its strategic plans. One of the essential strategic questions involved the following: if the United States attacked Afghanistan, where would surviving or fleeing members of al Qaeda seek sanctuary? There were a number of considerations: Pakistan, select states within the Middle East, or safe havens in Africa.

The administration focused intensely on each of the aforementioned contingencies, but observers were surprised at the rhetoric and then subsequent use of US and allied efforts in Africa. For starters, the administration persistently recognized the importance of failed or collapsed states. *The National Security Strategy of the United States*, however, formalized administration policy regarding the dilemmas associated with these states: "Weak states can pose as great a danger to our national interests as strong states" but the administration recognized another verity: that weak states left unattended could become breeding grounds for terrorist activity. In short the administration made it clear that no state in Africa could be allowed to develop into another Afghanistan.

In the months after the United States launched Operation Enduring Freedom in Afghanistan, the administration quietly dispatched intelligence assets off the coast of Somalia to monitor al Qaeda's activities in this unstable East African state. In recognition of increasing terrorist activity the administration began considering a host of contingencies: dispatching US Marines, planning covert missions led by the CIA, use of SOFs, air strikes, or the use of another novelty—constructing a regional alliance whose purpose was to jointly confront the challenge of terrorism in the Horn.

That alliance culminated in the Combined Joint Task Force in the Horn of Africa (CJTF-HOA). As discussed above, the participant states of the task force have received training that has benefited the armed forces of all members. Similarly, the CJTF-HOA has fulfilled its mission to detect, disrupt, and eventually defeat transnational terrorist groups operating in the region, and in some cases succeeded beyond the planners' expectations.

Not only has al Qaeda has been contained, its missions and cellular activities disrupted, but rarely do we hear of its affiliates in the Horn. Worse, its one true sanctuary, Somalia, may now be a thing of the past. The Ethiopian invasion of Somalia and subsequent occupation of the capital, Mogadishu, represented the first phase of al Qaeda's defeat in that country. The second phase involved two dynamics: the defeat of the UIC and the capture and killing of al Qaeda operatives (with the rest on the run).

Though there have been setbacks, the strategic benefits associated with the containment of al Qaeda in Somalia are numerous. Given the multiple successes and the containment of terrorism in the region, the Pentagon has quietly redeployed the

Marines for use in Iraq or for some future contingencies. The Navy is now in charge of the CJTF-HOA.

A second strategic benefit is that, other than the use of the SOFs and the AC-130 Spectra Gunship, the US military has largely been dormant. Any US military involvement in Africa will be examined with suspicion, either as a neo-imperial or hegemonic expression of US power, neither of which will be looked upon favorably in the region.

Third, by all accounts the states in East Africa have "stood up" and prevented the establishment of an outside influence in the region. Similarly, given the cooperation and joint exercises, and growing military capabilities, the Horn states have something they lacked prior to the advent of September 11: confidence. The presence of this characteristic, along with experience, will in time, set the stage for the gradual reduction of the US presence in the region. For Africans this will be the single greatest barometer of the success of the containment of the al Qaeda threat.

The administration and its African allies have succeeded in other venues as well. The TSCTI is itself a success for a host of reasons. The terrorist threat, despite administration rhetoric to the contrary, has always been internal and susceptible to penetration by al Qaeda. Thus the threat within the Sahel region is largely due the GSPC, which has pledged its loyalty to bin Laden. The armed forces of the Sahel countries, in the form of Chad, Mali, and Niger, engaged the forces of the GSPC. In a firefight involving the GSPC and soldiers from Chad, with support from US SOFs, the armed forces of this Sahel country killed or captured 43 terrorists. In another example, the Algerian intelligence, backed up by its military, seized a convoy replete with weapons (mortar launchers, rocket-propelled grenade launchers, and surface-to-air missiles). Those weapons, according to experts, were intended for a large-scale terrorist attack, presumably against US interests.

In spite of some challenges the GSPC threat has been marginalized but it is one that may be reconstituted at any moment. Vigilance is the watchword within the Sahel, but there are other realities. The participant states in the TSCTI understand (though there has been much progress) that border security remains a concern. There have been a host of new multilateral systems that have been constructed to resolve this very problem. The systems have been successful but individual terrorists are still able to enter participant states and foment instability in the region; this dilemma is problematic in that many individuals either connected to al Qaeda or supportive of the Wahhabi faith may instill fundamentalist beliefs that will challenge local sects of Islam.

From another perspective, the participant countries of the TSCTI have worked to increase the counterterrorist capabilities of their armed forces and have improved the intelligence capabilities of states in the region. Though there are concerns about the pace of the training of the Malian military and others in the region, the participant militaries, by and large, have much to be proud of. Indeed, by all accounts the confidence of the soldiers tasked to protect the Sahel region unanimously agree the training under the TSCTI is head and shoulders above that received during the course of the Pan Sahel Initiative.

In the final analysis the twin partnerships—the CJTF-HOA and the TSCTI—represent the center of gravity of Africa's renewed strategic significance. The principal objective, preventing the establishment of terrorist safe havens, has been achieved. The presence of al Qaeda is minimal at best and the threat of the transnational network has been very much been contained. Past successes aside, there are troubling signs on the horizon. The most important of which concerns al Qaeda's call for a jihad in Somalia against the "infidel forces" of Ethiopia (the jihad almost certainly involves the US because it was the US military that trained and provided intelligence and guidance to Ethiopian troops to launch the invasion). The CJTF-HOA will have to contend with the brunt of the expected influx of jihadists from the Middle East and beyond. The TSCTI's involvement in this matter will be a peripheral one: prevent safe havens and instability within participant states. Dealing with this threat will provide a new measure of the success or failure associated with the strategic benefits of partnership for African states in the US-led war on terror.

Dilemmas: The Problems Associated with Partnership with the US-Led War

The war on terror in Africa has succeeded beyond the expectations of the military planners in CENTCOM and EUCOM, the two regional commands with responsibility for Africa.[8] That said there are a host of dilemmas that, left unchecked, could undermine the successes made in the region. This section examines a host of issues, to include the following: Africa's issue prioritization, the continuing problem of reciprocal intelligence sharing, the marginalization of the African Union, uneven distribution of training, and the anti-American backlash.

Africa's Issue Prioritization

Once states within Africa assumed a role or decided to become active partners in the first conflagration of the twenty-first century, a reality assumed center stage: the issues within the region would be eclipsed by the US-led contention that the war on terror is the pre-eminent issue "of our time." In one sense, the moment such a decision was contemplated and then implemented, skeptics began to argue African issues would formally lose what little international interest that may have existed. This point was viewed this way. In a discussion with a African colleague he made the following profound argument: "If Tony Blair, could not convince President Bush to keep his word (the alleged quid pro quo asserts that Blair argued that he would commit British troops to the war in Iraq in exchange for Bush's commitment to focus his energies in pursuing peace in the Middle East), how could African states force the remaining superpower to make a commitment to deal with a host of critical issues in the region"? This is what the states within Africa will have to confront as the war on terror continues to unfold.

The issues confronting the continent of Africa are diverse and continue to impact its states. The issues include the following: state status (failed, collapsed, and weak states), corruption, HIV/AIDS in the sub-Saharan states, authoritarian regimes, ethnic and religious divisions within states, political terrorism, genocide in Darfur, Sudan, underdevelopment, poverty, and famine.

Iraq and Afghanistan are both failed states and both have received significant US economic reconstruction assistance, yet both remain far from fledgling democratic states. Long before the war in Iraq commenced members of the Bush administration incessantly warned about the problems associated with failed states and that if extensive economic assistance did not flow to these states then terrorist safe havens would be the result.

The administration has worked to provide economic assistance to its partners in the Horn task force and to those in the Trans-Sahara Initiative. As is well known there are a host of other failed (weak and collapsed) states that have not received such attention and are not likely to receive any attention from the United States. The reason for the administration's policy is clear: states beyond the Horn, the Sahel, or the Maghreb regions of Africa are of no strategic value to US military.

Though this policy is understandable from the perspective of US military, it ignores the overall requirement to think long term and not short term. The terrorist threats to the Horn, Sahel, and Maghreb countries are current issues that confront the region, but the threat to western and Saharan states are on the horizon. States such as Liberia and Sierra Leone in the west remain targets of al Qaeda. Both states remain unstable and both were critical to links to bin Laden's strategy of using diamonds to fund the operations of the transnational network. Currently this link has been disrupted but al Qaeda continues its efforts to reinvigorate this once vital link. Thus, beyond the three regions formerly mentioned, the administration (or more likely its replacement) should consider a massive influx of investment opportunities as a means to reverse continental underdevelopment to stave off future terrorism. Until the US government, the UN, and AU work to confront the host of failed, weak, or collapsed states in the region, it is only a matter of time before terrorist groups penetrate these countries.

Corruption has been a historic problem for the vast majority of African states. Political corruption in Nigeria, the Democratic Republic of the Congo, and Zimbabwe symbolize the recent trends. There is another trend that has received little attention by the United States: money laundering. In a bid to eliminate terrorist financing this issue is critical. In Africa criminal enterprises with ties to the government have helped to sustain funding for al Qaeda and its regional affiliates. Similarly, the Bush administration, through the Department of the Treasury, has been unable to eliminate charitable donations from Islamic organizations that too have aided the cause of al Qaeda. These dilemmas are problematic in that the Bush administration (along with the UN) has ignored these issues. African states have complained that unless and until the US government or the international community engage local governments in Africa, both will remain issues that will continue to undermine the credibility of states on the continent.

On the matter of the HIV/AIDS pandemic, this issue dominates the region of sub-Sahara. States within the region, despite assistance from the United Nations (and from the West collectively, principally from the United States, however the world has not met its economic pledges) the rates of those affected by the virus continues to spiral upward, and the ever-present health crisis continues to impact local economies already on the brink.

In an interesting turn of events the pandemic has been perceived as a strategic issue (not necessarily an African one). Within the region, and for those concerned about the issue worldwide, the use of term "strategic" meant that regardless of the expansion of the war on terror in Africa, HIV/AIDS retained its priority. That priority, however, has not translated into a dramatic increase in funding. Rather, "strategic" has instead had military and not health connotations. The following statement is emblematic of the military or security implications of the disease:

> Deputy Commander of the US European Command (USEUCOM) General Charles F. Wald expressed concern that Africa's major health and humanitarian crisis, the HIV/AIDS pandemic, was becoming a "strategic" issue affecting security. Referring especially to South Africa, Wald said that HIV "limits the number of troops they can deploy at any one time." South Africa's military has received US$2.2mil from USEUCOM for "study, identification, education, prevention and treatment and follow-up," on HIV/AIDS. "It may be the first holistic approach in the world," he said.[9]

Linking a health issue with national security requirements on the surface is understandable from the perspective of US strategic needs. That said, the HIV/AIDS rates are far greater among the civilian population than within the military of all Saharan countries. Thus while the administration may be concerned about the issue, its perspective, at least as couched above, is problematic and has certainly affected the sensibility of Africans across the continent.

There are a host of other issues of significance to African states that have received little priority since the outbreak of the war on terror. Of those issues, the failure by the administration to move beyond rhetoric to advance democracy is problematic when so many countries are authoritarian and engage in political violence, issues that are exploited by Islamists for propaganda purposes. Similarly, conflict resolution has all too often taken a back seat to the war on terror. As we have learned in Somalia, Liberia, and in the Sierra Leone, al Qaeda has carved safe havens and thereafter recruited from within these and other safe havens in the region. Until Africa's issues receive prominence, few within the region will say the war on terror is successful. If the aforementioned issues retain their low priority status, many in the region will begin to recite a familiar refrain: continental states in the region were pawns in the Cold War; and now in a post-September 11 conflict (if and when it concludes) many assert that participant states may too be remembered as pawns in a "new great game": the war on terror.

The Continuing Problem of Reciprocal Intelligence Sharing

The issue of reciprocal training is one that will not dissipate. Though partners of the United States, those in the CJTF-HOA, TSCTI, and individual states (Kenya, Egypt, or Morocco, to name a few), receive intelligence, sharing remains largely one way: flowing in the direction of the United States.

This issue surfaced during the Cold War when the United States utilized select proxies in Somalia, Angola, Chad, and even in the Sudan, to provide intelligence to disrupt the Soviet Union's attempt to export communism in the region. The critical nodes of US intelligence in Africa during the age of the great ideological clash involved the use of "facilities" in Somalia, South Africa, Nigeria, and in Egypt to monitor Soviet proxies in select areas the region. In spite of uneven success in the region, the intelligence presence in the Saharan states declined considerably. The cuts in US intelligence assets along with the closure of CIA stations dramatically increased in the wake of the precipitous Soviet collapse.[10] There were two issues that surfaced following the dissipation of the Soviet threat: did US allies in the region benefit from reciprocal intelligence sharing? And, as the post–Cold War era emerged, did those same allies retain their role with the US government? The answer to both questions is no.

To underscore US intelligence dilemmas consider that the Clinton administration was unaware of al Qaeda's activities in southern Somalia; these failures paved the way for the deadly firefight in Mogadishu in 1993. Additionally, experts within the region have argued that the al Qaeda terrorist attacks against US interests in Kenya and Tanzania saliently illustrate the American "intelligence blind spots" in the region. Similarly, the attack on the *USS Cole* is also indicative of this trend. As one official in the Defense Intelligence Agency (DIA) lamented, the attacks "explain how the US intelligence assets were blinded to this embarrassing attack." It was further noted that not only was it problematic that there was no intelligence collection via Djibouti or in Yemen; worse, US traditional allies (France or Egypt) were equally circumspect in the failures to recognize or transmit any known information to the CIA or DIA. Beginning in 2001 US intelligence officers visited their counterparts in Nigeria, Kenya, Tanzania, Sudan, Ethiopia, Uganda, and Eritrea and the CIA even worked with elements (warlords) inside the transitional governmental controlled territories to monitor events in Somalia. There was indeed sharing among allies. The concern for American allies in Africa is that US intelligence platforms—the CIA, DIA, SOFs, the use of the Predator Drone, Naval ships that monitored communications, occasional satellite photography, and other assets—often conducted surveillance without the approval of its regional partners, performed military operations without the consent of its partners, and worse, long after many missions ended, the US officials refused to share critical information with their African allies.

On the surface coalition leaders do not publicly express their displeasure regarding this issue. Instead numerous complaints are sent through private channels. Making matters worse for US regional partners, these complaints, on balance, have received little attention and more often than not have been ignored. There are two issues at work: the US has taken its allies for granted; and there is a view within the region that the failure of reciprocal intelligence sharing is another illustration that the Africa partners in the war on terror have not received the benefits commensurate with other American allies, most notably Pakistan. Even after consultations with the State Department, though there has been an increase in military assistance to some frontline states, the US government remains indifferent to direct intelligence sharing with most of its African partners.

In the short term the US is concerned that many rogue elements will likely develop (as was the case with Pakistan's ISI) within African intelligence services that will work to aid the cause of al Qaeda or indigenous terrorist organizations. This perception, though understandable, is nonetheless problematic. Accordingly, throughout the continent Africans cannot understand how the US government promotes cooperation among states within the region but simultaneously refrains from sharing critical intelligence with its partners. This "one way" intelligence relationship has engendered mistrust and remains an issue that could potentially lead to a split between the US and selected coalition allies.

The Marginalization of the African Union (AU)

Historically the Africa Union (AU) has been inundated with intra-state rivalries and regional bickering. Such rivalries preceded the war on terror; however, these rivalries have been renewed and the bickering has intensified among states from dissimilar regions. In addition, with the states in the Horn of Africa backing US-led interests in the region, and the Sahel and Maghreb countries doing likewise, the AU's marginalization has intensified. These realities undermine Africa's identity and its ability to resolve its own problems.

As tensions increased in Somalia during the summer of 2006 after the UIC seized control of Mogadishu, the AU seemed destined to play a significant role. In the wake of the takeover by Islamists loyal to bin Laden, the AU said little and did even less, prompting external entities—the European Union, the United States, and the United Nations—to intervene. The marginalization of the AU increased in the wake of the organization's failure to provide a solution to ever-increasing regional tensions.

As the threats of intervention increased throughout November and December of 2006, the voice of the AU was further diminished following the Ethiopian government's threat to intervene. In the midst of such threats the EU and UN pushed the use of African peacekeepers (an objective of the AU) to prevent another Ogaden-like clash between Ethiopia and Somalia. After Prime Minister Meles Zenawi ignored warnings by the EU and the UN (and after receiving a "green light" by the Bush administration to intervene and destroy the UIC), the Ethiopian government succeeded in meeting its national security objectives. In the occupation's aftermath the AU launched a brief protest, which was promptly ignored by all players. Commentators were again quick to illustrate the continuing decline of a once promising regional organization:

> The AU split with many sub-Saharan countries backing Ethiopia's intervention against the Islamists in Mogadishu while North African states backed the Islamic Courts. The Arab League was sympathetic to the Islamists in Mogadishu, and several of its members supplied them with arms. It is dangerously reminiscent of the Cold War era when the US backed Ethiopia in the Ogaden war against Somalia, which was then backed by the Soviet Union.[11]

The excerpt provides a sense of the regional and external forces that have affected the leadership capabilities of the AU. That said, other commentators were quick to illustrate the sheer fecklessness of the regional organization: "As the African Union stands by, silently and perhaps helplessly watching Somalia's return to anarchy, the Bush administration has claimed another 'victory' for its discredited 'war on terror.'"[12]

It is this point that became prominent in the wake of the AU's dismal showing in the crisis in the horn. Consider the following: "What these spin doctors won't reveal is the fact that by disregarding multilateral institutions such as the African Union, the Bush administration has ulterior motives in igniting a war in the Horn of Africa."[13] This point continued to gain traction in the region:

> According to Salim Lone, a highly respected Kenya-based commentator, the United States has cast this as a war to combat terrorism, but its real goal is to obtain a direct foothold in a highly strategic region by establishing a client regime there. The Horn of Africa is newly oil-rich and lies just miles from another strategic US client-state Saudi Arabia, overlooking the daily passage of large numbers of oil tankers and warships through the Red Sea. Interestingly, Lone also indicates that General John Abizaid, the current US military chief of the Iraq war, was in Ethiopia a few weeks ago. What was he doing there if not to get all of Zenawi's ducks in a row in preparation for destabilizing Somalia?[14]

From the perspective of the United States the Ethiopian invasion and subsequent occupation achieved its objective: the defeat of the UIC, the presumed departure of al Qaeda operatives responsible for the Kenyan and Tanzanian Embassies bombings, and movement (hopefully long term) towards national reconciliation. From the African perspective, the overt use of force by Ethiopia and subsequent occupation is too reminiscent of the large scale US action in Iraq. There is another quality that too is problematic: the US invasion of Iraq resulted in the marginalization of the UN; the Ethiopian invasion of Somalia has caused a similar outcome: the reduction of the AU's responsibility and the loss of confidence of that organization within the region. Such a reality has diminished any success felt among the participant states of the CJTF-HOA from their involvement in the Ethiopian invasion.

Uneven Distribution of Training

As mentioned in Chapter 9, the American military training of African troops has largely been a successful venture. The Bush administration, perhaps overly aggressively, seized control of the humanitarian dominated program known as African Contingency Operations Training Assistance (ACOTA) initiative formerly operated by the European Command (EUCOM). In the wake of the tragic events of 9/11 the Pentagon reorganized the program, requiring a greater integration of the African armed forces with those of the United States.

On the surface ACOTA has been a highly successful venture. Thirteen African states are participants in this program, the bulk of which come from the Horn and the Sahel regions, states that are primary US partners in the war on terror. By and large the training of these states has been impressive (but such training is by no means comprehensive) and the Bush administration has invested significant funding to ensure that the program is sustainable. Finally, most of the countries that are participants in ACOTA have received new equipment and have vastly upgraded counterterrorist training and border patrol policing.

These successes aside, the training is problematic on a number of fronts. First, the training is uneven; and second, the administration has failed to elevate the training to the next phase: the training of local police. In Chad for example the administration has been forbidden to train the country's larger ethnic groups out of fear that it may eventually revolt against the Zagawa-led government. The Pentagon suggests it has no choice; that is the US has selected stability over majority rule in this case but history has shown it is only a matter of time before "blowback" occurs.

On another front, soldiers in Djibouti's armed forces have complained about the extensive presence of US SOFs in the country and that despite the relatively large military presence, the relationship between the US–Djibouti forces does not match that of the US–Kenyan military relationship. Privately the government of Djibouti has expressed this view to the Pentagon but there is little activity to illustrate that the training procedures have changed in any meaningful way. Within the US military there is concern that the country that serves as the operational headquarters has expressed such views, but elements within CENTCOM argue it does not take much to increase the training of the units within Djibouti or to increase the number of joint exercises to ease the concerns of a major ally in the Horn.

In Niger its troops have made dramatic strides in the size and training of its military but the force remains too small to protect the country from an influx of external terrorist groups, which could easily cause considerable damage and threaten the existence of the ruling government. This is equally true of the forces of Mali, which have asked for but have yet to receive an increase in the training regimen as well as an increase in equipment. If the Bush administration, or subsequent administration, does not recognize that uneven training is an issue, then many of the administration's initiatives will collapse from within without any threats or attacks from terrorist groups, whether indigenous or external.

The second issue is similarly problematic. At the time of this writing the Bush administration has done next to nothing in the area of trained local police forces in many of the countries of the TSCTI. The reason for this policy is the fear expressed by the administration that in select countries such training may produce or lead to an increase in human rights abuses at the hands of the police. The administration's policy is indeed understandable to the extent that the police forces in many of its allied partners in the war on terror (more often then not roaming gangs on the government payroll) kill or intimidate the local population. Ironically in the age of terror, again within many of same allied countries, human rights abuses have increased not decreased. The reason for the increase involves the use of the local police to beat, detain, and in some cases kill opposition political elements that the ruling elite claims are terrorists.

In reality the training of such forces in counterterrorism tactics (along with the respect for the rule of law) will assist in the "professionalization" of local police units and therefore reduce the "unlawful and untrained elements." Additionally, there is another point overlooked by US strategic planners: the greater the number of African states that can confront terrorists (from within or externally), the closer they can get to meeting a major objective—ensuring an African presence (and a reduction and eventual elimination of the American "boots on the ground" in the region). The opportunity now exists for the administration to lay the groundwork through the training of the local police to achieve this objective.

Anti-American Backlash

The greatest threat to the US-led war on terror concerns the regional perception of American objectives as well as the outcomes of its missions. Similarly, if the Bush administration, or a subsequent administration, remain true to their objective of preventing al Qaeda from establishing new bases in the region, or preventing the transnational network from using "local affiliates" to foment instability within individual states, then the majority of Africans will find this policy acceptable in the short term. There are additional elements associated with the administration's war on terror that are attached to its policy—the strategy of keeping a "low signature" or the use of the least amount of US troops necessary to achieve administration objectives—that are acceptable to the majority of Africans.

Unfortunately, the administration is beginning to meet the "emerging" and some would say the "inevitable" anti-American backlash in Africa. The anti-American backlash remains the single greatest threat to the war on terror in the region. It is interesting that this is ironically a dilemma largely of the administration's own making. The anti-American backlash is a function of a host of variables. Those variables include the proverbial "expectation game" and two disparate regional dynamics that illustrate there are additional dangers on the horizon for the war on terror in Africa.

A growing dilemma awaiting the Bush administration and its African allies in the war on terror is the "expectation game." Both the Bush administration and its allies have made major promises about ending poverty, corruption, advancing democracy, and ending the cycle of underdevelopment that have symbolized African states since liberation. The ongoing rhetoric about the influx of economic assistance and the ever-present chorus that "change is coming" will likely produce an altogether different backlash if these expectations in the short term are not sustained or met. Should the administration fail in any combination of the aforementioned areas, indigenous terrorists groups (regardless of size) will use them against the local governments to foment instability. On another level, al Qaeda continues to propagandize about the "neo-colonial" or US attempts to "secularize" the region; in those areas where Muslims reside this continues to gain traction, whether through Friday prayers or in messages from bin Laden or Zawahiri. The administration's failure to counter these arguments (through public diplomacy, which is a major failing of the administration) has only provided credibility to the propagandists. In the final analysis the administration is losing the "hearts and minds" contests that if left unchecked will affect the overall effort in Africa.

There are two regional dynamics that illustrate the dilemma associated with the war on terror. In North Africa, for example, states within this region share a natural affinity to the plight of the Palestinians or to the people in Iraq. The dynamics associated with the anti-Americanism in the region are highly complex but the end result offers a clear sense of the realities confronting the war on terror in the region. The dynamics may be viewed this way:

Anti-Americanism in North Africa is a complex phenomenon that can be analyzed at two levels. The first level relates to the Maghribi governments' relationship—cooperative or hostile—with the United States. Traditionally, Tunisia and Morocco have maintained steady cooperation with the US, while for Algeria and Libya cooperation has only recently become a strategic choice. The second level relates to Maghribi public opinion. Although opinion polls and popular demonstrations often show a high degree of anti-Americanism, public opinion is not as homogeneous as it may appear. Indeed, there is a paradoxical twin movement of, on the one hand, real repulsion (animosity) towards the US government due to US policies, mainly toward the Arab and Muslim world, and, on the other hand, an obvious attraction for some American values and products, as well as for America's technological prowess. In order to avoid being alienated from their popular base, North African governments do their best to adjust their views to those of their public opinions. Hence, they criticize US policy towards the Palestinian issue or the Iraqi war, but at the same time cooperate fully with the US administration to obtain more direct investments for economic development, and for political support, in the name of security, to assure the survival of the regimes in place.[15]

This statement provides a sense of the complexities associated with the anti-Americanism in North Africa. That said there are two additional dynamics that are clear manifestations of the increasing backlash against US policies in the war on terror. In each case Iraq is the source of ongoing anti-American repercussions. The first dynamic is the large American footprint and the ongoing occupation in Iraq. As a result of both many Muslims in North Africa have answered bin Laden's call to launch a jihad to drive the "infidels" from Iraq. In the last two years the Bush administration has claimed that it has detained or killed over the 500 North Africans throughout Iraq, the bulk of which were in Al Anbar province or Baghdad. The ever-increasing presence of North African jihadists is an unwelcome revelation for the US military, indicating that within allied countries of the war on terror its citizens are willing to confront US troops in Iraq.

The second revelation is equally troubling. North Africans, and those from other regions, are returning to their home states, taking with them training in the use of tactics employed against US forces in Iraq (suicide bombings, Improvised Explosive Devises (IEDS), the use of mortars, and other tactics), and will likely employ them against government forces in Egypt, Algeria, Morocco, and Tunisia. Worse, the countries in the Sahel (Chad, Mali, Niger, and Mauritania) have discovered that its citizens have not only participated in attacks on US forces in Iraq but have returned from the "jihad in the Middle East" and are now attacking government troops as well. The Pentagon, in the form of EUCOM, is bracing for the inevitable attacks against US troops.

Another regional dynamic is playing out in the Horn of Africa. Strategically, as has been stated earlier, in the short term, from the perspective of the United States, ending the brief run of authority of the UIC in southern Somalia was indeed a success. Even in success there are consequences. The Bush administration is now bracing for the "blowback" in Somalia. Before delineating the burgeoning anti-Americanism, not just in the Horn in the wake of the Ethiopian intervention, but the growing surge throughout the continent, it is important to examine US efforts to put a "regional face" on the occupation of southern Somalia. Long before the troops from the transitional government arrived in the capital to assist Ethiopia's forces, the Bush administration made calls throughout the Horn and elsewhere in Africa to secure peacekeeping troops, not just to stabilize capital but to use the momentum to help unite the country. The administration's "preemptive diplomacy" failed almost as soon as it commenced. Thereafter the administration dispatched Assistant Secretary of State for Africa Jendayi Frazer to the Horn and to meet with officials within the ineffectual African Union. Her efforts too ended in failure, as the AU was unable to have member states agree on a timeline to introduce African troops to the capital to supplant those of Ethiopia.

With the diplomatic initiative faltering, the administration bolstered the forces of the Ethiopian government (and of those of the United States) by dispatching a carrier off the coastal waters of Somalia and privately sent in additional SOFs to assist Ethiopian and transitional government troops to capture fleeing UIC forces and those of al Qaeda that hid in enclaves near the Somali–Kenyan border. Similarly, to increase the pressure on UIC and in a bid to kill al Qaeda operatives deemed responsible for the bombings of US embassies in Kenya and Tanzania, CENTCOM dispatched and then utilized the deadly C-130 Spectra Gunships. The missions launched in southern Somalia were deemed successful even though the US military did not capture or kill the suspected senior al Qaeda members.

During this period of diplomacy, and both during and in the wake of the military operations to crush the UIC, anti-Americanism continued to rise in Somalia, the Horn, and elsewhere in the region. A host of commentators have endeavored to capture the increasing "blowback":

> The US blunder in Somalia could not be more humiliating to Somalis: Washington has delegated to its Ethiopian ally, Mogadishu's historical national enemy, the mission of restoring the rule of law and order to the same country Addis Ababa has incessantly sought to dismember and disintegrate and singled Ethiopia out as the only neighboring country to contribute the backbone of the US-suggested and UN-adopted multinational foreign force for Somalia after the Ethiopian invasion, thus setting the stage for a wide-spread insurgency and creating a new violent hotbed of anti-Americanism. The US manipulation is there for all to see; a new US-led anti-Arab and anti-Muslim regional alliance is already in the working and not only in the making; the US-allied Ethiopian invaders have already taken over Somalia after the withdrawal of the forces of the United Islamic Courts (UIC), who rejected an offer of amnesty in return for surrendering their arms and refused unconditional dialogue with the invaders; the withdrawal of the UIC forces from urban centers reminds one of the disappearance of the Iraqi army and the Taliban government in Afghanistan and warns of a similar aftermath in Somalia in a similar shift of military strategy into guerilla tactics.[16]

In the wake of this statement a participant state in the US-led CJTF-HOA has distanced itself from the perception of the Ethiopian–US intervention. According to the Eritrean Information Minister Ali Abdu, "This war is between the Americans and the Somali people."[17] This statement symbolized the growing discontent with the Ethiopian occupation and the perception of United States' involvement.

The administration has another issue to deal with: al Qaeda's Ayman al-Zawahiri has called for a jihad against the Ethiopian forces in the capital and against its US handlers. The UIC has promised to adhere to request by the al Qaeda leader to mount an insurgent campaign against the infidels.[18]

One thing is clear: the administration is in throes of a difficult situation. First, the protests continue against the US and its Ethiopian allies in the Horn. Similarly, the crisis has stirred up Muslim passions throughout the Horn, elsewhere in Africa, and around the world. Third, the administration has to contend with discord within the taskforce as Ethiopia and Eritrea, each of which is supporting dissimilar elements in Somalia, continue to engage in negative discourse. Fourth, the administration has both a short-term and a long-term dilemma to contend with: how will anti-Americanism manifest itself within Somalia and among its allies? How many "Arabs" or Muslims from other regions within Africa or around the world will flock to Somalia to participate in the latest jihad? The answer to these questions will offer benchmarks about the success or failure of the US-led war on terror in Africa.

Africa—Into the Future

This study has attempted to examine the successes and dilemmas associated with Africa's role in the war on terror. The results of the examination illustrate that, despite a host of strategic benefits, the dilemmas associated with the long-term health of the war on terror are plentiful. The point in this concluding section is to offer some recommendations to ensure the sustainability of the war in the long term. Thereafter, of equal significance, as we look "into the future" the point is to address the following questions: What are the some the major problems that, left unattended, could undermine the war on terror? What are the recommendations and, if implemented, how would they affect participant African states in the war on terror?

Recommendations for Sustaining Africa's Participation in the War on Terror

The section below endeavors to provide a list of recommendations followed by a brief discussion of some of the internal issues that are essential for the long-term success of the war on terror and similarly for the health of African states and the region's identity. The recommendations stretch the spectrum from issues relevant to state or regional identity, security concerns, and economic concerns.

African Prioritization

Recommendation #1:   As discussed earlier, until African issues are given priority the long-term viability of the war on terror in Africa is problematic. Besides the obvious, African issues such as poverty, rampant corruption, "state instability" (failed, weak, or collapsed), HIV/AIDS, underdevelopment, ethnic and tribal enmity, porous borders, the ever-present neo-colonial impulse, and the need for democratic governance, are just a few problems that are central to establish stability within nearly all African states. Within Africa, until these issues receive the appropriate attention, again the long-term health of the war on terror remains problematic.

No one expects that all of the aforementioned issues will be resolved overnight; indeed issues such as HIV/AIDS and ethnic-tribal tensions, may take a generation.

However, if most or some of these issues are resolved, then the expectations of change will resonate among the peoples of each state. This sets the government on a firm footing in the ongoing battle of "winning the hearts and minds." Just as important, as these issues gain traction African states will be in better shape with respect to their relationships with the United States (and its people) in the war on terror. The partnership among African states with the Bush administration is a classic dependency relationship. The vast majority of the benefits of the relationship accrue to the United States. There are lessons to be learned. During the Cold War, African states participated in a series of proxy wars and a number of states provided bases for the United States. When the "war on communism" dissipated, the United States declared victory and ushered in the "unipolar movement." Its African allies envisaged abandonment, which left the people of those states to deal with corrupt regimes, sprawling economic dysfunction, and ethnic violence, each of which set the stage for state failure. If African states are to avoid the negative lesson of the past, the leaders of its states must move to reassert their own identity.

Ending Political Violence

Recommendation #2:   Political terrorism remains a critical issue in every region of Africa. Political terrorism dominates the landscape: a few examples include Liberia, Rwanda, Somalia, Sudan, Sierra Leone, and the Democratic Republic of the Congo, to name a few. Without venturing into a history of political terrorism in the aforementioned states, the point herein is to list the commonalities. They include the following: corruption, human rights abuses, the development of virulent opposition groups, civil wars, and failed states. A question begs: How can Africa succeed long term in a war not of its making when the same variables remain in place? If African states do not address these issues the long-term prospect of the war on terror is not a positive one.

Ending the Marginalization of African Institutions

Recommendation #3:   As the US presence, and that of NATO and even the UN, has increased during the war on terror in the region, there has been one notable consequence: the decline or marginalization of African institutions. There are a host of institutions, each requiring a chapter unto themselves for a detailed discussion. The institutions include the following: the African Union (AU), the New Partnership for Africa's Development (NEPAD), Economic Community of West African States (ECOWAS), the Southern African Development Community (SADC), and the Intergovernmental Authority on Development (IGAD). Each of these institutions has been eclipsed by the US. If one were to add the increasing international presence (NATO/UN) that has supplemented the American presence on the continent, they too have assisted into in the marginalization of African institutions. In spite of a host of successes, the continuing problem of the marginalization of African institutions is and remains a negative consequence of the war on terror in the region. These institutions are both security and developmental and were erected to confront dissimilar challenges.

As events in Mogadishu in December 2006–January 2007 have illustrated, the AU, for example, has failed to deliver when it comes to laying the foundation for providing African peacekeepers to provide stability in Somalia. The US and western Europe reported the failure and then suggested that the institution should be overhauled. Irrespective of the criticism, the perception was that the AU was tasked to put a face on the Ethiopian-US supported invasion/occupation of Somalia. When the expected internal rivalries resurfaced within the AU the outcome was predictable. The AU at some time in the near future should act to assert its authority over its states. This, however, can only happen if the rivalries among member states dissipate and if its states are willing to accept a decline in sovereignty.

With respect to terrorism in general the AU has been unable to enforce (or have member states implement) member agreements regarding terrorist financing, harboring terrorists, or exchange of intelligence, to name a few. Thus, while US efforts have overshadowed those of the AU, the organization's inability to resolve its own internal problems is equally troubling. If the war on terror is to provide an African face, the AU must accelerate its authority, power that can only come if its participant states are willing to grant it.

The Need for More Economic Assistance

Recommendation #5:   In the words of Marcel Kitissou, "terrorism is a technique not an ideology. Military means may be used to combat its immediate effects. However, the ideology behind it can only be defeated through political action and development programs."[19] The United States has provided assistance but that funding has been primarily for military-related programs. Until more funding arrives to end the cycle of poverty, underdevelopment, and political violence, the war on terror may go the way of the war on communism: the United States defeated Soviet Communism but the seeds that created this ideology still exist. It is interesting that even in the areas of Africa where there has been success the underlying issues that could spawn terrorism still remain. Unless the Bush administration, the EU, or the other entities avail themselves with consistent economic assistance to states with a plethora of internal issues, numerous states within Africa will continue to drift toward instability.

Anti-Terrorism Measures

Recommendation #6:   States throughout Africa, not just those in the Horn or the Sahel, should move to enact and then implement anti-terrorist measures. This process will assist in the war on terror. Moreover, it will provide a clear sense of the "African face" as each of its states, with their own disparate issues, will enact and then implement measures that are consistent with their own individual problems.

Though anti-terrorism measures are badly needed throughout the region, there are a number of attendant issues or consequences. First, as the US and other developed states have learned, implementing such measures is a costly venture. Second, within each African state, issues such as poverty, HIV/AIDS, corruption, underdevelopment, and political violence are considerably higher priorities. Similarly, if the vast majority of states are unable to afford the costs of dealing with the above, it therefore follows that most states will be unable to afford the costs associated with implementing anti-terrorism measures. There is a third problem that was expressed by Adekeye Adebajo:

> Anti-terrorism, like anti-communism during the Cold War, should not become the new conditionality for receiving future American assistance, with Uncle Sam rewarding states that are seen to be fighting terrorism and punishing those whose efforts are perceived to be lackluster.[20]

Confronting this issue will be a major challenge for participant African states in the war on terror. With a plethora of internal issues requiring economic assistance from the US, many African states have made anti-terrorism a high priority. The problem, as discussed above, is that as important as anti-terrorism may be, for many people within African states, it is viewed as a US priority and not an African one. This dilemma highlights the long-term problems associated with the war on terror.

Sudan and Somalia: State Failure

Recommendation #7:   There are a host of examples of state failure in Africa. The situation in Sudan and Somalia are symbolic of the connections of failed states to terrorism. As is well known, both were havens for al Qaeda in the past and each retains linkages today.[21] Similarly, "within each country sympathies for militant Islam persist in security institutions as well as among warlords, mullahs and imams, and ordinary citizens."[22]

In Somalia, the Ethiopian invasion affords the international community with an opportunity and momentum to end the poverty, end the tyranny that has been established by the clan warlords, and lastly, end the violence and absence of national governmental authority. The opportunities arise at a time when al Qaeda and UIC are both fleeing the southernmost areas of the country, and the US and the UN are exercising authority. If these two entities do not work, along with the AU, to rebuild the country, one must ask how long before the violence resumes and the safe havens return?

In Sudan the on-going political terrorism in Darfur illustrates the division between the northern and southern areas of the country. Until and unless the international community is willing to end the ethno-religious terrorism, one of the more essential states cannot fulfill its leadership role. The ultimate absurdity currently exists where an outlaw regime continues to indiscriminately kill its people, and then is afforded the latitude to dictate to the AU, the UN, and NATO when and how many of their troops can police the Darfur region. Until these issues are resolved the US or its African partners cannot clam any real or long-term success in the war on terror.

Neither issue will end soon but both will require an abundance of international attention and resources. There has to be a renewed focus not just by these aforementioned entities but by the people of Somalia and Sudan. Until the people of these two states taken it upon themselves to end the tyranny and exploitation, regardless of the solutions offered by outsiders, such remedies stand little chance of sustainability.

Conclusion

In conclusion, the war on terror holds much promise for Africa, but as the recommendations illustrate, there are a host of problems that, left unattended, could easily undo the foundations for preventing terrorism in Africa. Similarly, the Horn and Sahel regions have taken an active role both in partnership with the US or with member states of the respective coalitions. If the war on terror is to produce long-term sustainability, the Bush administration must lay the foundation for a framework that implements some, if not all, of the aforementioned recommendations. The failure to do so ensures a war with unceasing violence; a war that again renews proxies—US-supported governments in the regions against indigenous terror groups that support al Qaeda's agenda—to fight a war in whose benefits in the long term will almost certainly diminish. Preparing for that eventuality requires attention to the internal and regional security priorities. If it is the case that globalization of the war on terror continues, few will write or talk about the role of African partners of the US in the war on terror. Rather, internally what is likely to be mentioned are the attendant consequences of the war to African issues—a reference to their marginalization.

There is a great irony afoot as the war on terror continues to unfold. The Bush administration has not received much in the way of accolades when it comes to its successful strategy in preventing al Qaeda's expansion into or its access to safe havens in Africa. The problem is largely of its own making. That is, its strategic blunder to invade and subsequently occupy Iraq has prevented any media coverage of the administration's successes elsewhere. In the case of Africa, particularly those states in the Horn and the Sahel, whatever gains have been made have subsequently been overshadowed by events in Iraq. Worse, because of the international focus on the suffering of the people of Iraq, little attention by the local or international press to the issues that have long affected African states have been sidelined as well. The verity is clear: the future of Africa may now be invariably linked to the war on terror.

Notes

1 "Camp United." http://www.globalsecurity.org/military/facility/camp-united.htm. The site was accessed on January 2, 2007.
2 Robert I. Rotberg, *Battling Terrorism in the Horn of Africa* (Washington, DC: Brookings Institution Press, 2005), pp. 2–5.3 "Trans-Sahara   Counterterrorism   Initiative." *GlobalSecurity.org*. http://www.globalsecurity.org/military/ops/tscti.htm. The site was accessed on January 3, 2007.
4 "Country Reports: Africa Overview." http://www.state.gov/documents/ organization/65468.pdf. The site was accessed on January 4, 2007.
5 Jeffrey Gettleman, "More Than 50 Die in US Strikes in Somalia," *New York Times*, January 9, 2007, p. A4.
6 Ibid.
7 "US 'Targets Al Qaeda' in Somalia." *BBC News*. January 9, 2007. http://news.bbc. co.uk/2/hi/africa/6245943.stm. The site was accessed on January 9, 2007.
9 A note to the reader: the CENTCOM has responsibility for the Horn countries (Djibouti, Kenya, Ethiopia, and Eritrea). EUCOM by contrast has responsibility for the rest of the 48 African states.

10 Charles Cobb Jr., "Africa: Trained African Armies Key to Terror Fight in Africa, Says US European Command Deputy," *AllAfrica.com*. March 8, 2004. http://allafrica.com/stories/200403090576.html. The site was accessed on January 9, 2007.

11 Ted Dagne, "Africa and the War on Terrorism," *CRS Report*, January 17, 2002, p. 22. http://fpc.state.gov/documents/organization/7959.pdf.

12 Patrick Smith, "Africa's Year of Terror Tactics." *BBC News*, January 2, 2007. http://news.bbc.co.uk/2/hi/africa/6217895.stm. The site was accessed on January 9, 2007.

13 Iqbal Jassat, "Horn of Africa: Latest Victim of War on Terror" December 29, 2006. http://world.mediamonitors.net/content/view/full/39199. The site was accessed on January 9, 2007.

14 Ibid.

15 Ibid.

16 Yahia H. Zoubir and Louisa Ait-Hamadouche, "Anti-Americanism in North Africa: Could State Relations Overcome Popular Resentment," *The Journal of North African Affairs*, March 2006, pp. 36–37.

17 Nicola Nasser, "Somalia: New Hotbed of Anti-Americanism." *Global Research*, January 3, 2007.
http://www.globalresearch.ca/index.php?context=viewArticle&code=NAS20070102&articleId=4308. The site was accessed on January 9, 2007.

18 Ibid.

19 Jeffrey Gettleman, "Across Africa, a Sense That US Power Isn't So Super," *New York Times*, December 24, 2006.
http://select.nytimes.com/gst/abstract.html?res=F40F17F93A550C778EDDAB0994DE404482. The site was accessed on January 9, 2007.

20 Marcel Kitissou, "Political Violence, Terrorism and Counterterrorism in Africa in the Global Context." http://www.hollerafrica.com/showArticle.php?artId=48&catId=1&PHPSESSID=4dc7f1ffdf6a573982b7dc28d4aa7c09. This site was accessed on January 10, 2007.

21 Adekeye Adabajo, "Africa and American in an Age of Terror," *Journal of Asian and African Studies*, 2003,vol. 38, No. 2–3, p. 185.

22 Stephen Morrison, "Somalia's and Sudan's Race to the Fore in Africa," *Washington Quarterly*, Spring 2002, p. 192.

23 Ibid.

Index